Hiking and Exploring the
Paria River

Including: The Story of John D. Lee and Mountain
Meadows Massacre

3rd Edition

Michael R. Kelsey

Kelsey Publishing
456 E. 100 N.
Provo, Utah, USA 84606
Tele & Fax 801-373-3327

First Edition November 1987
Updated Edition September 1991
3rd Edition January 1998
Copyright © 1998 Michael R. Kelsey All Rights Reserved
Library of Congress Catalog Card Number 97-092839
ISBN 0-944510-15-9

Primary Distributor   If you'd like to order any book, please call or write to the following address. All of Michael R. Kelsey's books are sold by this company.
Publishers Distribution Center, 805 West 1700 South, Salt Lake City, Utah, 84104, P.O. Box 27734, Salt Lake City, Utah, 84127. Tele. 1-801-972-6570, or for Book Orders 1-800-922-9681.

Many of Kelsey's books are sold by each of the following distributors
Alpenbooks, 3616 South Road, Building C, Suite 1, Mukilteo, Washington, 98275, Tele. 1-206-290-8587, or for book orders 1-800-290-9898, Fax 1-206-290-9461.
Anderson News, 1709 North, East Street, Flagstaff, Arizona, 86001, Tele. 1-520-774-6171, Fax 1-520-779-1958.
Big Horn Booksellers, 1813 E. Mulberry Street, Ft. Collins, Colorado, 80524, Tele. 1-970-224-1579, Order Line 1-800-433-5995, Fax 1-970-224-1394.
Canyon Country Distribution, P. O. Box 400034, Highway 50-6 West, #100, Thompson Springs, Utah, 84540-0034, Tele. 1-801-285-2210.
Canyonlands Publications, 4860 North, Ken Morey Drive, PO Box 16175, Bellemont, Arizona, 86015, Tele. 1-520-779-3888, or 1-800-283-1983, Fax 1-520-779-3778.
Crown West Books(Library Service), 575 E. 1000 S., Orem, Utah, 84058, Tele. 1-801-224-1455.
High Peak Books, PO Box 703, Wilson, Wyoming, 83014, 1-307-739-0147.
Many Feathers, 2626 West, Indian School Road, Phoenix, Arizona, 85012, Tele. 1-602-266-1043, or 1-800-279-7652, Fax 1-602-279-2350.
Nevada Publications, 4135 Badger Circle, Reno, Nevada, 89509, Tele. 1-702-747-0800.
Peregrine Outfitters, P.O. Box 1500, 105 South Brownell Road, Suite A, Williston, Vermont, 05495, Tele. 802-860-2977, or 1-800-222-3088, Fax 1-802-860-2978.
Recreational Equipment, Inc.(R.E.I.), P.O. Box C-88126, Seattle, Washington, 98188, For Mail Orders Tele. 1-800-426-4840 (or check at their local stores).
Treasure Chest Books, 1802 West Grant Road, Suite 101, PO Box 5250, Tucson, Arizona, 85703-0250, Tele. 1-520-623-9558, Fax 1-520-624-5888, or Order Toll Free Tele. 1-800-969-9558, or Fax 1-800-715-5888. Credit Cards Accepted.

For the UK and Europe: CORDEE, 3a De Montfort Street, Leicester, England, UK, LE1 7HD, Tele. 0116-254-3579, Fax 0116-247-1176.
For Australia and New Zealand: Macstyle Media, 20-22 Station Street, Sandringham, Victoria, Australia, 3191. Tele. Intl.+61-39-521-6585, Fax Intl.+61-39-521-0664

Printed by Banta IGS, 2600 North Main Street, Spanish Fork, Utah

All fotos by the author, unless otherwise stated.
All maps, charts, and cross sections drawn by the author.

Front Cover

Hiking and Exploring the
Paria River

| 1 | 2 |
| 3 | 4 |

Front Cover Fotos
1. Lower Buckskin Gulch
2. The Wave, Coyote Buttes
3. Pickup Wreck, Historic Bull Valley Gorge Bridge
4. Round Valley Draw

Back Cover

5	6
7	8
9	10

Back Cover Fotos
5. Narrows of Starlight Canyon
6. Mollies Nipple and Nipple Lake
7. Stone House at Jacob Pools, near Sand Hill Crack
8. Petroglyphs on Boulder, Lower Paria River Gorge
9. The Hoodoos in Bryce Canyon National Park
10. Castle Rock, left; and The Cockscomb

Table of Contents

Acknowledgments

Many people helped with information for this book, but special thanks should go to the following people. The most important person has been the late **Rod Schipper** (killed in a car wreck in September, 1997), more commonly known as **"Skip"**. Until 1990, he was the BLM ranger who lived and worked at the Paria Ranger Station. He had that job beginning in 1980 and knew the lower Paria River Canyon better than anyone. Skip spent hours proof-reading the hiking section of the first two editions of this book. See a small memorial to Skip at the Paria Ranger Station & Visitor Center.

Besides Skip, the BLM geologist in Kanab, Pete Kilborne also contributed in his specialty field. Other residents of Kanab the author interviewed were: Calvin C. Johnson, Jeff Johnson, Leola Scheonfeld, Merrill MacDonald, Mason Meeks, Merrill and Ramona Johnson and Dunk Findlay. Also the late Mel Schoppman and Bill Leach of Page, Arizona, and George Fisher, of Las Vegas. There were also Bryce Canyon ranger Nate Inouye; St. George BLM employees Tom Folks, Mike Small and Jennifer Jack; plus BLM employees in Kanab, Mary Dewitz and Mary Cassidy. Mike Salamancha, the Paria Ranger in 1997, proof-read and helped in updating this edition.

In the Bryce Valley towns, the author spoke with the late Ken Goulding, Layton Smith, Marian Clark, and Herm Pollock (all deceased), and Ralph Chynoweth, Bob Ott, George Thompson, Kay Clark, Joe Dunham, Wallace Ott, and Jack Chynoweth. Nearly all of these people were in their 70's when interviewed, and one, Marian Clark, was in his 90's; therefore lots of good information was gathered about the canyons and the early-day ranchers.

The Author

The author, who was born in 1943, experienced his earliest years of life in eastern Utah's Uinta Basin, namely around the town of Roosevelt. Then the family moved to Provo and he attended Provo High School, and later Brigham Young University, where he earned a B.S. degree in Sociology. Shortly after that, he discovered sociology was the wrong subject, so he attended the University of Utah, where he received his Master of Science degree in Geography, finishing in June, 1970.

It was then real life began, for on June 9, 1970, he put a pack on his back and started traveling for the first time. Since then he has seen 193 countries, republics, islands, or island groups. All this wandering has resulted in a number of books written and published by himself. Here are his books, listed in the order they were first published: *Climber's and Hiker's Guide to the World's Mountains(3rd Ed.)*, *Utah Mountaineering Guide(3rd Edition)*; *China on Your Own and the Hiking Guide to China's Nine Sacred Mountains(3rd Ed.) Out of Print*; *Canyon Hiking Guide to the Colorado Plateau(3rd Edition)*; *Hiking and Exploring Utah's San Rafael Swell(2nd Edition)*; *Hiking and Exploring Utah's Henry Mountains and Robbers Roost(Revised Edition)*; *Hiking and Exploring the Paria River(3rd Edition)*; *Hiking and Climbing in the Great Basin National Park(Wheeler Peak, Nevada)*; *Boater's Guide to Lake Powell--Featuring Hiking, Camping, Geology, History and Archaeology(2nd Updated Edition)*; *Climbing and Exploring Utah's Mt. Timpanogos*; *River Guide to Canyonlands National Park & Vicinity*; *Hiking, Biking and Exploring Canyonlands National Park & Vicinity*; *The Story of Black Rock, Utah*; and *Hiking, Climbing and Exploring Western Utah's Jack Watson's Ibex Country*.

He has also helped his mother Venetta Bond Kelsey write and publish a book about the town she was born and raised in, *Life on the Black Rock Desert--A History of Clear Lake, Utah.*

Grosvenor Arch at the head of Cottonwood Wash, as seen from the south.

Introduction to Hiking

This book is basically a hiking guide to the Paria River of southern Utah and northern Arizona. The Paria begins at Bryce Canyon National Park and nearby high plateaus and flows almost due south, across the Utah-Arizona state line, and ends at the Colorado River and Lee's Ferry. After the Grand Canyon, Zion Narrows and possibly the Escalante River system, this river drainage has more visitors than any other canyon on the Colorado Plateau. If you like narrow canyons, including one of the best slot canyon hikes in the world, this is the place for you. One can take day-hikes in some of the shorter tributaries, or go on a week-long marathon walk in the lower end of the Paria Canyon. The northern half of the area covered by this book is now included in the western part of the Grand Staircase-Escalante National Monument.

The Paria River drainage is located about halfway between Kanab, Utah, and Page, Arizona, and right in the middle of some of the best hiking parts of the Colorado Plateau. To the west is Kanab, St. George and Zion National Park; to the north is Richfield, Panguitch, and the Bryce Valley towns of Tropic, Cannonville, and Henrieville; to the northeast is Capitol Reef National Park, Torrey, Boulder, and Escalante; to the south is Flagstaff, and to the east is Page and Lake Powell.

Local Towns and Facilities

In these last few years, since tourism has been so important to the local economies, better accommodations have been built. Here's a run down on what's where in the immediate area. Population figures are for **1990**, but most of these towns have grown considerably since then.

Page, Arizona (population 6598) This town was built to house and accommodate the workers who built Glen Canyon Dam across the Colorado River creating Lake Powell. Today it's the southern gateway to Lake Powell and is the local headquarters for the National Park Service, which administers Glen Canyon National Recreational Area. Page has two supermarkets and a good shopping center. The town is full of tourists, as well as Navajos from the reservation, and seldom slows down. There are many motels and other facilities; and a good place to shop for about everything.

Kanab (population 3289) Kanab is a little smaller than Page, but this one is more quiet--mainly because the reservation and lake are farther away. Kanab has one huge supermarket, and another smaller one, plus numerous convenience stores. Its facilities are similar to those of Page, with many motels, gas stations and restaurants. It's the Kane County seat, and has two book stores, an airport, and golf course. Kanab has been the movie capital of southern Utah and it's the jumping-off point to the north rim of the Grand Canyon, which is open from about mid-May until late October. Kanab also has the nearest BLM office, Tele.435-644-2672.

Panguitch (population 1444) This town is located just northwest of Bryce Canyon National Park and is smaller than Kanab. Panguitch is the Garfield County seat and has moderately good facilities, including one small supermarket, and many motels and restaurants. Panguitch still depends on farming and ranching for support, but in the warmer half of the year it's busy with tourists.

Bryce Canyon Facilities Along the highway between Panguitch and Bryce Canyon National Park, are many motels, convenience stores, gas stations and independent campsites. On the Paunsaugunt Plateau, and just north of the entrance to the park, is Ruby's Inn. This is a huge complex, with gas station, store(including curios and books), restaurant, laundry center, campground, horseback rides, a rodeo three nights a week in season, and helicopter rides into the park. Most of this is open year-round

Inside the national park are two campgrounds, open in summers only. Bryce also has an historic old lodge and cabins for rent, and is open in early April through October.

Tropic (population 374) This is the biggest town in Bryce Valley, and it's where the area high school is found. Tropic has two gas stations; one with a small supermarket, the other with a convenience store; a couple of motels, a burger and malt shop(it's open from about Easter until after the deer hunt, at the end of October); and one garage, the only one in the valley. The burger stand, gas stations and motels are open on Sundays, everything else is closed. As time goes on, Tropic is becoming more dependent on tourism, less dependent on farming and ranching.

Cannonville (population 131) This small town in Bryce Valley has but one store which sells about everything--a general store. It used to sell gas, but no more. The old store will be closed in 1998, but will reopen in a new building along with a motel.

Kodachrome Basin State Park In 1987, Bob Ott and family from Cannonville, opened a small camper's store in the state park just south of the campground. They have horse and wagon rides, and are catering to senior citizens and campers. The store is about 13 kms southeast of Cannonville(with a paved road all the way now), and will be open from about Easter to early November.

Henrieville (population 163) Henrieville, which is also in Bryce Valley, no longer has any retail businesses in town.

Escalante (population 818) A town full of ranchers, farmers, lumbermen, and a growing number of BLM,

Forest Service and National Park Service personnel. It has two or more gas stations, several motels, two small supermarkets(general stores), a new restaurant or two, and one burger stand, which does a good business in the spring, summer and fall, with the hikers heading into the Escalante River country. It appears this town will see lots of growth in the near future because of the creation of the Grand Staircase-Escalante National Monument on September 18, 1996.

Road Report

For the most part, access to most of these canyons is reasonably good. If you're going down the Lower Paria River Gorge, you're in luck; you only have to drive about 3 kms on a graveled, all-weather road, and you're at the White House Trailhead. At the bottom end of the river, which is Lee's Ferry, you'll be on pavement all the way. For the rest of the hikes, with the exception of those inside Bryce Canyon National Park, you'll have to do some driving on dirt or sandy roads, but as a general rule almost all the hikes featured in this book are easy to get to with an ordinary car in dry weather.

Skutumpah Road This is a main link between the little community of Johnson, located about 16 kms due east of Kanab, and the Bryce Valley towns of Cannonville, Henrieville, and Tropic. The Skutumpah Road itself begins at the head of Johnson Canyon, where the road divides and the pavement ends; at that point one road goes northwest to Alton, while the Skutumpah Road heads northeast to Cannonville. It's 103 kms from Kanab to Cannonville, first along Highway 89, then up Johnson Canyon, and finally along the Skutumpah Road.

The road up Johnson Canyon is paved up to the Alton--Skutumpah Junction, then it's graveled up to about the Skutumpah Ranch. After that it's maintained and graded, but made out of what ever material the road passes over. In places it's just ordinary dirt, other places it's gravely, and still other places it's made of clay beds. When it rains only lightly, it seldom effects the road. All you have to do is wait 'till the sun hits it a few minutes, and away you go. **When heavy rains soak the area, it may be a one or two day wait in the warmer season; maybe a week's wait in the winter, before it's passable.**

For the most part, this road is closed in winter, but 4WD's do it at that time, especially during dry spells, or in morning hours when the road bed is frozen. However, on the dugway just south and above Willis Creek, is a seep right next to the road. This sometimes makes the road icy in winter, and 4WD's slide off it occasionally. For the most part, the Skutumpah Road is open for all traffic from about late March or the first part of April through mid-November, but each year is different. Because there are a number of ranches along this road, it's well-maintained, and carries up to 40 or 50 cars a day during the warm season when it's dry. Expect traffic to increase because of the newly created national monument.

Cottonwood Wash Road The Cottonwood Wash Road runs south out of Cannonville, to and past Kodachrome Basin State Park, to Grosvenor Arch, down the Cockscomb Valley(Cottonwood Wash Canyon), and eventually to Highway 89, at a point between mile posts 17 and 18.

This Cottonwood Wash Road was built back in 1957 by a cooperative organized by then-72 year-old Sam Pollock. It included people from Bryce Valley, Escalante and Antimony. This group of people wanted a shortcut to the Lake Powell area to increase tourism in their own little area. The $5500 for the road was raised by donations and sales of various kinds. The county loaned them one caterpillar and a road grader, and a mining company pitched in with a compressor. The project took 70 days to complete. Today it's a maintained county road.

That part of the Cottonwood Wash Road running from Cannonville to Kodachrome Basin is now paved all the way. East of the Kodachrome Turnoff, the road is made of dirt and clay and in the good weather of October, 1997, was used by maybe 200-300 cars daily. Expect traffic to increase because of the new Grand Staircase-Escalante National Monument. **For the most part, it's a warm weather, summer-time road, as there are slick spots in places when ever it rains hard making it impassable.** Those spots that become extremely slick are made of the gray colored clay beds of the Tropic Shale which are in the middle and lower end of the canyon.

Nipple Ranch Road This is a maintained county road to the Nipple Ranch just north of Mollies Nipple. It begins at Highway 89, right at mile post 37, and runs to an old drill site north of Kitchen Canyon. This is a good road, but it gradually deteriorates as you drive along it. In it's upper parts just west of Mollies Nipple, there are several big sand traps. If you don't have a 4WD, then take a shovel and lower your tire pressure in half when in the sandy areas. Because of the sand, this is one of the few roads which will be easier and safer to drive on if the surface is wet. The reason is, sand sets-up and becomes firmer when wet.

House Rock Valley Road This road runs from Highway 89 just west of The Cockscomb(between mile posts 25-26), south to Highway 89A(between mile posts 565 and 566) where an old ranch called House Rock, is located. This is the approach road to the Buckskin Gulch and Wire Pass Trailheads, and to the several entry points to Coyote Buttes. The road is about 50 kms long and is for seasonal use only. Normally it's open almost year-round, but in winter and when it's wet because of heavy storms, it's slick in places. The bad places are a result of the road running over clay beds, most of which are near the Utah-Arizona line. It's a maintained county road. Generally, the northern and southern ends are in very good condition--while the middle part is a little rocky & rougher. Road crews in Utah usually work the road over in April each year, or when there's a little moisture in the area. It's periodically closed during and right after flashfloods. During the warmer half of the year it has moderately heavy traffic--for such an out of the way road.

Pahreah Road The road to the old Pahreah townsite and the Paria Movie Set, begins between mile posts 30 and 31 on Highway 89, about halfway between Page and Kanab. This is a good 10 km-long road, which is well-used in the warmer half of the year. In winter it may be slick in spots, because most of it runs along the Moenkopi clay beds. It is definitely impassable during or just after heavy rains, but ordinarily it's a good road for all vehicles.

Cedar Mountain Road This road leaves Highway 89 between mile posts 17 & 18, right across the highway from the beginning of the Cottonwood Wash Road, but heads south, then east to the top of East Clark Bench, Flat Top and Cedar Mountain. This is the area north of the Lower Paria River Gorge and gives access to that rim country. This is a sandy road all the way, but it's graded occasionally up to the communications facility near where the road passes under the power lines. After that it gets even sandier and you'll normally need a HCV & 4WD to successfully get through the sandier places. Wet conditions makes this one better.

Here are some tips on how to drive the back roads of the Paria country. First, when you leave pavement, stop and reduce the air pressure in your tires. The author runs about 35 lbs on the highways, then reduces it to about 20 or 25 lbs for dirt or gravel roads. If the road gets real sandy and getting stuck seems eminent, then tire pressure is reduced again to about 10 or 15 lbs. Reduced tire pressure puts more rubber to the road and increases traction.

Emergency Provisions For Your Car

Everyone reading this book should remember, once you leave the paved highways, some parts of the Paria River Country can be rather isolated. Special care should be taken in planning for a worse-case emergency situation. Perhaps the thing you need most is a **reliable vehicle**, one you can depend on. Besides that, here is a list of things everyone should have in their vehicle before venturing out into remote areas. Take a **full tank of fuel**, and depending on where you're going, maybe **extra fuel**. Also, take most of the **tools** you own, plus a **tow rope** or **chain, battery jumper cable, shovel, tire pump, extra oil, matches** or **cigarette lighters**, some kind of **first aid kit, tire chains** for winter driving, and a **good spare tire** (check the air pressure before going).

Also, take more **food** than you think you'll need, and if you're heading to a far away place, take **lots of water** or liquids. This writer is always alone and during hot weather and in remote places, he starts out with as much as 35 to 40 liters of water, fruit juice and soda pop. That's about 10 gallons! In summer heat you'll drink about 2 or 3 times more than in the cooler months. Also, consider taking more clothing than you think you'll need. In spring or fall, weather can turn from summer to winter in a matter of hours. Also, always let someone know exactly where you're going and what time you expect to return. The thing to remember is, **GO PREPARED** for any problem that might arise!

Off Road Vehicles

In the spring of 1987, the Utah State Legislature passed four bills dealing with all aspects of Off Road Vehicle(ORV's) use. These new laws are written up as the **Utah Off-Highway Vehicle Act**, Title 41, Chapter 22, Utah code annotated 1953, as amended in April 1987. To make a long story short, here's the most important part.

41-22-12. (2) states: No person may operate and no owner of an off-highway vehicle may give another person permission to operate an off-highway vehicle *on any public land which has not been designated as open to off-highway vehicles.*

In a letter to this author from then Governor Norm Bangerter, he states, ...*'the statute specifies that all public land shall be presumed closed to the use of off highway vehicles unless designated as open by the agency or entity controlling said land."*

It sounds almost too good to be true. But in reality, Utah State laws do not control the Federal Agencies, which control most of the land in the state. They are the Bureau of Land Management and the Forest Service. The BLM, which administers almost all the land in the Paria drainage, continues to designate about 95% of it's land as open to Off Road Vehicles. So BLM policy is going contrary to the wishes of the Utah State lawmakers. The only areas safe from dirt bikes and three & four wheeled ATV's are places set aside as wilderness areas by law, or in national parks. In those places designated as Wilderness Study Areas(WSA's), ORV's are allowed on existing roads only.

Now this sounds good too, but the problem is, they don't always stay on the existing roads! This all adds up to nothing and a law without teeth and full of holes. *Please keep your vehicles on existing roadways.*

Best Time to Hike

For those heading into the Lower Paria River Gorge, the best time in the spring is from about late March through the end of May(but late May through June for the Buckskin Gulch). For some of the canyons higher in the drainage, April through mid-June is usually the best time. The biggest problem with going into the Lower Paria Canyon is that you'll be wading in water most of the time, and in the early morning hours your feet will feel like blocks of ice!

In the fall season and in the lower gorge, late September into late October is preferred, but higher in the drainage, early September through October is usually best, although snow can come during that time. For the high country hikes in Bryce Canyon and Table Cliff Plateau, the summer months, or from about late May through October are usually the best, but early or late season bad-weather spells can shorten the season. If you're not wading, then late February and March, and November can be reasonably good times to hike in various parts of this canyon country.

The time of year when the flash flood danger in the narrow slot canyons is highest, is from about mid-July through August(the worst time) extending to mid-September. Regardless of the time of year, one should always stay tuned to the local radio stations and have a generally good weather forecast before entering places like the Buckskin Gulch. The employee at the Paria Ranger Station & Visitor Center, always has the latest weather forecast posted in front of the ranger station at the information-bulletin board. Always stop there and check things out before entering the narrow canyons.

With increased visitor use, especially during late April and May, and October, consider going in the hotter summer months of June, July and August. There's lot of good dry weather then, and if you're going into the slot canyons, the temperatures there are cool.

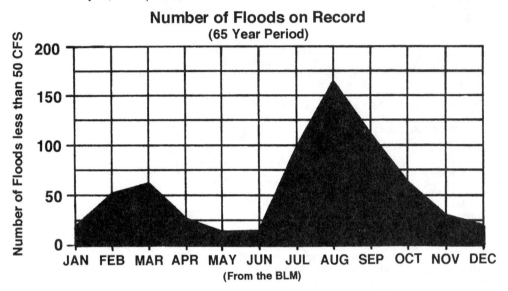

Number of Floods on Record
(65 Year Period)

(From the BLM)

Drinking Water

In recent years there seems to be great controversy over what is and is not suitable drinking water in the backcountry. The US Public Health Service requires the National Park Service and the BLM to inform hikers to boil all surface water, including water coming out of springs. This seems to leave little room for using common sense. The chief reason they do it, is to save themselves from possible law suits.

Here are some steps the author has taken to prevent getting the belly ache while hiking in the Paria River country. On day hikes he always carries a plastic bottle full of "city" water. However, if he passes a good spring which is obviously unpolluted, he normally drinks from it because it's often colder. An unpolluted spring is basically one which cattle cannot get into. If it is free flowing, comes right out of the ground or rock wall, and has no fresh cattle sign nearby, then it should be good to drink as-is.

When it comes to some of the small side canyon streams, the thing you'll have to look for are any fresh sign of cattle. If there are cattle in the area, then you'd better purify or filter any running water. If there are cattle around, the risk is higher. But if it's summer, and the cattle have been taken out of the canyons to higher summer ranges, and the water is free flowing, then the risks are lower. The Giardia cysts cannot swim; they can merely float downstream. After a flash flood, most side canyon streams have better water than before.

The chief reason for taking precautions is to escape the intestinal disorder called Giardiasis. This is caused by the microscopic organism, Giardia Lamblia. Giardia are carried in the feces of humans and some domestic and wild animals. The cysts of Giardia may contaminate surface water supplies. The symptoms of this stomach problem include diarrhea, increased gas, loss of appetite, abdominal cramps and bloating. It is not life threatening, but it can slow you down and make life miserable. If you take the precautions mentioned above and below, and under each hike, you'll surely miss out on this one.

If you're still not convinced, you can buy a water filter for from $30-$40 and up. You can also buy small bottles of Iodine tablets for about $3(containing 50 tablets-one per liter). On all overnight hikes the author carries a bottle of Iodine tablets, but has only used these tablets once in the Paria drainage, and 7 or 8 other times in his life while hiking or climbing.

Here's a tip for those who will spend several days in the lower Paria Canyon camping. Take along one or more large water jugs--3.75 liters or one US gallon. This will enable you to carry water from a spring to your campsite, which may be a ways from a good water supply. The local water availability and possible hazards are discussed under each hike.

Insect Season

The insect season seems to begin in late May, and continues to about mid-July in most of the Paria River country. In the wider parts of the canyons above both Lee's Ferry and old Pahreah, there are small gnats which get into your hair and bite. One remedy for this is to wear a hat of some kind. Sometimes insect repellent helps. In these same open areas are large gray deer flies which bite the back of bare legs. Wearing long pants takes care of this problem. These deer flies are always found around areas where there's water and tamaracks and other brush. For some reason they mostly disappear in about mid-July, or about when the first monsoon rains begin. In the fall there seems to be a general absence of these pests, especially from mid-September on.

The author can't remember any of these pesky insects in the narrow canyons, such as the Buckskin; nor can he remember any mosquitoes, except in swampy places, such as around Adair Lake. He can't remember any mosquitoes in the Lower Paria River Gorge either, where he has made 9 trips over the years, and in all seasons. For the most part, insects are not a serious problem in the Paria River Country.

Equipment for Day-Hikes

For those with less experience, here's a list of things the author normally takes on day-hikes. You may want to add to this list. A small to medium sized day-pack, a one liter bottle of water(maybe 2 or 3 liters on hot summer days), camera and lenses, extra film, a short piece of nylon rope or parachute cord, toilet paper, pen and small notebook, map, chapstick, compass, altimeter, pocket knife, a walking stick for probing deep waterholes(perhaps a ski pole with a camera clamp on top which substitutes as a camera stand), a cap with a "sun shield" or "cancer curtain" sewn on around the back, a pair of long pants(for colder temperatures or possibly deer flies or other insects) and a lunch for the longer hikes.

In warmer weather, he wears shorts and a "T" shirt; in cooler weather, long pants and a long-sleeved shirt, plus perhaps a jacket and gloves. In cooler weather and with more things to carry, a larger day-pack may be needed.

Equipment for Overnight Hikes

Here's a list of things the author normally takes on overnight hikes. You may add to this list too. A large pack, sleeping bag, sleeping pad(Thermal Rest), tent--with rain sheet, small kerosene stove, several lighters(no more matches!), 10 meters or more of nylon cord, camera and lenses, extra film, walking stick with camera clamp on the top end, one large water jug, a one liter water bottle, a stitching awl and waxed thread, small pliers, canister with odds and ends(bandaids, needle & thread, patching kit for sleeping pad, wire, pens, etc.), maps, notebook, reading book, chapstick, compass, altimeter, toilet paper, pocket knife, rain cover for pack, small alarm clock, candles for light & reading, tooth brush & tooth paste, face lotion, sunscreen, cap with cancer curtain, soap, small flashlight, long pants and long sleeved shirt, perhaps a lightweight mini-umbrella and maybe a light-weight coat and gloves. Also, a plastic bowl, cup, spoon, small cooking pot and extra fuel for the stove.

Food usually includes such items as oatmeal or cream of wheat cereal, coffee or chocolate drink, powdered milk, sugar, cookies, crackers, candy, oranges or apples, carrots, Ramen instant noodles, soups, macaroni, canned tuna fish or sardines, Vienna sausages, peanuts, instant puddings, bread, butter, peanut butter and salt & pepper.

Boots or Shoes

Because many of the canyons you'll be hiking in have running water, you'll surely want some kind of a boot or shoe which can be used when wet--some kind of a wading shoe. Many people just use an old pair of running or gym shoes. But here are some precautions. (1) If the shoes are too worn out, you may lose them before the hike ends, especially if taking in all of the Lower Paria Gorge. (2) If the running shoe is too old, it may lack proper support for the foot--a tip for older hikers. (3) A shoe made of canvas and rubber will last longer in a watery situation, than one with leather parts. (4) Leather shoes should be treated with oil after a wading hike, such as through the Upper or Lower Paria Canyon. (5) One last tip, you might consider starting out wearing an older pair of shoes, but have an extra light-weight pair in your pack.

Hiking Rules and Regulations

Bryce Canyon National Park

There are some rules to backpacking in Bryce Canyon, as there are in any of our national parks. Here are some of them. If you're planning to camp out in the backcountry, then you'll need a **camping permit**. Pick this up at the park visitor center, along with any other last minute information. If you're just day-hiking, no permit is needed. You must camp in designated campsites only, and use a stove of some kind--no camp fires allowed. Camping is limited to three days in any one site. No wheeled vehicles of any kind are allowed on the backcountry trails. Get all the latest information at the visitor center just as you enter the park.

For many reasons, there aren't too many hikers camping in the backcountry of Bryce Canyon. One big reason is, there is very little live running water in the park. Largely because of this, most people do day-hikes only.

Paria Canyon--Vermilion Cliffs Wilderness Area

Here's a list of regulations pertaining to the Lower Paria River Gorge between the White House Trailhead and Lee's Ferry. It also includes the popular Buckskin Gulch, main tributary to the Paria.

Regulations--1997 Handout

1. Group size is limited to 10 people. Groups larger than 10 are required to split into smaller groups and begin hiking on separate days. These groups are not permitted to rejoin during the trip. Minimum distance is two miles--3 kms apart. (if you have more than four groups of five or more persons, contact the BLM about more appropriate areas to use.)
2. Visitors must register at White House, Buckskin, Wire Pass, or Lee's Ferry Trailheads when entering or leaving the canyons.
3. The wilderness is closed to motorized or mechanized transport and equipment, including bicycles and hang gliders.
4. Campfires or burning of trash/toilet paper are prohibited.
5. Carry your trash and toilet paper out of the canyons.
6. All camps, latrines, and animals must be at least 200 feet(60 meters) or as far as possible from springs.
7. Wrather Canyon is closed to camping.
8. Leave archaeological sites, such as petroglyphs, potsherds and ruins, undisturbed.
10. Leash your pets or leave them at home. Remove and bury your animal's feces from trails and campsites. Private use of horses, while not recommended, is allowed. Horses must stay on the shoreline terraces. Restrictions apply on the use of pack animals. Contact the BLM for more information.
11. Commercially guided trips require a Special Recreation Permit

Other Recommendations

1. Use existing campsites rather than creating new ones.
2. Trenching around tents is not needed in the canyons.
3. Deposit human waste 6 inches(15 cms) deep, as far from water sources and away from camps as possible. Cover with soil. Urinate on wet river banks or in the river (to prevent stinky campsites).
4. Wash without soap to minimize water contamination or use a biodegradable soap away from water sources.

As of 1997, the BLM began a user-fee policy for hiking the Lower Paria River Canyon and Buckskin Gulch. Money collected will be used for upgrading facilities in this area. Here's the **Fee Schedule for 1997:**
1. For overnight camping in the canyon, $5 per person, per night.
2. For day-hiking, $5 per person per day (a second day is free).
3. Whitehouse Trailhead Campground, $5 per night, per site. Limit of 5 people. There is no water at this trailhead campground; get that at the well & tap 75 meters west of the Paria Ranger Station & Visitor Center.

You can pickup a **Recreation Fee Permit Envelope** for overnight camping or day-hiking at the Paria Ranger Station & Visitor Center. Or you can fill in the same permit envelope at the self-service pay station & information bulletin board in front of the visitor center, then drop the envelope & money in the metal box provided. Be sure to have the correct change upon arrival. You can use the self-service pay station 24 hours a day, 7 days a week as it is well lit at night and only 125 meters from Highway 89.

Coyote Buttes Information

To get into Coyote Buttes in 1997, you were obligated to not only get a permit, but had to have a reservation on a specific day as well. Read about the **Coyote Buttes Special Management Area** in the **Hiking Section, Map 28, page 165.**

New Management Plan for 1998

As this book goes to press, the BLM is in the process of establishing a new management plan for the Paria River & Buckskin Gulch, as well as the Coyote Buttes. Don't be surprised if they go to a **reservation system** for hiking the Lower Paria River Gorge & the Buckskin Gulch.

Here's what's happening regarding the use of this canyon. It seems that campsites in the lower Buckskin Gulch and those just below The Confluence of the Paria River, have very heavy use as this is the most popular part of the canyon. During times of heavy use, April, May and October, campsites are often used to capacity and there's a problem of smelly latrines or toilets nearby.

The BLM has been wrangling with this one for years, and now with new arrivals at the BLM of recreation specialists under the heavy influence of the radical fringe of the Southern Utah Wilderness Alliance(SUWA), new draconian plans have been put forward. One plan is to leave things basically the way they are as of 1997; the other three alternative plans all incorporate a reservation system for overnight camping. To get a reservation similar to what is used presently in the Coyote Buttes, you'd have to apply by letter or fax at Northern Arizona University in Flagstaff with 3 dates you'd like to go on. If the dates are filled, you'll have to try again. It could be that you'll have to apply for a reservation 6 months or a year in advance! All this to satisfy a small group of people in the environmental movement so they can have a "true wilderness experience", as defined by SUWA.

In the opinion of this writer, it would seem better if the BLM would take user-fee money and do some stabilization work on the Buckskin Gulch & Confluence campsites and construct a couple of solar-powered toilets, and have campers live in more crowded conditions for one night; rather than be required to set a hiking date 6 months or a year in advance. But some of these wilderness radicals think building a toilet or two, or constructing trails, or rehabilitating campsites, is somehow sacrilegious. Every wilderness area this author has seen, has improvements made to handle more traffic and bigger crowds. So why can't that be done here? If you agree(or disagree) with this writer, you're urged to write to the **BLM, 345 E. Riverside Drive, St. George, Utah, 84790**, Tele. 435-688-3230; or **BLM, Paria Team, 318 N. First East, Kanab, Utah, 84741**, Tele. 435-644-2672.

This is your land, not theirs, and these people work for you and me. Generally speaking, the BLM is about as good as any government agency when it comes to listening to peoples' concerns, which in the end, helps them set policy. The bean counters in St. George and Kanab do count letters, especially if the writer has legitament and thoughtful proposals--not just complaints.

For more detailed up-to-date information about soon-to-change policies, contact the BLM office, Kanab, Utah. Their fone number is 435-644-2672. You'll have to listen through a recording first before you can talk to a live person. Their address in the north part of town is 318 North, First East, Kanab. Office hours are 7:45 am to 4:30 pm weekdays.

There will always be a BLM employee or volunteer at the new Paria Ranger Station & Visitor Center, located between mile posts 20 and 21 just south of Highway 89, about halfway between Kanab and Page. There is usually someone staying or living in the trailer behind the office. This visitor center will be open 7 days a week from 8:30 am to 5 pm, but will likely be closed from mid-November through February. They presently sell books, maps, post cards, etc. About 75 meters west of the visitor center is a well & tap where you can fill water bottles. The Paria Ranger Station & Visitor Center has somekind of radio telefon contact with the Kanab office but can only be used in emergency situations. The person manning this ranger station or a roving Paria Ranger will always post an updated weather forecast and the latest information on hiking conditions on the new night-lit bulletin or information board in front of the office.

In emergencies after hours, drive west up the highway about 2 kms to where you see some homes to the south near the Johnson Store Butte. There are 6 or 8 or more new homes in that area which is now known as **New Paria**. Those people commute to Page or Kanab and most will likely have a cellular or radio telefone; or drive 11 kms east on Highway 89 to Church Wells.

Car shuttle service for hikers walking all the way through the Lower Paria River Canyon to Lee's Ferry is available at Marble Canyon, Arizona, not far from the end of your hike. Contact the Kanab BLM office for their latest list of shuttle people. Tele. 435-644-2672. In 1991, one couple paid US$80 to be driven from the parking lot at Lee's Ferry to the White House Trailhead. They of course walked right to their car at the end of the hike. The price is likely closer to $100 for this service now. This is one good reason to do days-hikes only, or return the same way back to your car.

Bureau of Land Management (BLM) Offices
St. George, Utah--345 E. Riverside Drive, 84790, Tele. 435-688-3230.
Kanab, Utah--318 N. First East, 84741, Tele. 435-644-2672.

Visitor Use--Lower Paria River Gorge
The diagram below shows the number of visitors to the Lower Paria River Gorge and the Buckskin Gulch in the 1994 through 1996 seasons. These figures should give you some ideas on when to go to avoid the biggest crowds.

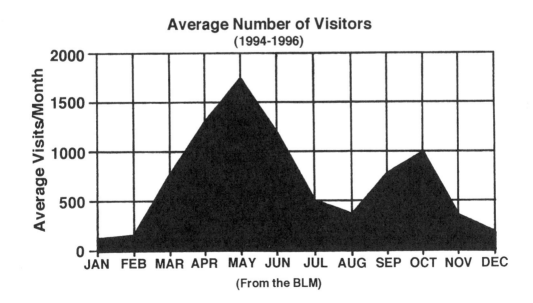

Average Number of Visitors
(1994-1996)

(From the BLM)

Hiking Maps for the Paria River Country

Included here is an index map showing most of the USGS topographic maps of the region. Any serious hiker should get one or several of the maps shown on this index.

There are basically three sets of maps for the area. They include: the newer metric maps at 1:100,000 scale; and the other USGS maps at 1:62,500(15 minute), if still available, and 1:24,000(7.5 minute) scale.

The author prefers the newer metric maps, and uses these almost exclusively. If you buy the three most important maps--**Kanab, Smoky Mountain,** and **Glen Canyon Dam,** you can hike and tour almost the entire region. Other than these, you'll need the **Escalante** map for a couple of hikes, and the **Panguitch** metric map covers the northern end of the Skutumpah Road and Bryce Canyon. Also, the **Fredonia** map covers the House Rock Valley Road and part of the Coyote Buttes. For those people who want to hike the Upper Paria River Gorge, Hackberry Canyon, The Cockscomb and all the tributaries, then the Kanab and Smoky Mountain maps just about cover it all. Only one small corner of the Panguitch map might help with the upper Paria River hike.

One reason the author likes the metric maps is they are relatively new, all dating after 1980. So virtually all present-day roads are shown on these maps. Many other maps date from the 1950's, and lack the newer roads. Another reason, just one map may cover several hikes; whereas with the larger scale maps(1:24.000), you may have to have several maps to cover one hike. The metric maps also fold up and fit in your pocket.

For those who don't understand metrics, you can still get along with these maps because they're laid out in one square mile sections, the same as on all USGS maps. Since all land was surveyed in these section and townships grids, it seems we will never get away from this old system entirely.

For the Lower Paria River Gorge, you might find three USGS maps at 1:62,500 scale, **Paria, Paria Plateau** and **Lee's Ferry.** These are no longer being printed, so if you see them buy them! For this hike, these maps are the very best.

Or you might buy the USGS publication titled **MF-1475--Miscellaneous Field Studies.** In this series of four maps, **A, B, C,** and **D,** are covered Geology, Geochemical Data, Mines and Prospects, and Mineral Resource Potential. Map C or D might be the two best for hiking the canyon. These maps are at 1:62,500 scale, and are based on the regular USGS maps at the same scale. The great thing about these maps is, each one includes all the Lower Paria River Gorge, Lee's Ferry, the Sand Hills-Paria Plateau and the House Rock Valley Road. All on just one map.

Probably the single best map for those hiking the lower canyon, if you can find one, is the old BLM publication, **Hikers Guide to Paria Canyon.** It's presently not being printed, but many BLM employees hope it will have a comeback. It's based on the 1:62,500 scale maps, but concentrates on just the lower gorge with numbers indicating springs, abandoned meander, campsites, etc, but omitting the Paria Plateau or Sand Hills. This map has been replaced by a newer plastic log-book-type booklet map titled **Hiker's Guide to Paria Canyon.** It shows the entire canyon in 30 short segments. It has labeled river miles, campsites, abandoned meanders and springs. Its disadvantage is that it doesn't show the entire canyon on one map; that's the reason some would also like the return of the other BLM map mentioned above.

The last set of maps you might consider are the USGS maps at 1:24,000 scale or 7.5 minute. The maps needed to cover the area from old Pahreah down to Lee's Ferry are: **Eightmile Pass, Fivemile Valley, Pine Hollow Canyon, West Clark Bench, Bridger Point, Glen Canyon City, Coyote Buttes, Poverty Flat, Wrather Arch, Water Pockets** and **Ferry Swale.** The Index to Topographic Maps(next page) shows the ones you'll need in the Upper Paria River Canyon. These maps are all rather new and are very detailed. The only problem the author has with this scale is they cover a small area and you may have to carry 2 or 3 maps to do just one day-hike.

Wilderness Areas of the Paria River

There is one officially designated wilderness area in the region covered by the Paria River. This is the **Paria Canyon--Vermilion Cliffs Wilderness Area**. This is one very long and almost circular wilderness, surrounding the Sand Hills or Paria Plateau.

In the middle and upper parts of the Paria River drainage, there are 4 Wilderness Study Areas, and parts of another. The smallest of the four is **The Cockscomb WSA.** It lies between Highway 89, the Cottonwood Wash Road, and The Box--where the Paria River flows through The Cockscomb. It, for the most part, covers the part of The Cockscomb between The Box and Highway 89. The Hattie Green Mine is found in this section.

Between the townsite of old Pahreah, and the Cottonwood Wash and Skutumpah Roads, is another very large WSA. This one is called the **Paria--Hackberry WSA.** It covers virtually all of the Upper Paria River Gorge and Hackberry Canyon. Also included is Mollies Nipple, No Mans Mesa, Bull Valley Gorge, Upper and Lower Death Valleys, and the lower part of Round Valley Draw.

There are problems with including this vast region into Americas Wilderness System, one of which is the fact that for more than a century, early settlers(and now cattlemen) have used vehicles in the washed-out upper Paria River bottom. Cattlemen still take cattle into the middle parts of this Upper Paria River Gorge with the help of 4WD's. There are also recreationests in that canyon just out joy-riding and test driving their ATV's. (This might be OK, except they don't always stay on the river floodplain.) Since this was an old road, they are doing this legally, at least through 1999. At that time the new management plan for the Grand Staircase-Escalante National Monument may call for an emergency closure of the canyon to motorized vehicles, at least for all except cattlemen. Until 1999, you might try mtn. bikes along the river.

A third area under consideration for wilderness status is **The Blues WSA.** This covers the blue-gray colored clay hills to the southwest of the tip of Table Cliff Plateau. The formations exposed there are: the

Index to Topographic Maps--Paria River Country

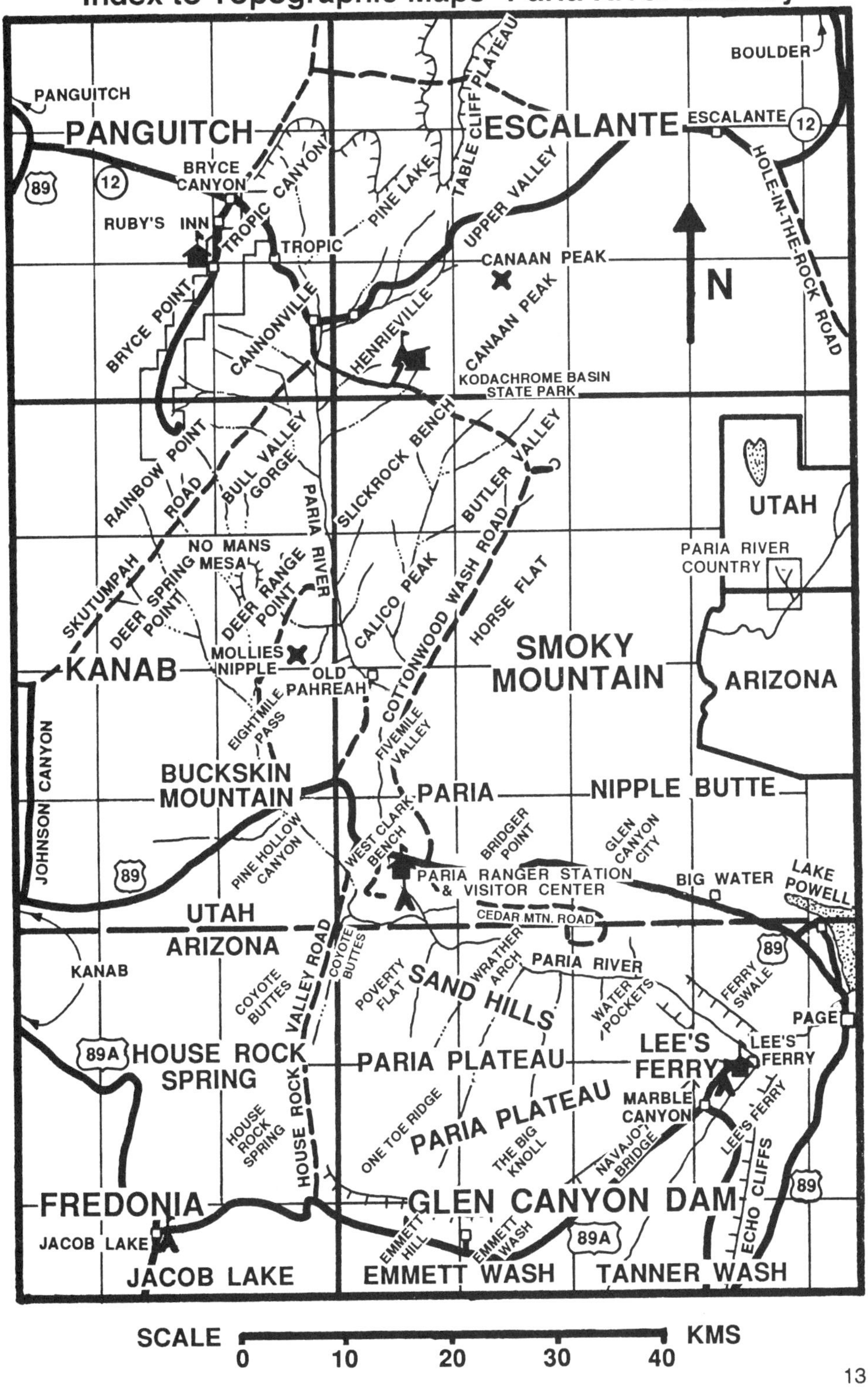

BOULDER

PANGUITCH

PANGUITCH

BRYCE CANYON

ESCALANTE

ESCALANTE 12

89

12

RUBY'S INN

TROPIC

TROPIC CANYON

PINE LAKE

TABLE CLIFF PLATEAU

UPPER VALLEY

HOLE-IN-THE-ROCK ROAD

BRYCE POINT

CANNONVILLE

HENRIEVILLE

CANAAN PEAK ✗

CANAAN PEAK

N

KODACHROME BASIN STATE PARK

RAINBOW POINT ROAD

BULL VALLEY GORGE

PARIA RIVER

SLICKROCK BENCH

BUTLER VALLEY

UTAH

PARIA RIVER COUNTRY

SKUTUMPAH

NO MANS MESA

DEER SPRING POINT

DEER RANGE POINT

CALICO PEAK

COTTONWOOD WASH ROAD

HORSE FLAT

SMOKY MOUNTAIN

ARIZONA

KANAB

MOLLIES NIPPLE ✗

OLD PAHREAH

EIGHTMILE PASS

FIVEMILE VALLEY

JOHNSON CANYON

BUCKSKIN MOUNTAIN

PARIA

NIPPLE BUTTE

PINE HOLLOW CANYON

89

WEST CLARK BENCH

BRIDGER POINT

GLEN CANYON CITY

BIG WATER

LAKE POWELL

PARIA RANGER STATION & VISITOR CENTER

UTAH

ARIZONA

KANAB

CEDAR MTN. ROAD

89

VALLEY ROAD

COYOTE BUTTES

COYOTE BUTTES

POVERTY FLAT

SAND HILLS

WRATHER ARCH

PARIA RIVER

WATER POCKETS

FERRY SWALE

PAGE

89A

HOUSE ROCK SPRING

HOUSE ROCK SPRING

HOUSE ROCK

PARIA PLATEAU

ONE TOE RIDGE

PARIA PLATEAU

THE BIG KNOLL

LEE'S FERRY

LEE'S FERRY

MARBLE CANYON

NAVAJO BRIDGE

LEE'S FERRY

ECHO CLIFFS

89

FREDONIA

JACOB LAKE

JACOB LAKE

GLEN CANYON DAM

EMMETT HILL

EMMETT WASH

89A

EMMETT WASH

TANNER WASH

SCALE

0   10   20   30   40

KMS

13

Wilderness and Wilderness Study Areas (WSA's)

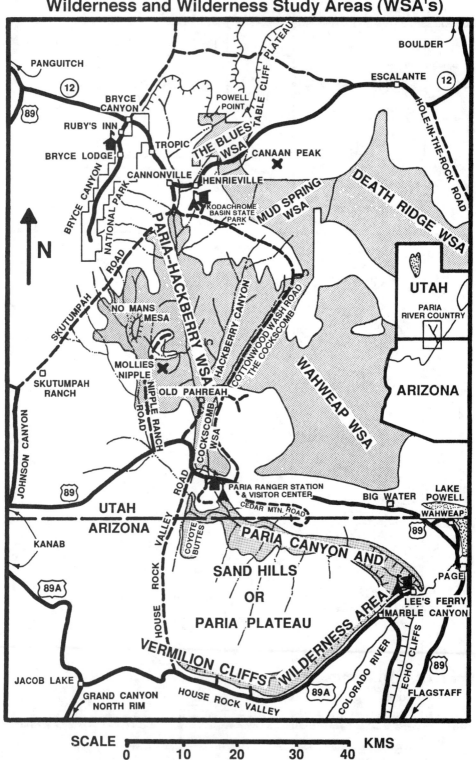

SCALE

0   10   20   30   40   KMS

Kaiparowits, Wahweap, Straight Cliffs and Tropic Shale. Much of the area has a resemblance to the Mancos Shale beds west of the towns of Green River and Hanksville. Next to The Blues WSA and just to the southeast is **Mud Spring WSA**. This one is just south of Canaan Peak, part of which is not in the scope of this book.

The last WSA included in the Paria Basin is the **Wahweap WSA.** It extends out of the area covered in this book and almost to Lake Powell. Part of it covers the upper parts of The Cockscomb, which is just to the east of the Cottonwood Wash Road. The Cockscomb is one of the more spectacular and fotogenic features on the Colorado Plateau.

In Arizona, many new wilderness areas have been set aside in the last few years, but Utah is lagging behind. All the BLM controlled WSA's in Utah are still floundering in Congress.

As this book goes to press, no one is sure what will happen to the WSA's within the boundaries of this book, or any others within the confines of the newly established Grand Staircase-Escalante National Monument. By 1999 we should know. Stay tuned.

Fotography in Slot Canyons

If you've talked to anyone who has tried taking fotos in some of the deep, dark, narrow canyons of the Colorado Plateau, and especially slot canyons like Buckskin Gulch, Bull Valley Gorge and Round Valley Draw, they'll likely tell you their pictures weren't worth writing home about. Since most of these hikers have tried taking fotos in such places only once or twice in their lives, failures are understandable. Here are some tips on how to make your pictures better on your first trip.

Some of the more common problems are these. Maybe the worst thing that happens is that the fotos turn out far too dark; there being very little light in the narrow canyon. One obvious reason for this is the camera doesn't have the capabilities to take a good picture in dark places.

Another common problem is the pictures are fuzzy or blurred or simply out of focus. This can be caused by a combination of low light, a slow shutter speed, and no tripod. Still another problem is, half of a foto may be very bright or totally washed out, while the other half is dark, sometimes black and shows almost nothing. This is caused by taking a picture with half of the area in bright sunshine; the other half in the shade or shadows. These are the more common problems. Below are some suggestions on how you can correct the situation.

Camera and Lens

The most common type of camera used by hikers these days is the 35 mm, with a through-the-lens metering system. Others may still use the instamatic-type.

The recommended equipment to take is a 35 mm camera and two lenses; one the normal 50 mm which comes with the camera, and a moderately wide angle lens, such as a 24 mm, 28 mm or 35 mm. A lens wider than about 24 mm, will distort the foto more than most people want. If only one lens could be taken, the author would likely choose a 28 mm or 35 mm. A serious fotographer will take at least two lenses, perhaps more.

Most of these 35 mm cameras have a shutter speed range from one full second up to 1/1000 of a second. In the darker canyons, you'll likely be using shutter speeds of 1/30 to 1/15 of a second, or lower, depending on your film speed.

The author now carries a Pentax K-1000, a totally mechanical camera, with a through-the-lens metering system, and a screw-on self-timer. He would prefer a built-in timer, because he uses it often.

Mechanical cameras, of which there are very few on the market today, are much more sturdy and can withstand more bumps and abuse than the newer electronic models. Mechanical cameras are also more likely to work after they've been dropped in water than the electronic ones. They are also easier and less expensive to repair. With electronic cameras, you may have a developing minor short in the electrical system, but which the repairman can't find or fix. The mechanical camera is easily diagnosed and repairs made quickly.

The author carries at all times a 50 mm lens, a 28 mm, and a 70-210 mm zoom lens. The zoom lens is seldom used in the canyons, but was used often when fotographing more open areas in this book. In the past, zoom lenses have been pretty poor quality, but the newer ones are much improved. There are new models out now which range from 28 mm to 70 mm, or there a bouts. This would be a good lens to have, except that it would be rather slow; that is, the F stop would be no better than about 2.8, and likely closer to 3.5, which makes it difficult to take good fotos in dark places unless you have a tripod. A lens with an F stop of 1.4 or 1.7, allows much more light onto the film than a 2.8 or 3.5 lens. Try to have a lens of F 2.0, or faster, if you can.

Film Type

Besides using a fast lens(F1.4 or F1.7), you can also compensate for the darkness by using a faster film. Film speeds range from a slow 25, 50, or 64 ASA, up to a fast 400 or 1000 ASA. If you're out on the ski slopes on a bright sunny day, you'd want a film with a slow speed, such as 25 or 50 ASA. But if you're in darker places such as Buckskin Gulch, you'll want one of the faster films such as 200, 400 or 1000 ASA. The author now uses mostly 100 ASA color slide film, and it works well in bright sunny scenes, but only moderately well in the darkest canyons.

Another technique you can use, is to "push" the film. For example, if you use 200 ASA Ektachrome (color slide film), you can set your camera ASA setting on 400 or 800 ASA, which is one or two full stops ahead. This higher setting(say two full stops) will change your shutter speed from 1/15 of a second, to 1/60 of a second. In this example, instead of using a tripod, you can hand hold the camera and still get good results.

When it comes time to develop the film, you'll have to take it to a lab which specializes in film finishing and tell them you pushed the film either one or two stops. They will then leave it in the developer for a longer period of time, thus compensating for the adjustment you made with the ASA setting on the camera.

You can use this "pushing" technique on Ektachrome 200 or 400 ASA film(or any color slide film which uses the E-6 processing method, such as Agfachrome 200 ASA), or B+W 400 ASA film. If using the B+W 400 film, you can push it as far as 1600 ASA, or two stops, which would virtually eliminate the need for a tripod. Lab people have also told the author this technique does not work for color print film, such as the new 1000 ASA Kodacolor print film. But that's plenty fast anyway--and grainy as hell! Before you try this method of "pushing the ASA", better call a local lab first, to get everything straight in your mind.

Tripod or Camera Stand

Carrying a tripod or camera stand down a long canyon is asking a lot for most people, but it will pay off with better results. Actually, if you have a fairly fast lens(F1.4 or F1.7), a fast film(200, 400 or 1000 ASA), and compensate by pushing the film(one roll of film in the darkest narrows only) one or two full F-stops, you can sometimes get by without the tripod.

In the past the author often used an old ski pole as a walking stick which was modified to double as a camera stand. You can use a walking stick to probe for deep holes in murky waters, and stick it in the mud or sand and with the aid of a small camera clamp on top, use it as a tripod too. One thing to remember though; when using a contraption like this in a very dark part of the narrows and with the shutter speed at perhaps 1/15 of a second or less, be sure to lean your camera against the canyon wall. Otherwise, you'll get a swaying motion in the single leg, which will blur your foto.

If your camera indicates the shutter speed is below 1/30 of a second, use a stand of some kind--either a rock, tripod, or walking stick. Sometimes you can lean against a wall and get moderately good results by hand-holding it at 1/15 of a second, but rarely.

Also remember, that the lower the F-stop number(F-2), the smaller the field of focus will be; a higher F-stop number(F16) means more of your picture will be in focus. This is where a tripod is indispensable. By having your camera firmly mounted, you can leave the shutter open for up to one full second on most 35mm cameras. With these very low shutter speeds, you may then have the F-stop up to 8, 11 or 16. If you can get numbers like this in a dark canyon, then all or most of everything in your picture will be in focus. If on the other hand, you have to hand-hold your camera at a 30th of a second, you may have an F-stop of 2, 2.8 or 3.5, which means very little of your picture will be in focus.

More Tips

When in a dark place like the Buckskin Gulch, never take a foto where there's a streak of sunlight in your subject area. If you do, part of the picture will be washed out with too much light; the other part will be dark or totally black. Instead, take a picture where the sunlight is being bounced off the upper wall, and diffused down into the slot bottom.

Another way would be to wait for a cloud to cover the sun, then the light is diffused, thus eliminating the harsh contrasts between sun and shadow. The best time to take fotos in the slot canyons is often in mid-morning or mid-afternoon. This way you can easily find places where the sun isn't shining directly down into the narrows, but instead is shining on an upper wall, and is bounced or diffused down into the dark corners.

If you should slip and fall into water, or somehow drop your camera in a stream, here are the steps to take. Immediately take the camera battery out. Quickly roll the film back into the canister, and remove it. Open the camera and shake and blow out any water. Allow it to sit in the sun to dry, turning it occasionally to help evaporate any water inside. If you're near your car, start the engine, turn on the heater, and hang the camera in front of a heat vent. The warmer the camera gets, the better. This helps the water evaporate more quickly. The quicker the water evaporates, the less corrosion there will be on the electrical system; and less rust will be on any metal parts.

If your camera is under water for just a second or less, there likely will not be any moisture inside the camera. In this case, by following the above steps, you will likely be fotographing again in half an hour, especially if the water is clear, no sand has gotten into the camera, and if the sun is warm. The author has had a number of little accidents and with each of his cameras. The last several times, no repair work was needed because he did the right things to get the camera dry fast.

Here are some tips for those going to **Coyote Buttes**. Take plenty of film. Use film that's heavy on reds and yellows like Kodak Gold or 3M Company film such as K-Mart's Focal brand. Under exposing a little seems to bring out the colors better. A Polaroid filter may help(?). The Wave is one place you don't want shadows, so be there between 10:30 am and 1:30 pm solar time--not daylight savings time--for best results. Be there on a day with 100% pure clear unfiltered & unadulterated sunshine--something that's difficult under the present booking & reservation policy!

The Grand Staircase-Escalante National Monument

Our newest national monument was established September 18, 1996 by President Clinton. It will be the only national monument in America to be administered by the BLM.

Here are the approximate boundaries of the GSENM. On the west is Johnson Valley or Canyon; on the south it's roughly US Highway 89 or the Utah-Arizona line and Lake Powell; on the north it's Bryce Valley, Escalante and Boulder; while on the east it's Capitol Reef National Park and Glen Canyon National Recreation Area. In the Paria River drainage, it begins at the wilderness boundary south of the Whitehouse

Trailhead and includes all land north up to Kodachrome Basin State Park and all of the land along the Skutumpah Road below the boundary of Bryce Canyon National Park.

As this book goes to press, BLM planners in Cedar City are working on a 3 year management plan for the GSENM. That should be finished in the fall of 1999.

<u>Warning:</u>

<u>Don't blame me if you get into trouble in some canyon or out in the desert!</u>
<u>It's Your Choice and Your Responsibility!</u>

This writer has tried his best to inform readers of potential dangers or problems that might occur if they visit some far away place in Utah. He has done his best to advise the reader of road conditions, weather patterns, and the best time of year to travel or to hike. He has also tried to make the maps as accurate and as easy to read as possible. He has done his best to inform readers about some of the more important items to take in their car, and where someone might get a safe drink of water. However, roads can be washed out by a sudden thunderstorm, or a big snow storm might make it impossible to drive a section of road. Things change! So it's up to each person to anticipate problems and go as well-prepared as possible.

If you go out along the Skutumpah Road in mid-winter without proper clothing or tire chains, and get stuck and freeze to death, don't blame this writer! If you go somewhere in mid-summer without enough water and your vehicle breaks down, and you choke to death, don't blame this book! If you go ill-prepared, don't take the proper maps, or do something stupid, and perish or have to be rescued, don't blame anyone here! No one is being forced to go into the wilderness; nobody is twisting your arm. You make the decision to go on your own! **This writer bears no responsibility for mistakes you might make or for your own stupidity or neglect!**

Charcoal pictographs in a cave in Starlight Canyon.

Colorful red & white rocks at the beginning of the hike into the Upper Cottonwood Wash Narrows.

Navajo Sandstone jointed rocks located just west of Castle Rock.

Metric Conversion Table

1 Centimeter = 0.39 Inch
1 Inch = 2.54 Centimeters
1 Meter = 39.37 Inches
1 Foot = 0.3048 Meter
1 Kilometer = 0.621 Mile

1 Mile = 1.609 Kilometers
100 Miles = 161 Kilometers
100 Kilometers = 62.1 Miles
1 Liter = 1.056 Quarts(US)
1 Kilogram = 2.205 Pounds

1 Pound = 453 Grams
1 Quart(US) = 0.946 Liter
1 Gallon(US) = 3.785 Liters
1 Acre = 0.405 Hectare
1 Hectare = 2.471 Acres

METERS TO FEET (Meters x 3.2808 = Feet)

100 m = 328 ft.	2500 m = 8202 ft.	5000 m = 16404 ft.	7500 m = 24606 ft.
500 m = 1640 ft.	3000 m = 9842 ft.	5500 m = 18044 ft.	8000 m = 26246 ft.
1000 m = 3281 ft.	3500 m = 11483 ft.	6000 m = 19686 ft.	8500 m = 27887 ft.
1500 m = 4921 ft.	4000 m = 13124 ft.	6500 m = 21325 ft.	9000 m = 29527 ft.
2000 m = 6562 ft.	4500 m = 14764 ft.	7000 m = 22966 ft.	

FEET TO METERS (Feet ÷ 3.2808 = Meters)

1000 ft. = 305 m	9000 ft. = 2743 m	16000 ft. = 4877 m	23000 ft. = 7010 m
2000 ft. = 610 m	10000 ft. = 3048 m	17000 ft. = 5182 m	24000 ft. = 7315 m
3000 ft. = 914 m	11000 ft. = 3353 m	18000 ft. = 5486 m	25000 ft. = 7620 m
4000 ft. = 1219 m	12000 ft. = 3658 m	19000 ft. = 5791 m	26000 ft. = 7925 m
5000 ft. = 1524 m	13000 ft. = 3962 m	20000 ft. = 6096 m	27000 ft. = 8230 m
6000 ft. = 1829 m	14000 ft. = 4268 m	21000 ft. = 6401 m	28000 ft. = 8535 m
7000 ft. = 2134 m	15000 ft. = 4572 m	22000 ft. = 6706 m	29000 ft. = 8839 m
8000 ft. = 2438 m			30000 ft. = 9144 m

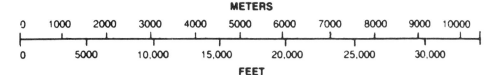

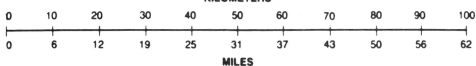

Map Symbols

Town or Community.................. ☐ ☐

Peak and Prominent Ridge ..... ━✕━

Building, Cabin or Home .... ◻

Stream or Creek, Desert .... 〰

Backcountry Campsite................ ▲

Stream or Creek, Mountain......... 〜

Campsite with Vehicle Access .... 🏠

Large River .... ▓▓▓

Campground............................. 🏕

Stream--Intermittent or Dry........ ─··─

Cemetery or Grave Site .... ⊞ †

Canyon Narrows.................... ▨▨▨

Ranger Station, Visitor Center..... 🏚🏠

Lake or Pond...................... 🌑 ◁

Airport or Landing Strip................ ✈

Waterfall or Dryfall.................. ─┼┼

U.S. Highway & Mile Posts ... ━┼━(89)
20 21

Spring, Seep or Well.................... ○

Utah State Highway .... ━━(24)

Canyon Rim, Escarpment........... ⌐⌐⌐⌐

Road--Maintained................. ≡≡≡

Natural Arch, Corral .... ∩ ⌐

Road--4 Wheel Drive(4WD)...... ═════

Mine, Quarry, Adit, Prospect .... ✖↗

Track--Road, Unusable.......... ━ ━ ━

Geology Cross Section.............. ⌐_⌐

Trail, Foot or Horse .... ─ ─ ─

Pass................................. ⌇

Route, No Trail...................... ••••••

Pictograph .... (PIC)

Cowboyglyph or Campground........ (CG)

Petroglyphs .... (PET)

Elevation in Meters......................1490

Abbreviations

Canyon ....C.	Campground & Cowboyglyphs........CG.
Lake..L.	Campsites ....CS.
River..R.	Two Wheel Drive Vehicle or Road...2WD
Creek...Ck.	Four Wheel Drive Vehicle or Road..4WD
Peak...Pk.	High Clearance Vehicle or Road......HCV
Waterfall, Dryfall, Formation ....F.	Spring...Sp.
Kilometer(s) ....km, kms	Sandstone......................................S.S.

United States Geological Survey... USGS
National Park Service..NPS
Bureau of Land Management ....BLM

Reference--Index Map of Hikes

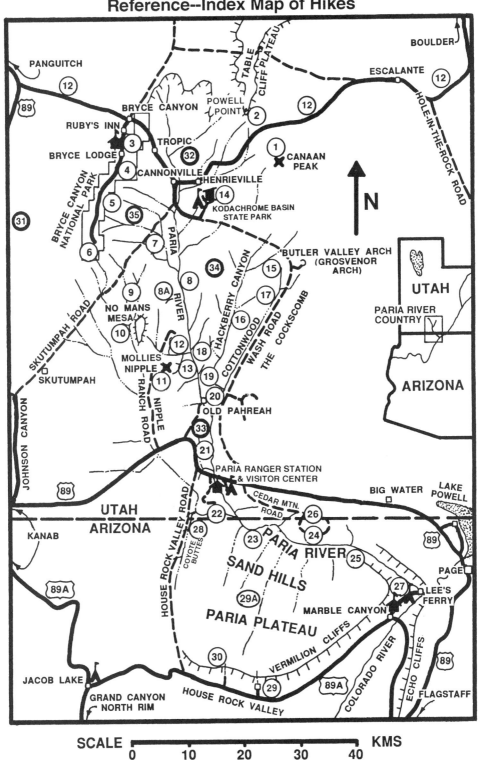

SCALE ⊢━━━━━━━━━━━━━━━━━━━━━⊣ KMS
0   10   20   30   40

21

Canaan Peak

Location and Access Canaan Peak, which rises to 2833 meters, is located about mid-way between the Bryce Valley towns of Tropic, Cannonville and Henrieville; and Escalante. It's also just southeast of Highway 12 as you pass through the area. The top part of Canaan Peak is made up of the same formation as is found at Bryce Canyon N.P. and Table Cliff Plateau, but its bright red limestone caprock is almost eroded away. All other surrounding hills or mountains have lost this Wasatch Formation cap, except Table Cliff Plateau, which isn't far away to the northwest. To get to the trail and trailhead on this mountain hike, drive along Highway 12, the link between Bryce Canyon and Escalante. Just northeast of mile post 45, turn south at the sign stating, *South Hollow and Canaan Peak.* Drive south about 8 kms on a rather good and well-maintained dirt road. The starting point is just before you cross the upper part of Willow Creek. You can either park right on this main road--if you can see or find the trail markers on the trees; or drive the short dirt track to the metal stock trough, as shown on the map. Near this stock trough is a good place to camp.

Trail or Route Conditions It's probably easier to find the trail(which isn't used that often) if you'll use the little insert map to find and locate the metal stock trough just below Pole Spring. Best to park there, then head due south up the minor canyon towards the spring. After the dirt road peters out, watch closely for trail markers on the trees, which look like an "i". Once on the trail, it's easy to follow, but the Forest Service doesn't remove dead-fall very often, so you'll have to jump over some downed trees occasionally. When you arrive on the west side of the main peak, the horse trail then intersects a very old logging road, which was unusable for vehicles in 1997. At about that point, you can walk straight up the slope to the top-most ridge, then south to the summit; or continue around to the southeast side of the mountain and climb from there. The south face of the peak is very rugged.

Elevations Trailheads, about 2560 and 2600 meters; the summit, 2833 meters.

Hike Length and Time Needed Length to the top is about 3 to 4 kms, and will take only 3 to 4 hours to climb, round-trip.

Water At Pole Spring, but none on the mountain above that point, so take your own.

Maps USGS or BLM map Escalante(1:100,000), or Canaan Peak and Upper Valley(1:24,000).

Main Attractions A short day-hike in a cool and little known mountain region, with many good camp sites. A nice place to visit in the heat of summer.

Ideal Time to Hike From about mid-May until the end of October, but each year is a little different. Get there too early or too late, and you'll find muddy roads.

Hiking Boots Any dry weather boots or shoes.

Author's Experience The author had to hunt around for the trailhead on his first trip, but after locating it, went quickly up the trail, and to the summit from the southeast side. He came down the west slope and returned to his car in less than 3 hours. In 1997, he re-hiked roughly the same route in about 2 hours round-trip.

Canaan Peak, as seen from an old logging road just to the south.

Map 1, Canaan Peak

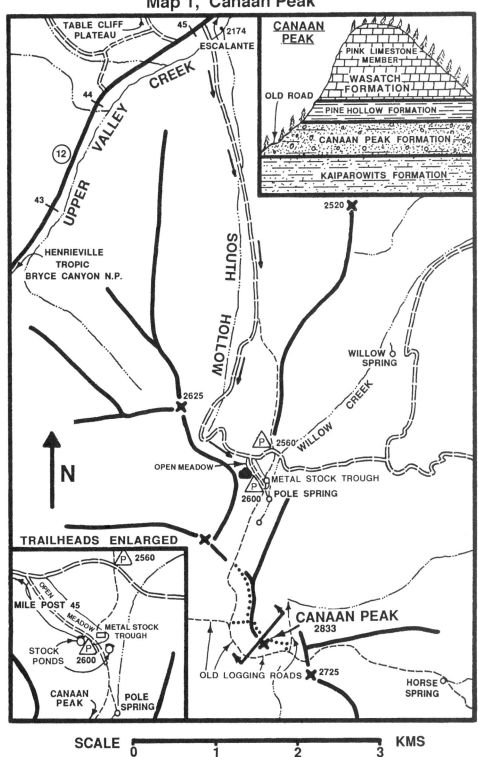

TABLE CLIFF PLATEAU

45

2174

ESCALANTE

CREEK

44

(12)

43

UPPER VALLEY

HENRIEVILLE
TROPIC
BRYCE CANYON N.P.

SOUTH HOLLOW

CANAAN PEAK

PINK LIMESTONE MEMBER

WASATCH FORMATION

OLD ROAD

PINE HOLLOW FORMATION

CANAAN PEAK FORMATION

KAIPAROWITS FORMATION

2520

WILLOW SPRING

WILLOW CREEK

N

2625

P 2560

OPEN MEADOW

METAL STOCK TROUGH

P

2600

POLE SPRING

TRAILHEADS ENLARGED

P 2560

OPEN

MILE POST 45

MEADOW

METAL STOCK TROUGH

STOCK PONDS

P

2600

CANAAN PEAK

POLE SPRING

CANAAN PEAK
2833

OLD LOGGING ROADS

2725

HORSE SPRING

SCALE

0   1   2   3   KMS

23

Table Cliff Plateau & Powell Point

Location and Access Table Cliff Plateau is located about halfway between Escalante and the Bryce Valley towns of Tropic, Cannonville and Henrieville. Table Cliff Plateau, or at least its very southern tip known as Powell Point, is one of the most prominent landmarks in southern Utah. To reach this hike, drive along Highway 12 between Henrieville and Escalante. The shortest route to Powell Point, can be found by leaving the highway very near mile post 44, and driving towards Pine Hollow; but this road is rough in places and you'll likely need a HCV of some kind to make it to the trailhead at 2400 meters. To reach the much better normal driving route, continue along the highway to near mile post 45, and head northwest from there to the Garden Spring area; or leave the highway halfway between mile posts 46 & 47. Again drive northwest toward Garden Spring. This loop-road was in very good condition for all vehicles in October of 1997. Just southwest of Garden Spring is the sign pointing out the trail, but if you go just a bit south of the sign, you'll see a rough road heading toward Water Canyon. Most vehicles can probably make it up this old logging road to the trailhead at 2500 meters.

Trail or Route Conditions From the trailhead at 2500 meters, there's a fairly well-marked, but little-used trail, to the top of Table Cliff Plateau. Once on this trail it should be easy to follow. It heads up the steep escarpment of the Plateau, then meets the rather good "home made" vehicle track running south to Powell Point. Once on this track, walk to where the road ends and a foot trail begins. Then it's a short walk through bristlecone pines to Powell Point. A shorter second route comes up from Pine Hollow. There are a number of old logging roads in that area, so follow which ever one seems to lead in the direction you're going. The track leading towards "running water" is an easy route, then the very steep(but not dangerous) slope up the escarpment to the top, and finally by road and trail to Powell Point.

Elevations Trailheads, 2390, 2400 and 2500 meters; the highest point on top is about 3125 meters.

Hike Length and Time Needed The sign at the Garden Spring Trailhead reads "6 miles", or 10 kms, to Barney Top and to Table Cliffs. This surely means it's 10 kms to Powell Point from that trailhead, making it about 8 or 9 kms from the upper trailhead in Water Canyon. It's about 7 kms to Powell Point from the Pine Hollow area, depending on where you actually park. If you park at Garden Spring, better plan on an all-day outing, round-trip. But it's a shorter day-hike, and a half-day hike for some, if you go in from Pine Hollow, or Water Canyon Trailhead.

Water In early June, the author found running water in upper Pine Hollow and in Water Canyon(a year-round flow). There's no water on top so always take some in your car and in your pack.

Maps USGS or BLM map Escalante(1:100,000), or Upper Valley and Pine Lake(1:24,000).

Main Attractions Splendid views, a cool summer hike, and quiet campsites.

Ideal Time to Hike From late May to late October, but each year is a little different.

Hiking Boots Any dry weather boots or shoes.

Author's Experience The author walked the Pine Hollow route from his camp near the highway. He came down Water Canyon, but failed to locate the top part of the trail. He later found it at the bottom of the escarpment near the upper trailhead. Then it was road-walking back to his car, all in 5 hours, round-trip. In October, 1997, he drove along this loop-road, but didn't hike.

The east face of Table Cliff Plateau. Powell Point is to the left.

Map 2, Table Cliff Plateau & Powell Point

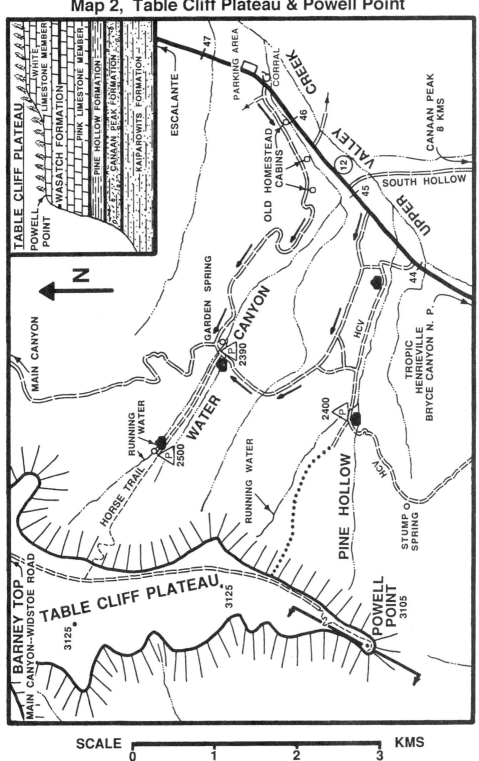

Fairyland Trail, Bryce Canyon National Park

Location and Access Included in this book are four maps covering the trails in Bryce Canyon National Park. This is the most northerly of the four, and is the most northerly of all trails in the park. The Fairyland Trail winds its way down through canyons and *hoodoos,* and also follows the rim of Bryce Canyon for a good part of its length. This walking path is located about due east of the park visitor center and North Campground. One place you can begin is at Fairyland Point. To get there, take the first road running east just after you enter the park as you drive south from the Ruby's Inn area. This turnoff is *before* you arrive at the visitor center and entrance fee station. At Fairyland Point is a parking lot and view point only. At or near Sunrise Point is another place to begin. It's near the old historic Bryce Canyon Lodge. Once inside the park just follow the signs. Another starting point is anywhere within the confines of the North Campground.

Trail or Route Conditions The Fairyland Trail, as is the case with all trails in this national park, is a constructed walking path and well-maintained. You can't get lost, and all trail junctions and points of interest are well sign-posted. This trail makes for easy walking, for those accustomed to hiking. It's an up and down hike all the way.

Elevations From a high point of about 2465 meters, down to about 2200 meters.

Hike Length and Time Needed This hike is divided into two parts; the Fairyland Trail, running down into the canyons; and the Rim Trail. If you start at or near Sunrise Point and walk down along the Fairyland Trail, then it's just over 8 kms to Fairyland Point. From Fairyland Point back along the rim to Sunrise Point, is just over 5 kms. So the length of the loop is about 13 kms. Some people can do this loop-hike in as little as 3 hours, but for most it's a 4 or 5 hour walk. You can shorten it just a bit, if you begin at the campground or Fairyland Point, thus eliminating the short walk to or from Sunrise Point. You could eliminate the Rim Trail part between trailheads by using a mtn. bike on the paved roads.

Water There are no springs or running water anywhere along this trail, so if it's warm weather, be sure to take some water with you(up to 2 liters on a hot summer day). In cooler weather, and if you're a fast and fit hiker, you can likely make it OK without water or a lunch.

Maps Trails Illustrated map Paunsaugunt Plateau, Mount Dutton, Bryce Canyon(1:50,000); or Bryce Canyon National Park(1:31,680). Both maps can be bought at the visitor center.

Main Attractions Easy access, a good and well-maintained trail, very little other foot traffic, and at least the second best area of the park for walking through and seeing the *hoodoos.* See the geology cross section.

Ideal Time to Hike May through October. Mid-summer can be a bit warm, as the altitude is only moderately high. Winter hiking could be fun too, for the properly equipped hiker, but it's not marked for winter use. Snow cover is generally light in this section of the park during winter, but in some years it can be a meter or more deep.

Hiking Boots Any dry weather boots or shoes.

Author's Experience The author started at Sunrise Point and made the loop-hike in about 3 hours on a very cool May morning.

Typical scene along the Fairyland Trail, in Bryce Canyon National Park.

Map 3, Fairyland Trail, Bryce Canyon National Park

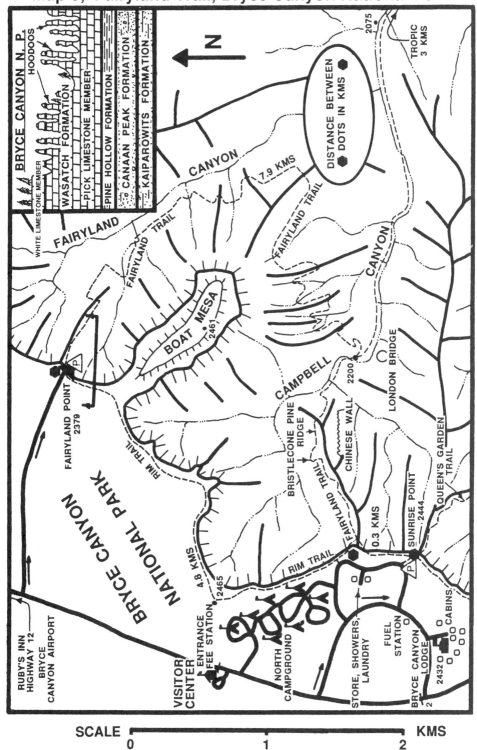

SCALE

0   1   2   KMS

The front or east side of the historic Bryce Canyon Lodge.

One of a dozen or so rustic cabins you can rent at Bryce Canyon. This one is located near the Bryce Canyon Lodge.

The Tropic Canal, seen just south of Ruby's Inn. It was built in 1892, to take water from the East Fork of the Sevier River, into Bryce Valley and Tropic.

Wall Street, along the Navajo Trail.

Navajo, Peekaboo & Queen's Garden Trails, Bryce C.

Location and Access The several trails on this map are near the center of Bryce Canyon National Park, and are in the area which has the most visitation. These trails may be the most touristy of all, but the scenery is also the best in the park. It's here you can walk right through the narrow canyons of *hoodoos,* the erosional spires so prominent in this section of the park and for which the park is famous. There are three possible starting points from the rim. They are: Sunrise, Sunset and Bryce Points. The first two are the most used, since they are very near the historic Bryce Canyon Lodge, cabins and campgrounds. There are paved roads to each trailhead, and now all the roads shown on this map are kept open on a year-round basis.

Trail or Route Conditions All trails on this map are in good condition and well-maintained. All junctions are signposted, and in some places there are benches to sit on for a rest. Walking is very easy and very enjoyable, especially for those visiting the park for the first time.

Elevations Sunset Point, 2431 meters; Sunrise Point, 2444; Bryce Point, 2529; and the lowest part of the Navajo Trail, about 2280 meters.

Hike Length and Time Needed On the map are some large dots and numbers in between. These numbers represent the kilomage between dots. None of the distances are very great. To walk down the Navajo, then along the Peekaboo Loop-Trail, and finish the hike by walking up the Queen's Garden Trail to Sunrise Point, and finally back to the starting place at Sunset Point, is to walk about 10.5 kms. This can be done in as little as 2 hours by a fast hiker, but most would want about 4 hours, or about half a day for the trip. Some would want to take a lunch and drinks and spend more than half a day on this hike, especially if one were to take in some short side trips, such as the walk up through Wall Street. A mtn. bike left at one trailhead would eliminate a tiresome road walk, especially if you start or end the hike at Bryce Point.

Water There is no running water anywhere in this area, so plan to take your own.

Maps Trails Illustrated map Paunsaugunt Plateau, Mount Dutton, Bryce Canyon(1:50,000); or Bryce Canyon National Park(1:31,680). Both maps can be bought at the visitor center.

Main Attractions The trails on this map give the hiker the best opportunity of any location in the park, to walk through and see at close quarters, the famous bright red spires of Bryce Canyon called *hoodoos.*

Ideal Time to Hike May through October, but mid-summer can be a little warm at lower altitudes. Because of relatively light snowfall, it's also possible to hike these trails in winter. However, in some winters the snow can pile up to more than a meter deep. Each year is different.

Hiking Boots Any dry weather boots or shoes.

Author's Experience The author worked at the lodge during the summer of 1965, so has been on these trails often. Later, he re-walked the Queen's Garden & Navajo Loop in a couple of hours.

Another look at the Hoodoos near Bryce Canyon Lodge. In the distance is
Table Cliff Plateau and Powell Point.

Map 4, Navajo, Peekaboo & Queen's Garden Trails, B.C.

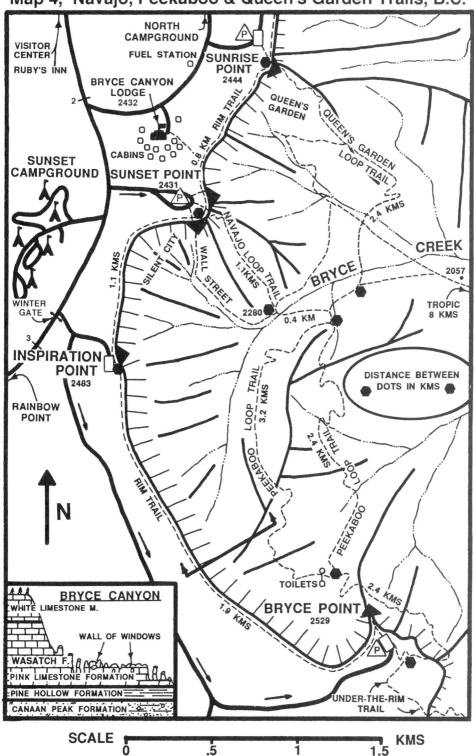

VISITOR CENTER
RUBY'S INN

NORTH CAMPGROUND

FUEL STATION

SUNRISE POINT
2444

BRYCE CANYON LODGE
2432

QUEEN'S GARDEN

QUEEN'S GARDEN LOOP TRAIL

SUNSET CAMPGROUND

CABINS

SUNSET POINT
2431

0.8 KM RIM TRAIL

2.4 KMS

CREEK

SILENT CITY

WALL STREET

NAVAJO LOOP TRAIL
1.1KMS

BRYCE

2057

1.1 KMS

2280

0.4 KM

TROPIC
8 KMS

WINTER GATE

INSPIRATION POINT
2483

DISTANCE BETWEEN DOTS IN KMS

RAINBOW POINT

PEEKABOO LOOP TRAIL 3.2 KMS

2.4 KMS

N

PEEKABOO LOOP TRAIL

RIM TRAIL

TOILETS

2.4 KMS

BRYCE POINT
2529

1.9 KMS

BRYCE CANYON
WHITE LIMESTONE M.

WALL OF WINDOWS

WASATCH F.

PINK LIMESTONE FORMATION

PINE HOLLOW FORMATION

CANAAN PEAK FORMATION

UNDER-THE-RIM TRAIL

SCALE

KMS

0   .5   1   1.5

31

Under-the-Rim Trail, Bryce Canyon National Park

Location and Access This rather long trail runs from Bryce Point near the center of Bryce Canyon National Park, south to Rainbow Point, which is at the very southern end of the park. This trail runs north-south along the eastern base of the Pink Cliffs, and offers both day and overnight hikes. In recent years, roads in the park up to Bryce Point have been kept open year-round. And if snow isn't too deep, and if graders are available, the road is sometimes plowed all the way to Rainbow Point.

Trail or Route Conditions Being in a national park, this trail is well-marked, so one can't get lost; it's well-signposted, especially at trail junctions, and there are signs along the way indicating campsite locations. Because this hike is so long, it's necessary for most people to camp one night. There are seven campsites along the way, all in the shade of giant ponderosa pines. Campsites are shown on the map. These campsites are never crowded, as very few hikers camp along this trail. This is a wilderness hike, even though it's near a busy highway. Be sure to get your camping permit at the visitor center before staying overnight on this trail.

Elevations Bryce Point, 2529 meters; low point on the trail, about 2050(but most is much higher), and Rainbow Point, 2776 meters.

Hike Length and Time Needed From Bryce Point to Rainbow Point is about 35 kms. This means the average hiker will need a day and a half, or two days. However, a fast hiker can do it in one long day with an early start and two cars(or perhaps the use of a mtn. bike). Water is scare along this trail, so day-hiking is worth considering. Also, consider doing the hike in stages, by using one of the connecting trails, thus shortening the hike, and eliminating the need to carry water for camping. The connecting trails are called: Sheep Creek, Swamp Canyon, Whiteman, and Agua Canyon Trails. On this map, distance between dots is in kms.

Water One major problem along this hike is lack of water. In Spring, just after the snow melts there's usually running water in most creek bottoms, but they dry up later on. Consult park rangers at the visitor center as to the whereabouts of water before hiking. Iron Spring has a good flow, but the water is undrinkable; Birch Spring has a small discharge, but may be dry late in summer. Lack of a good water supply is the reason this is not a real popular backpacking trail.

Maps Trails Illustrated map Pausaugunt Plateau, Mount Dutton, Bryce Canyon(1:50,000); or Bryce Canyon National Park(1:31,680). Both maps can be bought at the visitor center.

Main Attractions A forested trail hike along the base of the Pink Cliffs.

Ideal Time to Hike From about May through October, but there will be more water around in May or June.

Hiking Boots Any dry weather boots or shoes.

Author's Experience The author hiked the entire trail, but in four stages, using all connecting trails. This took two days to complete. On one hike from Bryce Point to Sheep Creek Trailhead, then the road-walk back to his car, took about 4 1/2 hours. A mtn. bike would eliminate a road-walk.

The middle part of the park is the best place to see the famous Bryce Canyon Hoodoos.

Map 5, Under-the-Rim Trail, Bryce Canyon National Pk.

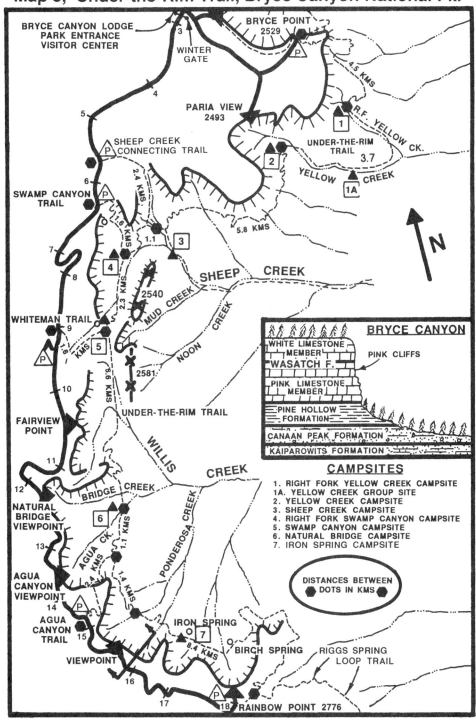

SCALE 0   3   6 KMS

Riggs Spring Loop Trail, Bryce Canyon National Park

Location and Access This is the last of four maps covering the trails of Bryce Canyon National Park. Shown here is the Riggs Spring Loop Trail at the extreme southern end of the park. The beginning of this hike is at Rainbow Point, which is at the end of the paved park road. In recent years, roads in Bryce Canyon up to Bryce Point have been kept open throughout each winter. And if the snow isn't too deep, the road to Rainbow Point is normally plowed, depending on availability of machinery. At Rainbow Point are toilets and drinking water.

Trail or Route Conditions The Riggs Spring Loop Trail is a well-maintained walking path and is used moderately often. Because of the availability of water at two locations along this trail, it's one of the better hikes in the park, and certainly one of the better areas for backcountry camping. From Rainbow Point, you can do the loop-hike either clockwise or counter clockwise, it doesn't matter. Once you get below the rim of the Pink Cliffs, then it's an up-and-down hike, until you once again walk back up to Rainbow Point. From the same trailhead, another short hike would be along the Bristlecone Loop Trail. Some of the nicest views around can be had from Yovimpa Point and from along this Bristlecone Loop Trail.

Elevations Rainbow Point, 2776 meters; Yovimpa Pass, 2548; Riggs Spring, 2269 meters.

Hike Length and Time Needed The total length of the Riggs Spring Loop Trail is about 14 kms. Fast hikers can do this hike in half a day, but for some it could be an all-day trip. However, of all the trails in the park, this one has some of the nicest campsites, so you might consider spending a night on the trail. Riggs Spring is the best campsite, with good water and lots of shade and grass.

Water Riggs Spring has a good, year-round flow. Yovimpa Pass has a good spring and some running water. However, the Corral Hollow Campsite(which is misplaced on all maps except this one) is normally without water, unless you arrive at the right time in spring, when some water is available for a short period of time in the creek bed. Water is pumped from the spring at Yovimpa Pass up to the parking lot at Rainbow Point.

Maps Trails Illustrated map Paunsaugunt Plateau, Mount Dutton, Bryce Canyon(1:50,000); or Bryce Canyon National Park(1:31,680). Both maps can be bought at the visitor center.

Main Attractions The highest and coolest part of the park is at Rainbow Point, making it a nice hide-out in summer. Yovimpa Point is a good place to see old bristlecone pine trees.

Ideal Time to Hike From about early to mid-May, until the end of October. Each year is a little different. Because of the higher altitudes, this can be enjoyed throughout the summer.

Hiking Boots Any dry weather boots or shoes.

Author's Experience As usual the author was in a hurry on this loop-hike, which included the short side trip along the Bristlecone Loop Trail; round-trip was about 3 hours on 3 different hikes.

This is the Riggs Spring Campsite. Riggs Spring is to the right about 40 meters.

Map 6, Riggs Spring Loop Trail, Bryce Canyon N. P.

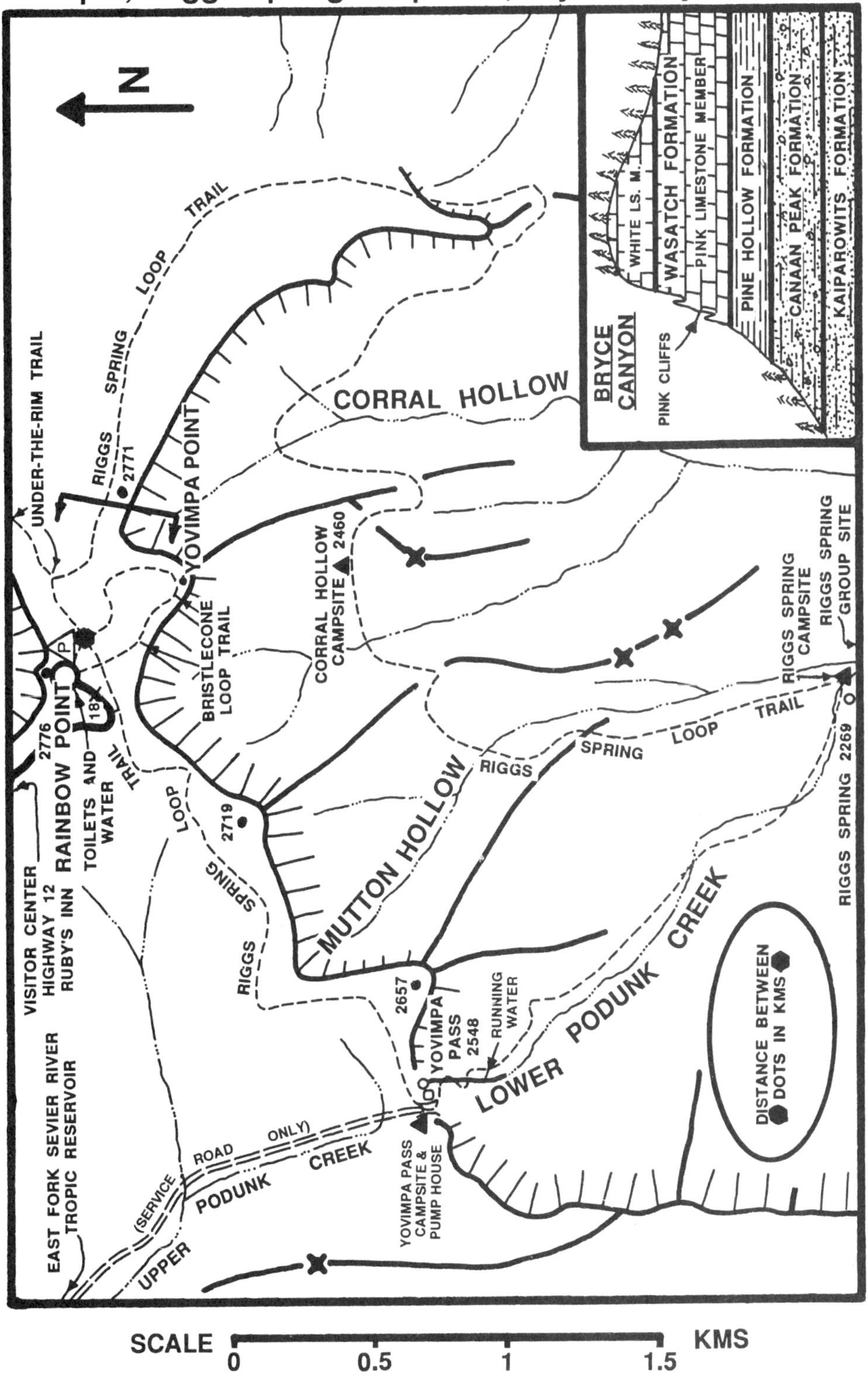

N

UNDER-THE-RIM TRAIL

RIGGS SPRING LOOP TRAIL

RIGGS 2771

YOVIMPA POINT

CORRAL HOLLOW

BRYCE CANYON

PINK CLIFFS

WHITE LS. M.

WASATCH FORMATION

PINK LIMESTONE MEMBER

PINE HOLLOW FORMATION

CANAAN PEAK FORMATION

KAIPAROWITS FORMATION

CORRAL HOLLOW CAMPSITE ▲ 2460

RIGGS SPRING CAMPSITE

RIGGS SPRING GROUP SITE

BRISTLECONE LOOP TRAIL

RAINBOW POINT 2776

VISITOR CENTER
HIGHWAY 12
RUBY'S INN

TOILETS AND WATER

182

2719

LOOP TRAIL

RIGGS SPRING

MUTTON HOLLOW

RIGGS SPRING LOOP TRAIL

RIGGS SPRING 2269

RIGGS

RIGGS

2657

YOVIMPA PASS 2548

RUNNING WATER

LOWER PODUNK CREEK

DISTANCE BETWEEN DOTS IN KMS

EAST FORK SEVIER RIVER
TROPIC RESERVOIR

(SERVICE ROAD ONLY)

UPPER PODUNK CREEK

YOVIMPA PASS CAMPSITE & PUMP HOUSE

SCALE   0   0.5   1   1.5   KMS

35

Bull Valley Gorge and Willis Creek

Location and Access This map includes two canyon gorges located not far to the southwest of the small town of Cannonville. The route of access is called the Skutumpah Road, which runs from the area south of Cannonville, in a southwesterly direction towards these two canyons, and on past the Swallow Park, Deer Spring and Skutumpah Ranches. The Skutumpah Road ends(or begins) at the upper end of Johnson Canyon northeast of Kanab. This is the shortest link between Kanab and Cannonville.

This road is generally open to all vehicles from around the first of April until sometime in November. But each year is different. During years with dry winters, it's possible to travel it all the time, except in the week or two right after a big storm. Parts of this road just south of the Bull Valley Gorge Bridge are made of clay, which become very slick when wet. Also, along the steep dugway just south of the old Clark Ranch on Willis Creek, it's sometimes icy in the coldest part of the year. In the winter of 1986-87, two 4WD's slid off this part of the road and had to be pulled out. In the warmer half of the year, the clay beds dry quickly after storms and it's a good road for all vehicles with a fair amount of summer traffic.

Trail or Route Conditions There are no trails what-so-ever in these canyons; you simply walk down the dry creek bed in Bull Valley, or along the small stream flowing through Willis Creek Gorge. If you make the loop-hike of these two canyons, using the middle part of Sheep Creek as a link between the two, then you will walk along a seldom used 4WD track in the bottom of the dry Sheep Creek. About twice a year, cattle grazing permit holders, take in or bring out cattle from the middle part of the Upper Paria River Gorge via Sheep Creek.

In Willis Creek, you simply walk in or out of the canyon with no obstacles what-so-ever. Bull Valley Gorge is a little different however. Park on the north side of the bridge, or at another site about 200 meters east. Then walk along the north side of the rim of the gorge west of the bridge about 350 meters or so. At that point you can step right into the dry creek bed. Just below where you enter, there used to be a big log jam, but that's gone now, washed a way in a big flood. In about the same area there are two short dropoffs caused by chokestones. Most people can get up or down these OK, but take a short rope for shorter or less-experienced hikers.

There's a second route, a rather steep rock climb, which begins along the north side of the gorge about 200 meters west of the bridge. This is called the Crack Route on the map. This route, up or down a crack in the Navajo Sandstone, is about 20-25 meters high and nearly vertical, but it's easier than it first appears. It has lots of hand and foot holds, but with some loose rock. The author has used this route three times, once with a large pack, which he had to pull up behind him on two pitches with a parachute cord. Use this route only if the main canyon above is somehow blocked. *This rock climb would be for experienced hikers only.*

There's also another route into or out of the gorge, located about 100 meters or so below, or east of the

One of two obstacles to get up or down in the upper part of Bull Valley Gorge.

Map 7, Bull Valley Gorge and Willis Creek

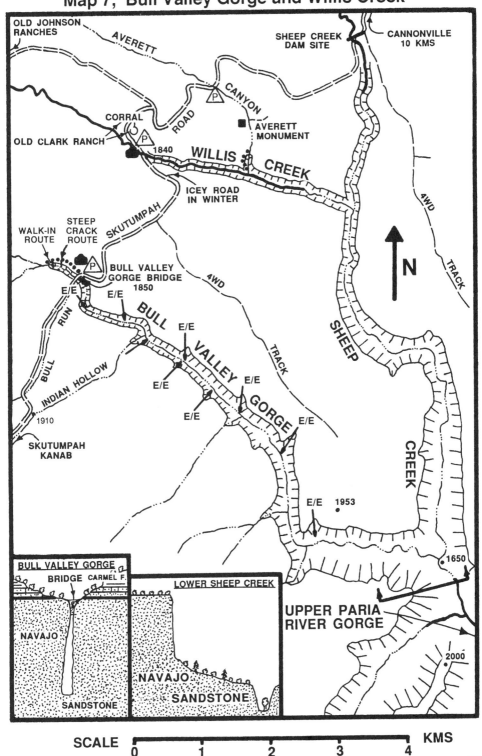

OLD JOHNSON RANCHES

AVERETT

SHEEP CREEK DAM SITE

CANNONVILLE 10 KMS

CANYON

ROAD

P

AVERETT MONUMENT

CORRAL

OLD CLARK RANCH

P

1840

WILLIS CREEK

ICEY ROAD IN WINTER

SKUTUMPAH

WALK-IN ROUTE

STEEP CRACK ROUTE

P

BULL VALLEY GORGE BRIDGE 1850

4WD

4WD

TRACK

N

E/E

E/E

BULL RUN

BULL

VALLEY

E/E

INDIAN HOLLOW

E/E

E/E

TRACK

GORGE

SHEEP

1910

SKUTUMPAH KANAB

E/E

E/E

CREEK

E/E 1953

1650

BULL VALLEY GORGE

BRIDGE CARMEL F.

LOWER SHEEP CREEK

UPPER PARIA RIVER GORGE

NAVAJO

NAVAJO SANDSTONE

2000

SANDSTONE

SCALE   KMS

0   1   2   3   4

37

bridge. The author came up this route once, but those unaccustomed to rock climbing may feel uneasy using this entry/exit(E/E) point. On the map are other *possible* entry/exit routes to the gorge.

Elevations Bull Valley Gorge Bridge, 1850 meters; trailhead on Willis Creek, 1840; and the junction of Bull Valley Gorge and Sheep Creek, the low point on a loop-hike, about 1650 meters.

Hike Length and Time Needed Most people just hike down each canyon about one km, which is where the best sections are, and return. Doing this may take one to 3 hours. Or for long distance hikers, the length of the walk down Bull Valley Gorge, then up Sheep and Willis Creek to the road, is about 20-22 kms. Combine that with the 2 1/2 km walk along the road between the two trailheads, and you have an all-day hike; a *long* all-day hike for some(a mtn. bike would eliminate the road-walk). Most hikers can do this in one day however. It's also possible to do the hike in two days, making an overnight camp in the lower part of Sheep Creek, near where it enters the Upper Paria River Gorge. There's running water, presumably year-round(?), and good campsites. If taking in big packs, it's likely easier to go down Bull Valley Gorge, rather than up.

Water There's running water in Willis Creek on a year-round basis. You could probably drink this water as-is in *winter*, as the land above the road is *summer range for cattle*. It's best to purify it first however. Bull Valley Gorge is dry, as is most of Sheep Creek. Water does begin to flow out of seeps in the lower part of Sheep Creek, as the red colored lower parts of the Navajo Sandstone begins to be exposed. This should be good water in summer, as the cattle at that time are up higher in the mountains.

Maps USGS or BLM map Kanab(1:100,000), or Bull Valley Gorge(1:24,000).

Main Attractions The upper two or three kms of each gorge have some extremely narrow passages, similar to the Buckskin Gulch. The scenery in the lower part of Bull Valley Gorge, with the huge Navajo Sandstone walls dotted with pine trees, is worth seeing too. Interesting also, is the unusual bridge over the upper part of Bull Valley Gorge, and the 1954 accident scene where 3 men were killed. Also, the Averett Monument, discussed below

Ideal Time to Hike From sometime in April on through October. This time period offers the best chance for the Skutumpah Road to be open and dry. May or June, and September or October, might be the ideal times to actually do the hiking.

Hiking Boots Willis Creek is small and you can usually hop right across, but it's best to have wading-type shoes for that part of the hike. Bull Valley Gorge has no running water, but just up the gorge from the bridge, are pools which can hold water and mud for a few days or a week after each storm. So for the entire loop-hike, wading-type shoes are recommended.

Author's Experience The author first tried the Bull Valley Gorge hike on a very cold mid-April morning, but found the big water & mud pool near the bridge, and turned back. A month later that pool was dry and he made two more trips into the gorge at that time. On another trip he went down Willis Creek on his way into Deer Creek, in the middle part of the Upper Paria River Gorge. His last trip into both canyons was in October, 1997.

History of Bull Valley Gorge Bridge

One of the more spectacular and unusual bridges you'll ever see is the one spanning the upper part of Bull Valley Gorge. The top part of this extremely narrow slot is only about one meter wide. One reader, whose name has been lost, measured the depth of the slot from the top of the bridge to the bottom at 44 meters. The rock involved is the famous Navajo Sandstone, perhaps the most prominent formation on the Colorado Plateau, and perhaps the most famous for making narrow slot-type canyons.

This bridge was first built sometime in the mid-1940's by Marian Clark, Ammon Davis and Herm Pollock. The first stage of that operation involved using a winch to drag several large logs across the gap to serve as a foundation for the bridge. Then planks were laid across the logs, making a rather simple bridge which was first used by local cattlemen. This was the first time Bryce Valley and the Kanab and Johnson Canyon areas were linked. A later event forced the county to upgrade the bridge which is safe and sound today.

That event was the accident which occurred sometime on Thursday, October 14, 1954. Three men died as their pickup got out of control and slid off the bridge and wedged in the upper part of the gorge. The victims were Max Henderson, 33, and Hart Johnson, 37, both of Cannonville, and Clark Smith, 32, of Henrieville. The *Garfield County News* carried the story in the October 21 edition.

Quoting from the newspaper report, *"They started out Thursday to set up a deer hunting camp on rangeland one of the men owned in Kane County. When they had not returned by Saturday, a search was started for them.*

A party led by Kendall Dutton of Cannonville, crossing the Bull Valley Gorge bridge, at 1 p.m. Sunday, sighted the pickup truck lodged in the narrow gorge about 50 feet[15 meters] below the bridge.

Bodies of two of the victims were still wedged into the truck, the third body had fallen clear and crashed to the Gorge floor almost 200 feet[60 meters] lower down"

The Highway Patrol and county Sheriff were called in and the rescue operation started. Garfield County Sheriff Deward Woodard was in charge of removing the bodies which was *"a hair-raising operation. His*

This is what the Bull Valley Gorge Bridge looks like when viewed from above and to the east.

The bottom of the Bull Valley Gorge Bridge and the pickup truck still stuck
in place. It's been there since 1954.

The narrows of Willis Creek, just below the Skutumpah Road.

The Averett Monument and gravesite in Averett Canyon. The smaller stone was placed there in 1866. The larger monument behind was erected in April, 1937.

son, Paul Woodard, with a rope around his waist, worked for hours sawing away parts of the truck--including the steering column--in order to free the bodies[Herm Pollock recalls they also used an acetylene torch for awhile]. He worked at the dizzy height above the canyon floor, with the swaying truck threatening to give[way] under him at any time[from the truck to the bottom of the gorge is 30 meters]. When one of the bodies was released from the truck, the weight almost pulled 22 men over the edge as the slack in the rope was suddenly snapped up.

According to the Sheriff, in reconstructing the accident, the light pickup truck the men were riding, stalled on the south side of the bridge and rolled backwards and into the gorge, dropping 50 feet[15 meters] before the narrowing sides crushed the cab and the men inside it."

Hart Johnson was buried in the Georgetown Cemetery, south of Cannonville; Max Henderson was buried in the Cannonville Cemetery, north of Cannonville; and Clark Smith was buried in the Henrieville Cemetery. Tombstones date from October 14, 1954.

Since the accident, the Bull Valley Gorge Bridge has been rebuilt. It appears workers simply pushed trees and large rocks down into the narrow chasm where they became lodged in the narrow upper part. Then a bulldozer must have pushed more rock and debris on top of that, making a very solid and much wider bridge than was first built.

When you stop there today, walk along the north side of the gorge to the west of the bridge, and from a view point you can see the pickup still lodged in the narrow slot. As you walk along the bottom of the gorge you have an even better view of the truck from below. Because the pickup is sitting high and dry and protected from rain and snow by the bridge, it will be there in the same position for a long time to come.

Averett Monument

Another interesting thing to see in the immediate area is the Averett Monument(some people spell it Everett). First the story behind the grave.

In August of 1866, a Mormon cavalry company from the St. George area was ordered by Erastus Snow, to go on an expedition to the Green River against Black Hawk and his marauders. This company, under the command of James Andrus, left the southern Utah settlements and went past Pipe Springs, Kanab, up Johnson Canyon, and northeast to the upper Paria River Valley. This was before there were any settlements in the area and traveling was rough.

By the time they reached the spot where Cannonville is today, many men were sick. It was decided to send these men back home. So six men and 14 head of disabled horses headed back. Along the way the small group was attacked by Indians. Elijah Averett Jr. was in the lead and he was shot and killed. The rest of the group escaped and managed to circle around and return to the main unit in the upper Paria. The Indians, presumably Navajos, were pursued, but escaped. Later, Averett was buried on August 27, 1866, where he died. This is in the bottom of what is now called Averett Canyon. The place is right on the old trail which was used by early-day stockmen and settlers before the present road was built.

Later in 1871, Frederick S. Dellenbaugh wrote about visiting the place in his diary. He stated he came across the grave marked by a sandstone slab with E. A. cut on it, which the wolves had dug out, leaving the human bones scattered around. Later, local cowboys reburied the bones and erected a cedar post with Averett's name on it. Many years later, the boy scouts of Tropic put that cedar post in their little museum in Tropic, and replaced it with a permanent stone marker that you see there today. According to Wallace Ott of Tropic, the new monument, the large one you see there today, was dedicated in April, 1937. About 15 people showed up and James L. Hatch, the local Stake President, conducted the dedication ceremony.

The best way to get to this monument, is to drive northeast on the Skutumpah Road from the old Clark Ranch on Willis Creek(in the direction of Cannonville). After about 2 or 2 1/2 kms, you'll drop down into the dry Averett Creek wash. Park on the road, and walk downcanyon about 600-700 meters(8 minutes of fast walking). You'll know you're there when you see water begin to seep out of the creek bed, and when you can see an old trail running up the east side of the canyon. The monument is about 8 or 10 meters above, and about 30 meters back from the creek bed, on a low bench on the right or west side. It's in a small clearing, surrounded by piñon-juniper trees. You can also come up Willis Creek. At the place is the original(?) round stone with E. A. carved on it, and the larger and newer monument nearby.

This is the slot part of Bull Valley Gorge just above or west of the bridge.

Another scene in Bull Valley Gorge, just above the famous bridge.

The second of two obstacles you must get around in the upper part of Bull Valley Gorge.

Upper Paria River Gorge

Location and Access The Upper Paria River Gorge is that part of the river between Cannonville and the old Pahreah townsite. Some might extend this upper gorge on down to Highway 89. The Lower Paria River Gorge is from Highway 89 down to Lee's Ferry and the Colorado River. Like the Lower Gorge, this upper part has rather good and easy access.

You can start at either end and walk all the way through, but you'd need two cars. Or you can park at either end and head for the middle part of the gorge, then return the same way. To reach the upper part, drive south out of Cannonville on the paved road in the direction of Kodachrome Basin and the Skutumpah Road. Cross over the Paria going toward Kodachrome Basin, then park at one of several little side canyons which can used to reach the main canyon. Little Dry Valley would be one, or even Rock Springs Creek. All routes in are easy walking.

Another possible way to get closer to the middle of the canyon, would be to drive east from the Kodachrome Turnoff about 1 km. At the first little rise, which is Watson Ridge, turn south, and drive past the BLM corral on the left. A little further along, you'll drop down into Rock Springs Creek where you'll see Wallace Ott's Corral. From there, continue south up the dry creek bed toward Rock Springs Bench, then along a rougher track to the end of the road on Rock Springs Point. The last 5 or 6 kms of that track is for HCV's, but the author managed to make it in his VW Rabbit Diesel--but just bearly. See *Map 8A, Deer and Snake Creek Canyons*.

From the Skutumpah Road, you can also enter or exit the gorge via Sheep or Willis Creek, or the more difficult and more exciting, Bull Valley Gorge.

To enter at the lower end of the gorge, drive along Highway 89, about halfway between Page and Kanab. Between mile posts 30 and 31, and at the sign stating *Paria Movie Set, 5 miles(8 kms)*, turn northeast and drive about 10 kms to near the old Pahreah townsite on a rather good dirt and clay road(which can be slick in wet weather).

Another possible way into the canyon, but one the author hasn't tried yet, would be to drive along Highway 89, then right at mile post 37, turn north onto the Nipple Ranch Road. Drive up to the pass marked 1825 meters with a 2WD vehicle, or on toward the old drill site marked 1937 meters with a 4WD. Near the end of this sandy road, you could hike north only 5 or 6 kms to reach Deer Trails in the middle part of the canyon.

Elevations About 1750 meters along the Upper Paria trailheads; about 1850 at Willis Creek and Bull Valley Gorge; and 1440 meters at old Pahreah.

Hike Length and Time Needed Old timers who talk about using the gorge as a road between Cannonville and Pahreah, say it was 30 miles, or 48 kms, between the two settlements. But you can shorten that by nearly 10 kms by beginning from one of the side canyon drainages such as Little Dry Valley. This entire distance can be walked in one very long day, but you'd need a car at both ends. However, it's recommended you take several days because there are many side canyons to see, such as Deer Creek, Snake Creek, and some old cattle trails to explore. In three or four days one could have a fun hike.

Almost all of this Upper Paria River Gorge or Canyon is within the Paria-Hackberry WSA, but since the main canyon corridor has been an old road since the 1870's, motor vehicles are presently allowed entry. This means you could take a 4WD or even a mtn. bike, which would save lots of walking. It also means ATV's are leaving the Paria River floodplain and trying to make their tracks into side canyons--which is definitely illegal.

However, this policy is likely to change when the management plan for the new Grand Staircase-Escalante N.M. comes out in 1999. The Kanab BLM office is recommending an emergency closure of the canyon to motorized vehicles, except for limited entry to stockmen who have cattle in the canyon.

Water There is a year-round flow in the Paria, but during the irrigation season, which is from sometime in late April until about the first of October, there's little or no water flowing downcanyon past Cannonville. Most or all of the water in the gorge at that time, seeps out from the bottom of the Navajo Sandstone or the top layers of the Kayenta Formation. This is in the area below the White Cliffs, which begins near the bend of the river known as the Devils Elbow.

There are many small seeps in the upper part of this map and in the gorge near Devils Elbow, which should be drinkable as-is. Also, most major side canyons have a small stream. If you walk up any of these canyons to where the spring or seep begins, then that water is normally drinkable as-is. In winter months there are cattle in the canyons, so some precautions should be taken, such as taking water directly from a spring, using Iodine tablets, or filtration. However, in the summer months, from about mid-May until the end of October or the first part of November, there are no cattle in the canyon. They are taken out during this time period and put on higher summer ranges in the mountains. With the rather steep gradient, the stream flows fast and will wash out the microbes which can give hikers stomach troubles.

It's during this time of year, and when there has been a long dry spell, that the water in this upper gorge is as clear as any mountain stream and which the author has drank many times. About the only sediment entering the creek at this time is the small amount of sand being washed down by Kitchen Creek. However, when you get into mid or late summer, and with the presence of thunder shower activity, the water is often times very muddy.

44

Map 8, Upper Paria River Gorge

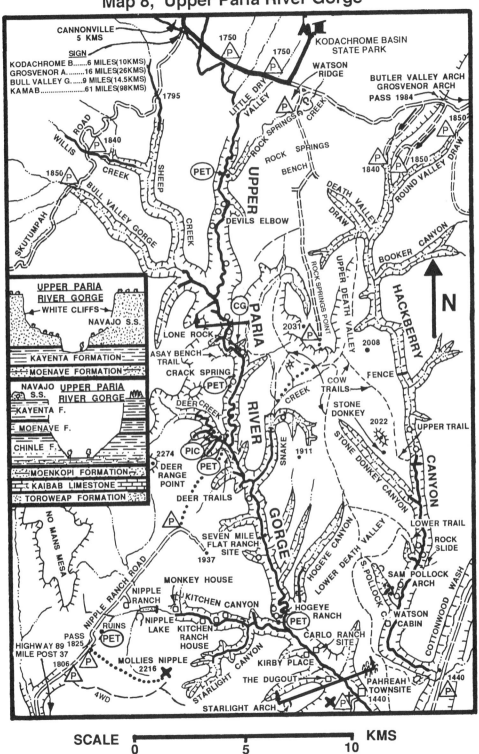

CANNONVILLE
5 KMS

SIGN
KODACHROME B.......6 MILES(10KMS)
GROSVENOR A........16 MILES(26KMS)
BULL VALLEY G.....9 MILES(14.5KMS)
KAMAB...............61 MILES(98KMS)

KODACHROME BASIN
STATE PARK

WATSON
RIDGE

BUTLER VALLEY ARCH
GROSVENOR ARCH
PASS 1984

1750
1750
1795

ROAD
WILLIS
CREEK
SKUTUMPAH
BULL VALLEY GORGE
SHEEP
CREEK

1840
1850
1840

LITTLE DRY VALLEY
ROCK SPRINGS CREEK
ROCK SPRINGS BENCH

UPPER

PET

DEVILS ELBOW

DEATH VALLEY DRAW
ROCK SPRINGS POINT
UPPER DEATH VALLEY

BOOKER CANYON
HACKBERRY

N

UPPER PARIA RIVER GORGE

WHITE CLIFFS
NAVAJO S.S.
KAYENTA FORMATION
MOENAVE FORMATION

NAVAJO S.S. | UPPER PARIA RIVER GORGE
KAYENTA F.
MOENAVE F.
CHINLE F.
MOENKOPI FORMATION
KAIBAB LIMESTONE
TOROWEAP FORMATION

CG
LONE ROCK
ASAY BENCH TRAIL
CRACK SPRING
PET

PARIA
RIVER

2031
2008

CREEK
COW TRAILS
FENCE
STONE DONKEY
2022
STONE DONKEY CANYON
UPPER TRAIL

DEER CREEK
2274
PIC
PET
DEER RANGE POINT
DEER TRAILS

SNAKE CREEK
1911

GORGE

NO MANS MESA

P
SEVEN MILE FLAT RANCH SITE
1937

MONKEY HOUSE
NIPPLE RANCH ROAD
NIPPLE RANCH
KITCHEN CANYON
NIPPLE LAKE
KITCHEN RANCH HOUSE

HOGEYE CANYON
LOWER DEATH VALLEY
S. POLLOCK

LOWER TRAIL
ROCK SLIDE
SAM POLLOCK ARCH
WATSON CABIN

COTTONWOOD WASH

PASS
HIGHWAY 89
MILE POST 37
1825
RUINS
PET
1806
P
MOLLIES NIPPLE
2216
4WD

STARLIGHT CANYON
KIRBY PLACE
THE DUGOUT
STARLIGHT ARCH

HOGEYE RANCH
PET
CARLO RANCH SITE
PAHREAH TOWNSITE
1440
1440
P

SCALE

0   5   10   KMS

Near the Devils Elbow, in the Upper Paria River Gorge.

The best waterhole in the Upper Paria River Gorge is at Crack Spring.

For those who want to be on the safe side and drink only spring water, there are two fine springs on the west side of the canyon about straight across from the mouth of Hogeye Canyon. Another good source, perhaps the best in the gorge, is the historic Crack Spring. This spring is about 2-3 kms upstream from the mouth of Deer Creek Canyon and about half a km downcanyon from Lone Rock. Walk close to the west wall and look and listen carefully for the water coming out of a cluster of small cottonwood trees.

Maps USGS or BLM maps Kanab and Smoky Mountain(and a small corner of Panguitch)(1:100,000), or Calico Peak, Deer Range Point, Bull Valley Gorge, Slickrock Bench, and Cannonville(1:24,000). Be sure and carry either of these sets of maps, as this hand-drawn sketch is not that accurate. The two metric maps at 1:100,000 scale are recommended.

Main Attractions The sites of the old Dugout, Carlo, Kirby, Hogeye and Seven Mile Flat Ranches. Petroglyphs at the mouths of Kitchen Canyon, Deer Creek, and Rocks Springs Creek. Pictographs inside Deer Creek are the only panels in the area. Cowboyglyphs at Crack Spring, Lone Rock and other sites. A number of old historic cattle trails, and many good campsites and solitude.

Ideal Time to Hike Spring or fall, with the very best times being from late March or early April to mid or late May, and from mid or late September to late October. Summers are hot, and late spring and early summer(late May through June and into July) bring the small gnats and large deer flies. If you go too early in the spring, or late in the fall, your feet will be blocks of ice.

Hiking Boots Wading boots or shoes. If you're planning to do the entire gorge hike, which is rather long, try to have a sturdy pair of shoes or boots. Many people take an old pair of shoes to "wear out" on a trip like this, but if they're too old or battered, they fail to give support to the foot and may not last to the end of the hike. So consider taking a pretty good pair of shoes, even though the wading will shorten their life.

Author's Experience The author has been upcanyon from old Pahreah 5 times visiting the old ranches and trails, and Hogeye, Deer Creek and Kitchen Canyons. These were all day-hikes, which took from 8 to 9 1/2 hours. Another day he walked from the side canyon west of Little Dry Valley down to Crack Spring, had lunch, and returned, in 7 1/2 hours. A mtn. bike would have shortened that trip. Another time he walked down Willis Creek to Deer Creek Canyon on a two day trip, which should have been at least three days. On one of the author's last visits, he walked from old Pahreah to as far as Deer Creek and the cow trails in that area, in less than 8 hours, round-trip. His last trip of 1997, was a hike off Rock Springs Point. He walked down past Sugarloaf and into the middle part of Snake Creek, then over the hump west and down the CCC Trail, and up Deer Trails to the west side bench. Then he returned to his car on Rock Springs Bench, all in about 7 1/2 hours.

Trail or Route Conditions There are no trails as such in this canyon, but as you begin or end your hike, and in the bottom part just above old Pahreah, you'll be able to use some of the original old wagon roads which went from Pahreah to some of the ranches up the canyon. The Smoky Mountain map shows the old road accurately to where it ends at the Kirby Place. Today there's an occasional 4WD or ATV using this track, which are scarring parts of the canyon bottom and illegally entering side canyons.

There are also grazing permit holders who go into the middle part of the canyon occasionally in 4WD's to take in or bring out cattle. This is usually in about mid-May, and in the period at the end of October or the first part of November. These permit holders have a reason to be there, and are not just out joy-riding, as are most recreation vehicle owners.

At about the Kirby Place and going north, these tracks fade away as the canyon narrows; then you'll be walking in the flood-gutted canyon bottom. Grazing permit holders now get into or out of the upper part of this gorge via Sheep Creek, but the early day wagon road was right down the Paria past Devils Elbow. Walking is easy all along this creek bed.

Beginning now in the upper end of the gorge. You'll first be walking in a shallow canyon, but soon it narrows and deepens as the river begins to cut down into the Navajo Sandstone. Remember, while the river is downcutting, the walls are rising; that is, the top of the Navajo is higher to the south than to the north. In other words the rock formations slope down to the north.

At the mouth of Rock Springs Creek, you'll see an isolated, lone standing butte, which must be a part of an old abandoned river channel. On the west side of this butte, and 6 or 8 meters off the ground, you'll see some pretty good petroglyphs. They must have been put there when the river bed was much higher.

Downriver from Rock Springs Creek, is a big bend in the canyon, which old timers call the **Devils Elbow.** At that point the canyon is rather deep and moderately narrow. The white sandstone walls are the Navajo Sandstone, which form the White Cliffs all across the region.

In the area of the Devils Elbow, you'll begin to see many small seeps along the sides of the stream channel, and the creek begins to grow in volume. In summer, the upper part is totally dry, or nearly so, and the water you often see in the Paria downstream, actually begins here.

As you near the place where Sheep Creek enters from the west, you begin to see red sandstone in the canyon bottom. This is the bottom part of the Navajo Sandstone. Then just a bit further downstream, and in the area of Lone Rock, you'll see the top part of the Kayenta Formation emerging. The Kayenta forms little benches or terraces. As you walk south, the river continues to downcut, and the beds rise at the same time. From the Lone Rock area on down, most of the major side canyons have some kind of water supply, either a flowing stream or good springs.

About 2 1/2 kms below the mouth of Sheep Creek, you'll see two fences come together part way across the canyon bottom. In between the fences, and on the west side of the canyon wall, is a cattle trail running up to the top of Asay Bench. The triangle-shaped fence allows the cattle to come down to the river for water, but doesn't allow them access to the rest of canyon. This is one route to the upper part of Deer Creek, where one can look for a very good panel of big horn sheep petroglyphs. One Cannonville cattleman mentioned this panel to the author, but the author never did find it.

Just a bend or two below the Asay Bench Trail, is a big rock standing out in the river channel. This is what old timers call **Lone Rock**. Look closely on its sides and you'll see numerous old signatures or cowboyglyphs. Some of these date back to the late 1800's, but some of the older ones are now becoming indistinct.

About a half km below, or south, of Lone Rock, and on the west side of the canyon, is **Crack Spring**. You'll have to walk close to the west wall and watch carefully to be able to see or hear the water coming out of a crack in the wall. It's on a narrow little bench, with many small cottonwood trees, and is hard to see unless you're close by. In the old days, when wagoneers and freighters were running from Cannonville to Pahreah, they always made this place their lunch stop, thus making the whole trip in one long day.

Years ago someone placed a 5 cm pipe into the crack, making it easier to get a drink. The pipe is still there, and it always has a good flow. Since the space right at the spring is rather small, it would be best to camp on the opposite side of the river under some big cottonwood trees. Camping over there would also leave the spring site clean and pristine.

Kay Clark of Henrieville, remembered a trip he took with his father in April, 1920. They started in Cannonville and headed for Pahreah. They were carrying several sacks of grain, evidently to be sold to sheep herders in the lower valleys. When they made their lunch stop at Crack Spring, there were several other wagons already there. Since they were riding in comfort in a White Topped Buggy with fringes, some of the other drivers made comments as to how *they were really traveling in style*. In those days, the White Topped Buggy was like a Mercedes, and the ordinary wagons used by most local people, were like Model T Fords.

On either side of Crack Spring and on the lower wall, are many very old cowboyglyphs or signatures of travelers. Those which are black in color, were made by placing axle grease on a finger, then writing a name. This grease prevented the sandstone from flaking away, so what you'll see there today are many raised letters or signatures which literally stand out on the wall like Braille writing. Other people carved their names into the sandstone with a sharp metal instrument.

About half a km below Crack Spring, you come to some tight turns of the river, and high above are four or five alcoves on the east side of the canyon. One or two seem to have developed into arches. Just below these goose necks, is the mouth of Deer Creek Canyon. This is one of the best side trips you can take while hiking the Upper Paria River Gorge, so plan to camp and spend time in this one.

Deer Creek Canyon

Deer Creek Canyon is moderately narrow, with the canyon walls being vertical and made up of the red colored lower Navajo Sandstone and Kayenta Formation. This canyon is similar to places in the Lower Paria Gorge or even the lower end of the Buckskin Gulch, where the campsites are located.

Inside the canyon is a crystal clear, year-round flowing stream, which begins flowing at the base of the dryfall about 2 1/2 kms up from the Paria. Someone told the author there was some running water above the dryfall but surely that would be seasonal. Along the stream are many fine campsites under large cottonwood trees. The walls of the canyon are red, but the benches you'll be camping on are white Navajo sands, which have blown off from the White Cliffs above.

As far as Deer Creek water is concerned remember; cattle will be in this canyon from about late October or early November, on through about mid-May. At that time the cows are taken to their summer ranges. After the cattle are gone the water should soon be drinkable as-is, as it flows quickly out of the canyon.

If you're interested in petroglyphs and pictographs, this is one of the best canyons around to see them. Right at the mouth of the canyon is one long panel of petroglyphs, including one glyph which is like a tit-tac-toe box. You'll have to climb a cedar tree to have a close look at this one.

Just inside Deer Creek about 100-150 meters, and on the north side, are several pictographs and petroglyphs. At one time, it looks as though someone tried to chop one of them out of the wall with an ax-- but was unsuccessful. About a km upcanyon from the Paria, is the best pictograph panel around. There are actually two panels: one you can crawl up to and see close-up; the other is out of reach. This second one faces west, and must have been made before part of the wall below it collapsed.

About two kms up Deer Creek Canyon you'll come to a blocking dryfall. This is as far as you go from inside the canyon. Below this dropoff is where the water begins to flow. It's in this upper part, that you'll find many white sand benches and large cottonwood trees, which combine to make some of the best campsites anywhere. If you wish to get upon top of the Cad or Asay Benches, you'll have to get there via the Asay Bench Trail or Deer Trails, just south of the mouth of Deer Creek. There could be some good foto opportunities in the area of Deer Range Point as the white Navajo Sandstone is streaked with red--at least

Map 8A, Deer and Snake Creek Canyons

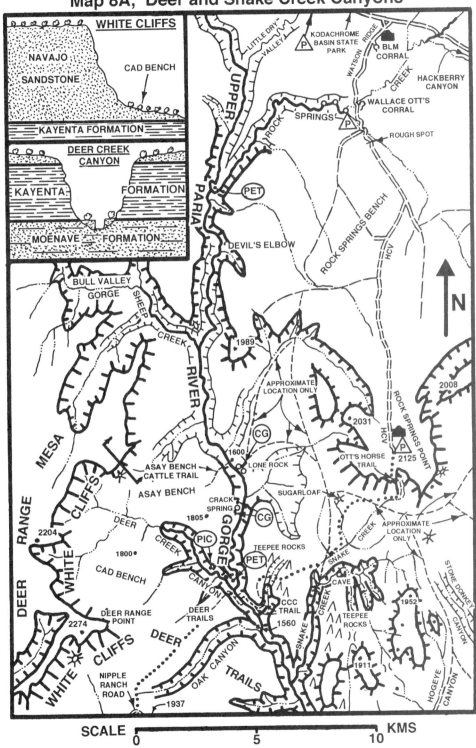

WHITE CLIFFS

NAVAJO
SANDSTONE

CAD BENCH

KAYENTA FORMATION

DEER CREEK
CANYON

KAYENTA FORMATION

MOENAVE FORMATION

LITTLE DRY VALLEY

KODACHROME
BASIN STATE
PARK

BLM
CORRAL

WATSON RIDGE

CREEK

HACKBERRY
CANYON

WALLACE OTT'S
CORRAL

ROCK SPRINGS

ROUGH SPOT

UPPER

PARIA RIVER

PET

ROCK SPRINGS BENCH

HCV

DEVIL'S ELBOW

N

BULL VALLEY
GORGE

SHEEP CREEK

1989

APPROXIMATE
LOCATION ONLY

2008

ROCK SPRINGS POINT

HCV

2031

MESA

CG

1600

LONE ROCK

ASAY BENCH
CATTLE TRAIL

ASAY BENCH

2125

P

OTT'S HORSE
TRAIL

RANGE

WHITE CLIFFS

2204

DEER

CREEK

CRACK
SPRING

CG

SUGARLOAF

APPROXIMATE
LOCATION
ONLY

1805

PIC

DEER

1800

CAD BENCH

GORGE

PET

TEEPEE ROCKS

SNAKE CREEK

CANYON

STONE DONKEY CANYON

CCC
TRAIL

CAVE

1952

DEER
TRAILS

1560

SNAKE CREEK

TEEPEE
ROCKS

DEER RANGE
POINT

2274

WHITE

CLIFFS

DEER

TRAILS

1911

NIPPLE
RANCH
ROAD

OAK CANYON

HOGEYE CANYON

WHITE CLIFFS

1937

SCALE

0   5   10

KMS

as seen from No Mans Mesa.

Continuing down the Paria Canyon now. About 200 meters below the mouth of Deer Creek, used to be a fence across the canyon bottom. About 100 meters below that, and on the east side, is the beginning of the **CCC Trail**. In the beginning, this trail is well-constructed, and was used to run cows from the Upper Death Valley and Snake Creek areas, down to water in the Paria Canyon. This one is easy to find and follow.

According to Wallace Ott of Tropic, this trail was built by the CCC's sometime in the mid-1930's. At that time, they had their main camp northeast of Henrieville at the old Smith Ranch, but while doing various projects along the Upper Paria River, they had a spike camp near the mouth of Deer Creek Canyon.

About 100 meters below the beginning of the CCC Trail, and on the west side of the canyon, is the beginning of the trail known by cattlemen as **Deer Trails**. This too is a constructed trail, at least up to the rim, and is easily seen from the other side of the canyon and from the bottom. If you follow this one up, you'll find yourself upon the rim of the lower end of Deer Creek Canyon. From one of several perches on the rim, you'll have fine views of both the White Cliffs and the canyon below. This trail was gradually built-up by cattle & sheepmen over the years beginning just after about 1900. Wallace Ott says a Jim Henderson was probably responsible for most of the rock-work you see there today.

Snake Creek Canyon

A half km below both of the above mentioned trails is *Oak Canyon*, a tributary coming in from the west, and about 1 1/2 kms below it is the mouth of *Snake Creek*. Snake Creek has a good, year-round flowing stream along all of its lower end. About 2 kms up from the Paria, you'll come to a waterfall or cascade. This one may be a little difficult to get around, but 2 or 3 people with a short rope should have no great difficulty. Above this first waterfall, is a narrow section with lots of trees, then you'll come to 2 more dropoffs. Climb the first on the left.

Between these 2 dropoffs, the water begins to flow, and there's an old constructed cattle trail down between the two. Wallace Ott once did some cement work between these 2 dropoffs to enlarge one pothole.

About 100 meters above these dropoffs, is where two main upper tributaries of Snake Creek come together. Coming down the point between the two is another constructed cattle trail. Wallace Ott says this Snake Creek Trail was first built by Eli LeFevre and Layton Jolley during the 1930's, but after Ott bought their grazing rights in 1945, he upgraded it.

There are two other ways you can enter this middle part of Snake Creek. One is to walk up the CCC Trail from the Paria. Once that trail reaches the rim, it disappears going north. From there, and with a compass in hand, continue north less than a km, then veer right or east and cross the upper part of a minor side canyon. When you come to the second drainage, turn right and head south downcanyon. When you reach a big dropoff, climb the east bank to find the Snake Creek Trail. Walk south and into the main canyon as described above.

Typical scene in the lower part of Sheep Creek near the Paria River.

Still another way into the middle part of Snake Creek, Upper Death Valley, or the upper end of Stone Donkey or Hogeye Canyons, is to drive to the end of the track on Rock Springs Point. From there route-find due south through the piñon-junipers until you come to the point where you'll have some great views. Then make your way to an east-facing part of the rim and look below for a big sand slide. Work your way down the ledges on a minor horse trail built by Wallace Ott in the early 1960's, then veer south, then west, and head for the prominent yellow Sugarloaf rock. From Sugarloaf, walk down the sandy drainage, or locate the Snake Creek Trail just to the west and follow it into the canyon as described earlier.

Where the Snake Creek Trail reaches the bottom, head up the main fork and after about one km, and immediately above a minor dropoff to the east, is an overhang and an unusual cave. If you continue upcanyon, there will be another fork. The author still hasn't been there, but Ott says if you turn into the drainage coming down from left or east, you can eventually get out and make your way into the upper end of Hogeye Canyon. Read about that well-watered canyon under Map 18.

Here's a fotographer's tip. Throughout the area from Rock Springs Point to Snake Creek and Hogeye Canyon, is the mostly-white Navajo Sandstone. However, much of it is streaked with yellow and red, much the same as what you find in Coyote Buttes. From a distance, the teepee-like rocks just above and east of the lower end of Snake Creek, looked interesting.

Seven Mile Flat Ranch

About 2 kms below the mouth of Snake Creek is a place where the canyon opens up a bit and becomes wider. This is Seven Mile Flat. It got its name because it was about 7 miles, or 11 kms, above the town of Pahreah. Kay Clark, an old time cattleman from Henrieville, was too young to remember much, but was told this is where a man by the name of John W. Mangum had a small ranch, which people referred to as the Seven Mile Flat Ranch. As the story goes, it was a summer time place, with a cabin and corrals. At the ranch, they raised, among other things, sugar cane, from which they made molasses. In winter the family lived in Pahreah.

Kay Clark does remember that at the northern end of the flat area and on the west side of the river, he saw the remains of a small molasses mill. There was some kind of a foundation and the old rollers, which were used to squeeze juice out of the sugar cane. It's possible you might find something there today.

No one can say for certain what the exact dates were when this ranch was occupied, but Kay thinks it must have been at about the same time Pahreah was prospering, which was in the late 1870's and up until about 1883. That's when the first of the big floods hit the Paria and started the migration out of the valley. It must have been one of these first floods(later floods occurred in 1884 and 1896) which took out the buildings, and started washing out the entire bottom of the canyon. Today, there is nothing more than a broad washed-out river flood plain.

One of several pictograph panels inside Deer Creek Canyon.

Hogeye Ranch

From the Seven Mile Flat area down to the mouth of Hogeye Canyon, there isn't much to see, except a couple of side canyons on the east. At the very mouth of Hogeye, is an abandoned meander or river channel. Right out in the middle of the rather flat area is a rounded butte, which apparently resembled a hogs eye, thus the name, *Hogeye Canyon*. Hogeye is another of the major side canyons of the Paria River, which is discussed in another hike. It does have a good year-round running water supply and many good campsites.

Right at the mouth of Hogeye Canyon and on the flats surrounding the Hogeye Butte, is the location of another old homestead, the Hogeye Ranch. The late Herm Pollock of Tropic thought it was first settled and used by an Ernest Mangum. But the late Marian Clark, who was in his 90's when interviewed in 1987, thought is was a John W. Mangum.

Both sources believed this summer ranch was occupied in the years after people started leaving Pahreah town, but no one knows for certain when it was first used. Herm remembered a small wooden shack on the north side of Hogeye Butte, and Marian remembered a small two-meter square stone storage building of some kind. Goats were raised, and some farming was done in summer. The big floods of 1883-84 or 1896 must have lowered the creek bed to the point they could no longer get water up to the farmland. Nothing remains today, except a lot of cheat or June grass, indicating the place was heavily used by someone at some period in time.

Just northwest of the Hogeye Butte is a good spring coming out of the west side of the canyon; and just to the southwest of the butte is another spring, which made the site a good one as far as water is concerned.

About a km below Hogeye is **Kitchen Canyon**, which is discussed in another hike. But right at the mouth of this canyon, is a good panel of petroglyphs and cowboyglyphs. Be careful of Kitchen Creek water; it drains the Nipple Ranch area which has cattle grazing year-round.

On the east side of the Paria Canyon, opposite the mouth of Kitchen Canyon, is where the Marian Mangum family(or perhaps one of his sons) had a dugout, and what must have been a garden and summer ranch area. The author was made aware of this place after all his hikes were finished and has not made an attempt to look over the site.

Kirby Ranch

About a km below the mouth of Kitchen Canyon, on a bench just west of the creek and under a large cottonwood tree, are the ruins of the Kirby Place or Ranch. The only thing left to see is a rock chimney. The old cabin was either burned down or the logs were hauled away to build another house or barn some place else.

As with the other ranches in the area north of old Pahreah, not much is known for sure about this ranch site. But everyone agrees that it is the Kirby Place, and that it was first occupied from the years of about the mid-1870's on through about the time of the first flood to hit the valley. Kay Clark says it was the typical summer ranch site. Apparently the Kirby family lived in Pahreah during the winters, then had cows and a

The only thing remaining of the Carlo Ranch home is this chimney.

small garden at the ranch in summer. Herm Pollock believes the Kirby family left for Arizona after the 1884 flood, which left their irrigated land high and dry.

Carlo Ranch

About 200 meters due east of the Kirby Ranch house chimney on the opposite side of the canyon, and sitting out in the middle of a sagebrush flat, is the foundation and chimney of the Carlo Ranch house. Herm Pollock remembered this family when he was just a boy of 12.

The year was 1922 and it was Christmas time. For most of that fall Herm and his father Sam Pollock, had stayed in the town of Pahreah. The Pollocks lived in Tropic, but they were in the Pahreah area with a sheep camp, and were also in the business of supplying food and supplies to other sheep camps in the region.

On Christmas morning with nearly half a meter of snow on the ground, Sam loaded up two boxes of food and other supplies, and put them on two mules. He instructed 12 year-old Herm to go up the canyon about 5 kms to the Carlo home, and present the family with the gifts of food. Herm vividly remembers the time, because it was the first time he ever played Santa Clause.

He also remembered the time well, because of how poor the Carlo family was. Their home was a one-roomed cabin made of logs and rocks. At that time it had no door, only a piece of canvas covering the opening. The only heat they had was from an open fireplace. When Herm first went in, he placed his hand on the inside of the door frame, which was covered with thick soot. When he pulled his hand back, it was covered black.

The several small children were dressed in rags, and were just filthy. Their normally red hair was black, because they had gone so long without bathing. Mrs. Carlo was dressed in flour sacks. Herm also remembered a story of one of the young boys. He had found an old blasting cap somewhere and was playing with it when it exploded. He had lost three fingers on one hand.

Herm Pollock went back home a week after this experience, but his father helped the Carlo family get through the winter. When spring finally came, Sam took a wagon to the ranch, and helped them get out. Later in the spring of 1923, the family left the country, and no one remembers if their old cabin was ever occupied again.

If looking for the old Carlo Ranch site, first find the Kirby Place, which is easier to locate. Then walk 200 meters due east across the creek, which is a low flood plain, then upon a sagebrush-covered bench. It must be about 30 meters or so from where the steeper canyon wall comes down to the tall sagebrush.

Going downcanyon from the Kirby Place, and on the west side of the river, you can get onto one of two of the old original roads and walk most of the way to Pahreah. At the mouth of Dugout Canyon(called Deer Range Canyon on the USGS maps), the two tracks meet. If you continue on this single track about half a km south or below the mouth of Dugout, you'll see on the right, just as you go down a little decline, several old logs, posts and a depression in the ground. This is believed to be what is called The Dugout.

The Kirby Place. All is gone but the fireplace chimney.

The Dugout

The Dugout is just one of several old ranch or homestead sites along the Paria River, just above the old Pahreah townsite The site was situated up against a low embankment; which was along the edge of an old river channel. First, earth was removed, then logs were built up on the sides and on the top. Dirt may or may not have been put on the roof, but inside it must have been rather cool in summer and warm in winter, because it was at least partly underground.

No one alive today seems to know who built The Dugout, or who lived in it first, but several old timers from Tropic and Henrieville, remember the time John (Long John) Mangum and family lived there. This was in the late 1920's and early 1930's, and may have extended to about 1934, according to Wallace Ott and Kay Clark. The wife of John Mangum was named Oma, and whose maiden name was Carlo. Mr. Carlo of the Carlo Ranch was her brother.

In about 1934 the Mangums, either John or brother Marian, had a cabin at the mouth of Kitchen Canyon. At that place, they once had a fine corn field out on the flat. Herm Pollock remembered this time period well, because the Mangums lived there for two years, then were washed out by a big flood which rolled down Kitchen Canyon and the Paria on July 10, 1936. During this same flood, Pollock was stranded for two and a half days on the Carlo Bench(surrounding the old cabin) with a herd of sheep. He had nothing to drink but muddy flood water.

Some time in the mid-1930's the Mangums began working on a ranch in Fivemile Valley south of Pahreah, which they homesteaded. Herman Mangum got title to it in June, 1937. This was at Cottonwood Spring and was called Fivemile Ranch by most people, but some called it Cottonwood Ranch. They lived there until 1942, then headed for Idaho. See the Hattie Green Mine story along with Map 21, for the location of Fivemile Valley & Ranch.

Continuing south from The Dugout. Perhaps the last thing to see in the Lower Paria River Gorge, besides the Pahreah townsite, is the line of cottonwood trees marking the original ditch or canal which provided water for Pahreah homes and gardens. This canal began about a km below The Dugout, and about two kms above Pahreah on the east side of the river. It's where the stream is pushed to the west by a rocky bend from the east. You can still see the very faint remains of the canal by following the broken line of cottonwood trees down to the townsite.

The end of the road to Pahreah is on the west side of the creek. This will either be the end, or the beginning of your hike. Read about the history of Pahreah in the chapter titled, *History of Ghost Towns of the Paria River,* in the back of this book.

The mouth of Deer Creek Canyon as seen from the rim on the east side.

If hiking up Snake Creek, this is the first waterfall you'll encounter. The top of the picture shows where you'll have to climb up.

Interesting cave in the middle part of Snake Creek.

Bullrush Gorge and Deer Range Canyon

Location and Access The location of Bullrush Gorge and Deer Range Canyon is about halfway between Johnson Valley and Cannonville. Johnson Valley is about 20 kms east of Kanab. If driving from Kanab on Highway 89, turn north into Johnson Canyon from between mile posts 54 and 55. At the north end of Johnson Canyon is the Skutumpah Road, which links the valley with Cannonville. Be sure and carry the *Kanab* metric 1:100,000 map to be sure and find the right valleys and roads. It's probably best to park right on the Skutumpah Road where it crosses Bullrush Hollow Creek. You could also park at the corral in Swallow Park, or if you have a HCV or 4WD, you could drive to the head of Deer Range or Tank Canyon.

Trail or Route Conditions There are no trails here, except for a few made by cows. So for the most part you'll be right in the dry creek bed of either canyon. The walking is easy. Just walk down one canyon and up the other. Between Bullrush and Deer Range Canyons, in the area called Park Wash, you'll be walking along a very sandy 4WD track which runs down to the LeFevre Cabin and on toward the Nipple Ranch and Nipple Lake. This road is so sandy in its lower parts, only a fool would attempt to drive it, even with a 4WD(it is possible to drive it in wet, or wet and cold weather--which makes sand-trap driving possible). There are no hiking obstructions anywhere except for one minor dryfall in Tank Canyon, which you can skirt easily by climbing the west-side slope.

Elevations From 2025 or 2075 meters, down to 1850 near the metal water troughs.

Hike Length and Time Needed If you park on the road in Bullrush Hollow, walk downcanyon and up Deer Range and Tank Canyons, then due west cross-country back to your car, it will be 25-26 kms. This is an all-day hike for anyone, and a very long all-day hike for some. You could also take in No Mans Mesa on the same hike, and spend 2 or 3 days in the area.

Water Both canyons are dry, except for running water in upper Bullrush G. in spring time only. Cattlemen have piped water from Adams Spring, southeast of Adair Lake, down to the water troughs, and to a tap just beyond the LeFevre Cabin. The author isn't sure if the water is allowed to run year-round or not, but it was there in late April, 1987, and in October of 1997. If there are cattle in the area, then water should be in the pipe. However, always have plenty of water in your car no matter what time of year it is.

Maps USGS or BLM map Kanab(1:100,000), or Rainbow Point and Deer Spring Point(1:24,000).

Main Attractions The gorges are only moderately narrow, but the best part is in the lower end of Deer Range Canyon. The walls are broken down and not sheer, allowing ponderosa pines to grow in the cracks and crevices, making a unique scene. It's similar in some ways to the Coyote Buttes country. So are the upper parts of Deer Range Point, as seen from No Mans Mesa.

Ideal Time to Hike Spring or fall, but it's possible in summer too because of the higher altitudes.

Hiking Boots Any dry weather boots or shoes.

Author's Experience The author parked on the road in Bullrush Hollow, walked down the gorge, then up Deer Range and Tank Canyons, and finally cross-country back to his car, all in 6 1/2 hours. You'll want more time than that.

Typical scenery in the lower Park Wash and Deer Range Canyon.

Map 9, Bullrush Gorge and Deer Range Canyon

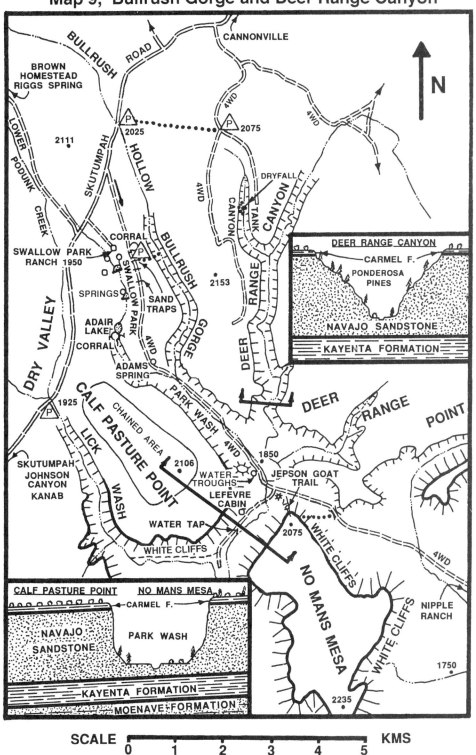

Lick Wash and No Mans Mesa

Location and Access All the canyons, cliffs and mesas on this map make for an interesting area, not only for hikers, but for geologists, botanists and historians alike. The main hike featured here is to the top of No Mans Mesa. You can reach it from several ways, but including Lick Wash in the access route, rounds out a description of all the interesting canyons in the immediate area.

No Mans Mesa is a remnant of the former plateau which extends to the north. At one time it was part of Calf Pasture and Deer Range Points, but erosion has left it high and dry, and surrounded by unclimbable cliffs. It's 6-7 kms long and about 2 kms wide. The walls you see are white Navajo Sandstone, which are part of the prominent feature of southern Utah known as the White Cliffs. The capstone is the Carmel Formation, a more erosion resistant rock than the Navajo. The top of the mesa is flat, except it tilts down to the north and northwest, as shown on the geology cross-section. The height of the cliffs range from 200 meters in the north, to about 400 meters at the south end. The altitude of the mesa ranges from about 2075 meters on the north end, to 2235 meters to the south.

The author has found two routes to the top. One is up the east side of the northern-most point; the other is the old *Jepson Goat Trail*. In 1927, a local rancher by the name of Lewis Jepson built a trail up the extreme northern end of the mesa. He had 800 Wether goats there in the spring and summer of the first year, and 1300 to 1500 goats on the mesa in the spring of 1928(one source states 3000). One story says the goats were taken to the mesa top to hide them from the bankers who had a lean on their owner. The goats did fairly well for the short time they were there, but lack of water prevented it from becoming a good pasture, and has prevented any further grazing of livestock there since. For the most part, No Mans Mesa is untouched by the hand of man and is very pristine.

The soaring White Cliffs make this one of the more scenic places in this book. To get to this area, use the Skutumpah Road which links the upper end of Johnson Canyon with Cannonville. Also, have along the *Kanab* metric map(1:100,000), which shows almost the entire Skutumpah Road. You can park where Lick Wash crosses the road; or in Swallow Park, perhaps at the corral east of the old Sears Riggs Ranch house. More on this later.

Trail or Route Conditions Starting at the road next to Lick Wash, you'll walk right down the dry creek bed, which has some short but interesting narrows, then use cattle trails near the bottom end, which will take you to the LeFevre Cabin. This old cabin was brought into the canyon from the East Fork of the Sevier River in the mid-1960's and placed on a corner of a state section. If you walk down Park Wash below Swallow Park and Adair Lake, you can use an old and very sandy 4WD track which runs to the LeFevre Cabin, and on south to the Nipple Ranch and Nipple Lake. This makes walking easy, but you'd better not try to take a vehicle down there, as it's one hell of a sand trap. That's 4WD country only!

The north end of No Mans Mesa. The Jepson Goat Trail runs up this prominent talus slope.

Map 10, Lick Wash and No Mans Mesa

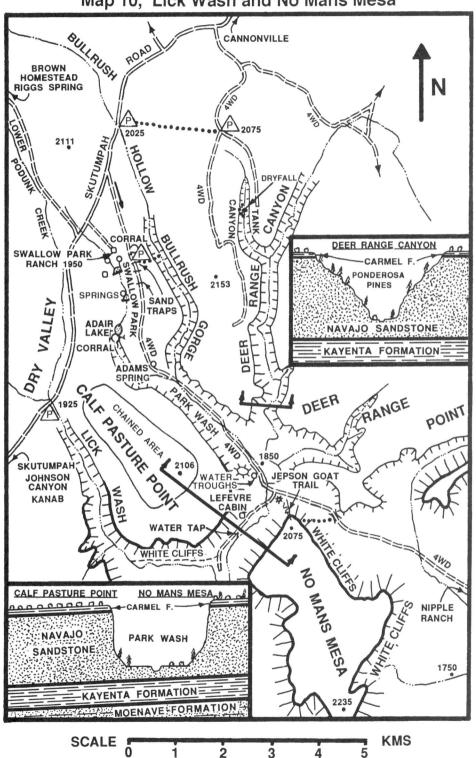

N

BULLRUSH ROAD
CANNONVILLE

BROWN
HOMESTEAD
RIGGS SPRING

4WD
4WD

P 2025
P 2075

LOWER PODUNK CREEK

2111

SKUTUMPAH HOLLOW

4WD

DRYFALL

TANK CANYON

CANYON

CORRAL
P
SWALLOW PARK
RANCH 1950

BULLRUSH GORGE

DEER RANGE CANYON

2153

SWALLOW PARK

SPRINGS
SAND TRAPS

DEER RANGE CANYON
CARMEL F.
PONDEROSA PINES

NAVAJO SANDSTONE

KAYENTA FORMATION

ADAIR LAKE
4WD

CORRAL

ADAMS SPRING

PARK WASH 4WD

DEER
RANGE
POINT

DRY VALLEY

P 1925

CALF PASTURE POINT
CHAINED AREA

2106
WATER TROUGHS
1850

LICK WASH

SKUTUMPAH
JOHNSON
CANYON
KANAB

JEPSON GOAT TRAIL

LEFEVRE CABIN

WATER TAP

WHITE CLIFFS

2075

WHITE CLIFFS

4WD

NIPPLE RANCH

CALF PASTURE POINT   NO MANS MESA
CARMEL F.

NAVAJO SANDSTONE

PARK WASH

NO MANS MESA

WHITE CLIFFS

1750

KAYENTA FORMATION

MOENAVE FORMATION

2235

SCALE   KMS
0   1   2   3   4   5

59

As you approach the north end of No Mans Mesa, which is in full view as you walk down Park Wash, notice the talus slope on the northern corner. This is where the goat trail is. You may have to go up this talus slope about halfway before you can see the trail. Once on the trail, it's easy to follow. The top part, which zig zags around some minor cliffs, is very obvious and is still in good condition. At the very top is a wire gate and short fence which kept the goats on top. About 100 meters from the top of the trail on the east side, is another way of getting up or down, but there's no trail on that slope.

Elevations From 1925 meters at Lick Wash car-park, to 1950 at the Swallow Park Ranch; the LeFevre Cabin, about 1850; top of the goat trail, 2075 meters.

Hike Length and Time Needed If you make the loop-hike of Park and Lick Wash, and include the side trip to the top of the goat trail, it'll take you all day--and a very long day for some. The distance, if you include the walk back to your car on the road is about 25-26 kms. A mtn. bike placed at one trailhead would eliminate a road walk back to your car.

Water There are several springs in Swallow Park, plus Adair Lake, but all the canyons are dry. Don't plan to use the water in Swallow Park, as there are livestock there all the time. However, ranchers and the BLM have constructed a water pipeline from Adams Spring southeast of Adair Lake, down Park Wash to 2 metal water troughs, and to a water tap just below the LeFevre Cabin. When there's cattle in the area, there should be water in the pipeline and troughs. Because of its moderate elevation, cattle may be there year-round.

Maps USGS or BLM map Kanab(1:100,000), or Rainbow Point and Deer Spring Point(1:24,000).

Main Attractions An old historic trail and grand views of the nearby park lands and White Cliffs from the top of No Mans Mesa. Lick Wash has some short, but interesting narrows, and some pine-clad cliffs near the bottom end. Adair Lake is interesting.

Ideal Time to Hike Spring or fall, but the moderate altitude makes it possible to hike in summer too.

Hiking Boots Any dry weather boots or shoes.

Author's Experience He parked where Lick Wash crosses the Skutumpah Road, walked down Lick Wash to the LeFevre Cabin, then around to the east side of No Mans Mesa, and climbed it along the route shown. He later came down the goat trail, and returned via Park Wash and the Swallow Park Ranch. This took a little over 7 hours, round-trip. In October of 1997, he parked at the corral east of the ranch, walked down the road and part way up the goat trail, then checked out the water tap & cabin. After that he headed back, but climbed up the east side of Calf Pasture Point. That allowed him some good looks right down on the LeFevre Cabin and No Mans Mesa. From there, back to his car, all in about 5 2/3 hours. You should plan on more time than this.

The History of Swallow Park Ranch

Swallow Park is a high valley, at just under 2000 meters elevation. It's located along the Skutumpah Road about halfway between the upper end of Johnson Valley and Cannonville. It's also just south of the southern end of Bryce Canyon National Park.

From the *Biography of John G. Kitchen*, it appears the first settler at Swallow Park was Frank Hamblin. This had to have been in the late 1870's, or more likely in the 1880's. Hamblin's occupancy extended into the 1890's to past the turn of the century. For several years, he was the only neighbor John G. Kitchen had while he was at the Nipple Ranch. Read more about Kitchen in the chapter on *Kitchen Canyon and the Nipple Ranch*.

If the memories of some of the old timers are right, the second owner of the ranch was a man named George Adam's. George married Minda, one of the daughters of Frank Hamblin, thus giving him a toehold on the ranch. George's name is on the spring, southeast of Adair Lake. Wallace Ott believes Adams got there sometime just after the turn of the century. Actually, it was November 23, 1917, when George first got official ownership from the government under the homestead act. There are no other records of land ownership prior to that time, but most early settlers just squatted on the land without having a deed. It also took 5 full years of homesteading to gain title officially. Frank Hamblin apparently never tried to get the patented deed to the ranch.

Adams owned the ranch only a couple of years, then sold the lower part of the valley, around what they called Swallow Park Lake, to Jackson Riggs, in December, 1919. Just prior to this sale, William Sears Riggs in November, 1919, settled and filed ownership on the northern part of the valley. In 1926, W. S. Riggs then bought more land from the Federal Government, which was an enlargement of his original 160 acres. Sears Riggs is the one who built the first house at the ranch, which is still there today. His name is also on the rather good spring near the head of Lower Podunk Creek, just south of the south tip of Bryce Canyon, and along the Riggs Spring Loop Trail.

Wallace Ott, who is now semi-retired and who lives in Tropic, bought the entire spread on December 11, 1940. He lived there part time, using it as a summer range or ranch until 1955. During his stay at Swallow Park, part of the property was sold to John H. Johnson in March, 1945. Then Wallace Ott sold out entirely to one of his relatives, Layton Ott, in December, 1955. Less than a month later, John H. Johnson sold his part of the Park to Calvin C. Johnson of Kanab, who still holds title to that parcel of land. So presently, it's Johnson and James D. Ott who own two different parts of

This is the very top of the Jepson Goat Trail on No Mans Mesa.

From the southeast side of Calf Pasture Point, one has a good look at No Mans Mesa and the talus slope where the Jepson Goat Trail is located.

the old Swallow Park Ranch and most of the land which is considered Swallow Park.

At the Park today, you'll see the old house built by Sears Riggs, and a couple of other old buildings just southwest of the house. In the valley are a couple of small dams and duck ponds which are always full of water, and which are fed by several springs. Near the largest pond is an old yellow camp wagon with the name, *Camp Burge*, painted on it. Perhaps the most interesting thing to see is Adair Lake. This was always known to old timers as Swallow Park Lake. It's at the southern end of the park, and right at the beginning of a little narrow section of upper Park Wash.

The lake is actually on a fault line, or just to the east of it. This fault line forms the cliffs you can see from upvalley. The west side has been raised, thus creating the lake just to the east. The lake and a swamp have always been there, but one of the early owners, and someone before Wallace Ott's time, put up a very low dam, maybe a meter or less in height, to create a slightly larger and deeper lake.

The lake is there year-round; throughout wet and dry years. On two occasions Wallace Ott attempted to plant bass there, but apparently it was too shallow to sustain them throughout the winter. Presently in the lake, and for as long as anyone can remember, are *salamanders,* or what the locals call *water dogs*. The lake also has an abundant waterfowl population for much of each year.

At the bottom end of the lake, and right on top of the low and almost invisible dam, is a corral. Wallace Ott used this corral to hold cattle for spraying, but other owners used it as a kind of trap. They would herd cattle or horses up Park Wash from the area of No Mans Mesa. When they reached the corral, they were automatically trapped in one easy operation.

Adair Lake is easy to get to, and although it's on private land, it seems the owner shouldn't worry about visitors walking to it, because there's nothing there to disturb.

From halfway up the goat trail, looking southwest at Park Wash and Calf Pasture Point.

The southeast side of Calf Pasture Point and Park Wash. This picture was taken from near the water tap.

The old Riggs Home, in the middle of Swallow Park. Pink Cliffs are in the background.

Mollies Nipple and the Burch Ranch

Location and Access Mollies Nipple is located just a few kms north of Highway 89, about halfway between Page and Kanab. On some older maps of the area, it's called the White Cone. This name comes from the white Navajo Sandstone which the cone, or nipple, is made of. At the very summit of the peak is the brown and more erosion-resistant capstone. The author believes it could be the Carmel Formation, but it could also be a harder iron-rich layer within the Navajo. The name Mollies Nipple, comes from the wife of John G. Kitchen, whose name was Mollie. Read more about John G. Kitchen and his ranch under *Kitchen Canyon and the Nipple Ranch.*

One hiking route to the mountain begins west of the peak. From Highway 89, turn north onto the Nipple Ranch Road right at mile post 37. This rather good road was built by an oil company which made a test hole near the point marked 1937 meters. It's now maintained by the county for access to the Nipple Ranch. This road is good, except right near the pass at 1825 meters, there's usually a sandy area. Going down the other side toward the ranch, there are even more sandy places too. Drive to or near the pass and park. Or better still, stop at the beginning of a very sandy track marked 1806 meters. This track heads east and ends at the southern base of Mollies Nipple. Most of this area is in a WSA, and in the future this could be closed to motorized vehicles. If so, it will make a good hiking trail.

You can also come in from old Pahreah and Starlight Canyon to the east and southeast. Leave Highway 89 between mile posts 30 and 31, and drive north to old Pahreah and the nearby Paria Movie Set. See the next map and the discussion on *Kitchen Canyon* for more details on that route.

Trail or Route Conditions From the pass marked 1825 meters, walk southeast up the slope to the top of the ridge. From there you'll see your objective. Walk east across the valley, and route-find up the peak from the southwest. After climbing a couple of steep pitches, you're on top. You could also come in along the sandy track south of the South Swag which is the best and easiest way. That ATV track ends right at the base of the peak where you'll see a number of ponderosa pines. Or route-find in from Starlight following the route symbols, or possibly Kitchen Canyon.

By using the Nipple Ranch Road and by parking at the pass of 1825 meters, you can also include in your hiking day, a quick look at the only cliff dwellings in the immediate area. From the pass, walk down the road about 700-800 meters to the northeast, and to the valley bottom. This is what is known as the West Swag. At the bottom, make a 180 degree turn to the right, and walk southwest in the bottom of the valley to the head of what could be called the south arm of the West Swag. Right at the southern end, and under the overhang are two cliff dwellings. These rock and mud structures have been partially damaged by time and cattle.

The strange thing about these ruins is they are under an overhang and facing north--the first of its kind this author has seen. The Indians who inhabited this site were likely a part of what archaeologists called the Virgin Anasazi. But the site is very near to the transition zone of the Sevier, Great Basin, or Fremont Culture area, and the Anasazi Cultures to the south. Just north of the ruins,

Mollies Nipple, as seen from the southern base.

Map 11, Mollies Nipple and the Burch Ranch

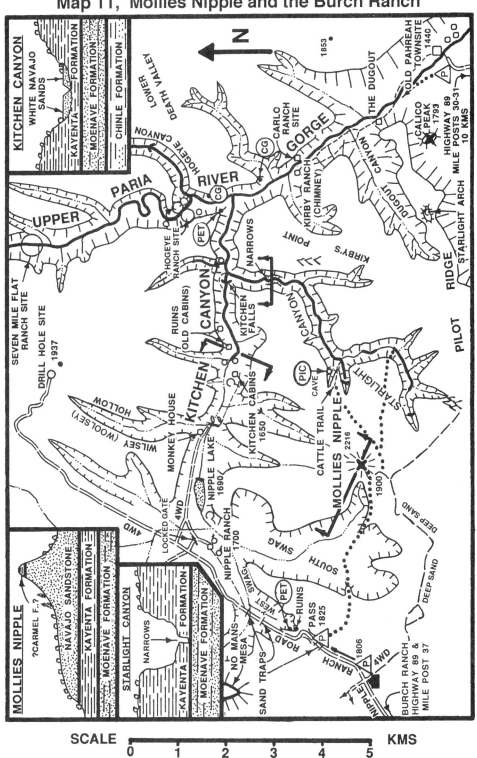

SCALE

0   1   2   3   4   5   KMS

A well-preserved matate. When used with a mono, this is where Fremont Indians used to grind seeds and corn.

Very little remains of the old Burch Ranch, near Kitchen Point Corral.

The caved-in roof of the cellar at the old abandoned Burch Ranch.

Part of a "Stake & Rider", or "Rip Gut" fence located at the old Nipple Ranch.
The Kitchen Cabin in the background.

and along the east facing wall, are some minor petroglyphs.

Elevations Mollies Nipple, 2216 meters; the car-parks at 1806 & 1825; old Pahreah, 1440 meters.

Hike Length and Time Needed From the pass on the Nipple Ranch Road, it's about 5 kms to the peak. A fit hiker can do this round-trip in about half a day; but others may want to take a lunch, water, and spend a day. It's a lot easier walking however if you stay on the old sandy track to the base of the peak. The time and distance is about the same as going in from the pass at 1825 meters. It's much further from old Pahreah, and some would have to do it on a two day trip, camping in Starlight Canyon. You could also go up Kitchen Canyon to the old Kitchen Cabins and climb from there, but you're supposed to get permission from the land owner, Calvin C. Johnson first(Tele. 435-644-2384-Kanab). No problem; he just wants to know who is on his land, which is from about the old cabin ruins to the Nipple Ranch Road, in the bottom of Kitchen Canyon.

Water Carry your own on the normal route.

Maps USGS or BLM maps Kanab and Smoky Mountain(1:100,000), or Deer Range Point and Calico Peak(1:24,000).

Main Attractions A beautiful peak, a fun half-day hike(normal route), and excellent views. Along the Paria are petroglyphs at the mouth of Kitchen Canyon and old ranch sites. And just northeast of the pass marked 1825 meters, are the Kitchen Canyon cliff dwellings.

Ideal Time to Hike Spring or fall, but it can be climbed year-round.

Hiking Boots Any dry weather boots or shoes(except, if you come up the Paria River, you'll need waders for that part).

Author's Experience From the pass, the author made it to the summit in 1 1/4 hours. He then went north to the Monkey House, Nipple Lake & Ranch, and road-walked back to his car. Round-trip was 4 1/4 hours. In November, 1997, he hiked the sandy track to Mollies Nipple, then explored Starlight Canyon and the cave, then returned the same way, all in 8 1/4 hours.

The Burch Ranch

On your way to climb Mollies Nipple via the standard routes from the west, you'll pass one of the abandoned ranch sites along the way. One of the last ranches to be built and used in the Paria River drainage, was the Burch Ranch. This old homestead is located in the northwestern corner of Section 33, R3W, T41S. To get there, turn north from Highway 89 right at mile post 37, which is the Nipple Ranch Road. Drive about 10 kms, to where you see the Kitchen Point Corral and old stone building on your right. This is an old CCC camp dating back to the mid-1930's. Across the road from the corral, look for an old track running due west. Follow this track west 100 meters, and park at the gate just before the wash. If the gate is unlocked, walk through to the southwest, then north in the wash bottom. Veer left along an old track to the west, then through a 2nd gate and north again. Finally veer northwest and walk past an old dam. The ranch site is just north of the old dam, and about 1 1/2 kms WNW of the Kitchen Point Corral.

Fremont Indian ruins just below the road and the pass at 1825 meters.

Part of the land you'll be walking over is private, belonging to Calvin C. Johnson of Kanab. To rightfully explore the site, you should first telefone him and get permission. There's really nothing out there to disturb, but as a matter of respect, call him first at 435-644-2384. It was Calvin Johnson who the author interviewed for this Burch Ranch story.

In the early 1930's, Dood Burch, his wife, and two young sons, Robert and Omer, migrated from Texas to the House Rock Valley area, which is just south of the Vermilion Cliffs and Paria Plateau. They lived there a couple of years, then homesteaded this ranch in about 1934 just below where Deer Spring Wash and Park Wash meet.

The first thing they did was to build a small house out of lumber and a storage cellar behind the house. The cellar was dug out of the hill side, and lined with rocks. It was likely a place for food storage, but they may have also lived in it. They built several corrals, a small dam to create a pond, and a blacksmith shop. Their water came from a small spring on a hillside about 200 meters south of the home and cellar. At one time they had water piped to the house, where they raised a small garden.

One interesting feature of their home was that Mrs. Burch built a special floor, like nothing the author has ever heard of. When she had collected enough old fruit jars, she turned them upside down and placed them in the floor of the cabin. They must have been packed very close together so they wouldn't break. On top of the bottles, she laid goat hides. This, according the Calvin Johnson who later bought the place. When the author visited the site, there were a number of old bottles around, but apparently at a later date they installed another floor made of wood.

The Burches were horse and rodeo people. They brought with them a number of quarter horses, and also ran goats in the hills around the ranch. They apparently supplied part of the stock animals during the rodeo season in southern Utah and northern Arizona.

Evidently the Burches had marital problems. They never officially got a divorce, but he took off for Texas not too long after they had settled in at this ranch. Sometime later he was killed when his horse threw him as it stepped in a gopher hole and stumbled. Mrs. Burch ended up raising the boys by herself.

County records show the patented land was obtained officially from the government in January, 1945. It was listed in the name of Omer Burch, the youngest of the two boys. Robert got married to a local girl and drove the mail truck for several years in the Kanab area before moving to Provo, where he lived for the rest of his life.

Omer and his mother moved to Oregon in late 1947, when they sold the land to Johnson. Omer ended up as a brand inspector and continued in the rodeo stock business. After their departure, Johnson used the place as a kind of line cabin for several years afterwards, until the house and facilities literally fell apart and decayed. Parts of the house, cellar, and corrals are still there today.

Corn cobs and potsherds are all that remain at the Kitchen Canyon ruins.

Kitchen Canyon and the Nipple Ranch

Location and Access Kitchen Canyon is located in the area north of Highway 89 about halfway between Kanab and Page. One way to get there is to drive north from the highway between mile posts 30 and 31, at the sign stating *Paria Movie Set, 5 miles(8 kms)*. You'll stop and park near the old Pahreah townsite about 10 kms north of Highway 89 on a good and well-traveled dirt road(but which is slick in wet weather because of the Chinle and Moenkopi clay beds). The movie set is about 8 kms from the pavement.

Another possibility is to leave Highway 89 right at mile post 37, and drive north about 25 kms along the Nipple Ranch Road to the Nipple Ranch. But the land downcanyon from the Nipple Ranch to just beyond John G. Kitchen's old cabins is private, and you'll need to call Calvin Johnson of Kanab to get permission to cross his land(435-644-2384). A simple fone call will insure permission.

The Nipple Ranch Road is very good, except it has sandy places beginning about 4 kms short of the ranch. For a nice hike, the route from old Pahreah is best. Even if you come up from old Pahreah, Calvin Johnson would prefer you call or let him know if you're planning to see the old homestead and the Monkey House, which are both on the lower part of his land.

Trail or Route Conditions After parking your car near the end of the road not far from the Paria River, simply walk upcanyon in the washed-out river bed. You'll be crossing the small Paria stream several times in the 8 kms or so to the mouth of Kitchen Canyon. Inside Kitchen Canyon, you'll be walking beside a small stream. When you arrive at Kitchen Falls(just where Starlight Canyon enters), head up the steep slope on the north side of the falls and pass through an old gate, which at one time was a wagon road down to old Pahreah. About a km above the falls(which is about where the private land begins), you can get out of the creek bed, and walk on cattle trails on the north side of the "V" shaped erosional gully so prominent in Kitchen Valley. It's easy walking all the way.

Elevations Old Pahreah, 1440 meters; the old Kitchen Cabins, about 1650; and Nipple Lake, 1690 meters.

Hike Length and Time Needed It's about 8 kms from old Pahreah to the mouth of Kitchen Canyon, then another 5 kms to Nipple Lake. Plan on taking a lunch and spending the entire day seeing the Kitchen Valley historic sites. You could also camp in Starlight Canyon, where there's a good water supply--and no private land.

Water Lower Kitchen Canyon has running water year-round, and several springs in the valley. There are cattle in this valley year-round, so be careful with that water. Starlight Canyon has the best possibilities for a safe drink.

Maps USGS or BLM maps Kanab and Smoky Mountain(1:100,000), or Deer Range Point and Calico Peak(1:24,000).

Main Attractions Kitchen Falls, Nipple Lake, the stone Monkey House, and the ruins of the oldest ranch in the entire region, the John G. Kitchen cabins and the Nipple Ranch. Along the Paria are petroglyphs and the chimneys of the old Kirby Place and the Carlo Ranch, as well as the ruins of the Dugout, once occupied by

Kitchen Falls, as seen in 1987. In 1997, the whole bottom of this canyon was washed away by the El Niño floods.

Map 12, Kitchen Canyon and the Nipple Ranch

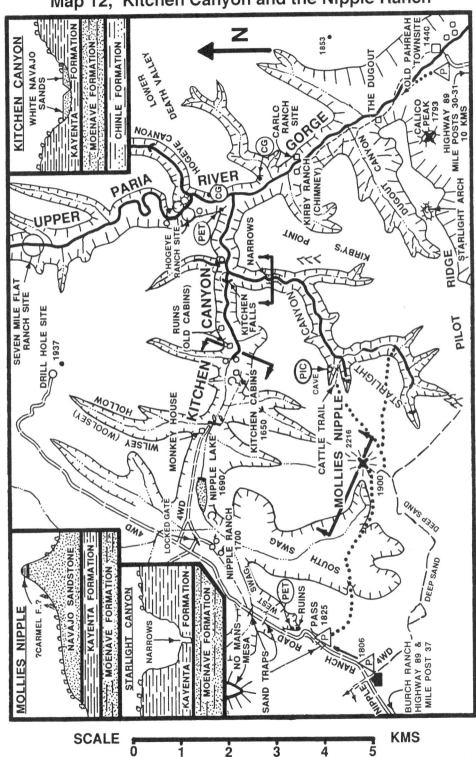

KITCHEN CANYON
WHITE NAVAJO SANDS
KAYENTA FORMATION
MOENAVE FORMATION
CHINLE FORMATION

N

1853

OLD PAHREAH TOWNSITE
1440
THE DUGOUT
CARLO RANCH SITE
CG
GORGE
CALICO PEAK 1793
HIGHWAY 89 MILE POSTS 30-31 10 KMS
LOWER DEATH VALLEY
HOGEYE CANYON
CG
KIRBY RANCH (CHIMNEY)
DUGOUT CANYON
STARLIGHT ARCH
PARIA RIVER
UPPER
PET
HOGEYE RANCH SITE
NARROWS
KIRBY'S POINT
RIDGE
SEVEN MILE FLAT RANCH SITE
DRILL HOLE SITE
1937
RUINS (OLD CABINS)
KITCHEN CANYON
KITCHEN FALLS
STARLIGHT CANYON
PILOT
WILSEY (WOOLSEY) HOLLOW
MONKEY HOUSE
KITCHEN CABINS
1650
PIC
CAVE
CATTLE TRAIL
MOLLIES NIPPLE 2216
NIPPLE LAKE 1690
1900
LOCKED GATE
4WD
4WD
NIPPLE RANCH 1700
SOUTH SWAG
DEEP SAND
DEEP SAND

MOLLIES NIPPLE
?CARMEL F. ?
NAVAJO SANDSTONE
KAYENTA FORMATION
MOENAVE FORMATION

STARLIGHT CANYON
NARROWS
KAYENTA FORMATION
MOENAVE FORMATION

WEST SWAG
PET
RUINS
PASS 1825
NO MANS MESA
ROAD
P
NIPPLE RANCH 1806
P 4WD
SAND TRAPS
BURCH RANCH HIGHWAY 89 & MILE POST 37

SCALE 0 1 2 3 4 5 **KMS**

John Mangum and family. At or near the car-park along the Paria River is the Paria Movie Set, old Pahreah townsite and Pahreah cemetery.

Ideal Time to Hike Spring or fall. Or, perhaps in winter warm spells if you had some good rubber wading boots. Summers are a little too warm for most people to enjoy.

Hiking Boots Wading boots or shoes.

Author's Experience He first visited the canyon on his Mollies Nipple hike and from the pass at 1825 meters, then made two more foto trips into the canyon from old Pahreah. One trip to Starlight, lower Kitchen and lower Hogeye Canyon, took about 9 1/2 hours, round-trip. Another trip to Seven Mile Flat and to the Monkey House, took 8 1/2 hours round-trip. His last hike was in October, 1997. He parked at the pass marked 1825 meters, walked to the ruins below, to the Kitchen Cabins and Monkey House, and returned, all in 4 1/4 hours. Starlight Canyon is covered in more detail under *Map 13*.

History of the Nipple or Mollies Nipple Ranch

One of the very first ranches to be built in the entire area is what most people call the Nipple Ranch. In researching the history of this old homestead, the author obtained a copy of the *"Biography of John G. Kitchen"*, from Adrian Kitchen(a great grandson) of Wahweap on Lake Powell near Page. This short history of the original founder of the Nipple Ranch, was compiled by a Nephi Johnson of Mesquite, Nevada, and Ramona Kitchen Johnson of Kanab. They got the information from John G. Kitchen, Jr. The following is the history of John G. Kitchen and the Nipple Ranch, which has been edited slightly for this book.

John G. Kitchen was born in Canada in 1830. Very little is known of his childhood or his early youth. The first anyone knows of him was during the gold rush days of California. There at the age of nineteen, his willingness to work and his determination to get along in the world, began to assert itself. Money was plentiful at that time in California. A gold mine was to be had almost for the taking, but young Kitchen was not interested in a gold mine. His heart was set on a cattle ranch in the Rocky Mountains. So he worked at the job that paid the best, and saved his $11.00 per day, to make that cattle ranch dream come true.

In 1873 he arrived in Johnson, Utah [in Johnson Valley east of Kanab], with a herd of heifer calves, which he had purchased in and around St. George. Sixtus Johnson was then running the Dairy Ranch, two miles [3 kms] north of Johnson, and he took the calves to manage while Kitchen went back to his job in California for the winter. This arrangement lasted for several years, with Kitchen returning each fall with more calves; or money to buy more.

In 1878 he took a herd of steers to Nephi, Utah, to sell. While there and waiting for the train to load his steers, he became acquainted with Martha or Mollie Grice. She was waiting tables at the Seely Hotel, and keeping house for her uncle, William Grice. John married Martha and brought her back to the Dairy Ranch, which he had leased. There the couple lived until their first baby, Rose, was born. The following spring[1879] with the assistance of Nephi Johnson, they moved their cattle into Mollies Nipple Ranch.

This is the original Kitchen home. It has two fireplaces, both still standing.

The ranch received its name because of the peculiar shape and coloring of a large knoll or peak located to the south of the ranch and Kitchen Valley. Martha's nickname was Mollie, because it's common knowledge around the country this peak was named after Kitchen's wife. This peak of course, is named Mollies Nipple. When you see it, you'll understand how it got the name.

Their life at the Nipple Ranch, though filled with hardships and disappointments, was successful. They started with meager beginnings, and built slowly as time and means would permit, while faced with drought years, crop failures, menaces of gophers, squirrels, and chipmunks. For several years, Kitchen did all of his own riding on an old mare, "Dolly", upon which he carried food and a quilt for a bed when he was forced to camp away from home for a night or two. In later years he brought back a few blooded horses each fall or spring when he shipped his steers and thus built up a fine band of horses, along with his cattle.

Those first few years at Mollies Nipple Ranch were never to be forgotten by the Kitchens. They had a new country to conquer, land to clear, buildings and fences to be built, and cattle to tend. The cattle were so well taken care of, that other cattle men said jokingly, that "Kitchen knew where every cow laid down each night." He knew his cattle so intimately that many of them were given names, such as Betsy, Posey, Kill Deer, Brin, Blue Neck, Red Rony, and Jennette.

Most of his cows were red Durham, branded with the box brand on the left ribs, and marked with a Kitchen Slit in each ear. The Kitchen Slit was a circular cut just above and following the vein in the lower part of the ear, and is so called because Kitchen was the first man in Southern Utah to use that mark.

To build up a better grade of cattle, he used to bring in blooded bulls each fall or spring when he returned from taking his steers to the railroad. One of these was a roan Durham named Paddy, that cost him $500. The original cattle were Hereford stock.

A John Mangum helped the Kitchens with the buildings at Mollies Nipple Ranch. The corrals and fences were made of cedar logs and posts secured there in the valley and constructed in the stake and rider[or rip gut] style, which consisted of two posts set in the ground so as to form an X every 8 or 10 feet [2 or 3 meters] with a cedar pole rider placed in the saddle of the X to connect the pairs of posts. [Only those who have tried to chop down a cedar tree with an ax, can appreciate the amount of work which went into this type of fence]

The buildings were of pine logs or native rocks laid up with mud. The roofs were of split pine logs. The split side was laid down, then covered with bark and about a foot [30 cms] of sand. It was on these roofs, warmed from the heat within, that the wild flowers first bloomed in the springtime.

The dwelling house, which consisted of two long rooms [actually two cabins and a store room placed next to each other], was constructed of hewed logs, in the shape of a "T". One room served as a kitchen, living and dining room, and was heated by the cook stove and fireplace. The other room had a large fireplace and it served as a bedroom and a school room. The floors of both rooms were unplained lumber, but Mrs. Kitchen kept them scrubbed clean and white; "So clean you could eat off them", was a familiar

Mollies Nipple as seen to the south of Nipple Lake. The floods of 1997, filled
up about half of Nipple Lake.

family expression.

After their children became old enough, the Kitchens had a school teacher who boarded with the family every winter. These private tutors, boarded with the family and assisted with the ranch labor when not teaching. Among these teachers were Robert Laws, Lydia Johnson, Jim Burrows, and a Mr. Ramsdale.

A little distance from, and at the back of the home, was the cellar and smoke house. These buildings were of much the same construction as the ranch house, except that the cellar was excavated about six feet[2 meters] in the ground. Here many bushels of fruit and vegetables were stored in winter, and milk and butter were kept cool in summer. The smoke house was constructed of rock, and here Kitchen cured beef, pork, and venison.

While their home was still being built, another child was born to them. For this occasion, Martha went to Pahreah, where she could have the assistance of other women during childbirth. The child was a boy and they named him John G. Kitchen, Jr. Their next two children were Rosena and Mattie, born at Nipple Ranch. Their fifth child, Una, was born in Kanab.

In addition to stock raising, Kitchen farmed and always had a garden to keep his family alive. There were several large springs that boiled up at the foot of the mountains, creating a meadow land for several miles up and down the valley. These springs he dammed up, and used for irrigation purposes. He would store the water for several days, and until the ponds were full, then run the water off onto his crops. It was on the hillside just above the ditches that he used to build his hot beds. Early in the spring he would level off a small space on the mountain side, where the sun shone early and late, and was protected from the cold. Here he would plant some of his seeds.

Before he began irrigating each spring he would carry water for the young plants. After he began irrigating, the hot beds were so located that he could scoop water from the ditches onto the plants with a shovel. He raised cabbage, cauliflower, squash, turnips, carrots, potatoes, corn, watermelon, rye, and hay. One year he raised over 800 bushels of corn. He had a span of oxen, Ben and Brady, to assist him with the farming, and other heavy work such as hauling wood and securing rocks for building.

Because of the lack of roads and long distances to any settlement, there was practically no demand for his produce, except what his own family, hired help, and stock consumed. He delighted in taking a pack load of vegetables to his Hamblin friends at Swallow Park some 7 or 8 miles [11 or 12 kms] to the northwest. And each fall he enjoyed taking part of a beef to Pahreah, and distributing it among his less fortunate friends.

As his cattle increased and financial conditions improved, Kitchen purchased the Meadows Ranch from Chet Patrick. [In Dunk Findlay's history of his family's ranch, he states that Alexander Duncan Findlay sold his squatters rights of the Meadows to Kitchen for 50 head of steers]. This ranch was northwest of the Nipple, not far below the Pink Cliffs on Meadow Creek. It's just to the northwest of the present-day Deer Springs Ranch. It was used primarily as a summer ranch. There he added dairying to his ranching

In about the middle of Kitchen Canyon, stands the Monkey House.

activities. Some summers he milked as many as 50 cows. From the milk, they made butter and cheese, which were packed and stored for winters use at the Nipple. [The late Dunk Findlay stated that a man by the name of Joe Honey lived in a dugout Kitchen had built as a shelter at the Meadows for one winter, to preserve Kitchens claim to the land].

At the Meadows Ranch, with the assistance of Edwin and John Ford and Thomas Greenhalgh, he built a dugout shelter [it's still at the upper end of the Meadows today] and large corrals and fences. One night the cowboys had five hundred head of three and four year old steers ready to drive to the railroad the next morning. About two o'clock in the morning something frightened them, and they stampeded. The cowboys were camped only a short distance from the corral and when they heard the cattle running and bellowing, they rushed to the scene. The corral was built on a sidehill, and on the downhill side, the cattle were piling up and being trampled. Fear seized the cowboys, lest so many would die, so they spent the rest of the night fighting the steers back from the downhill side of the corral. The next morning revealed one steer dead, and several lame and bruised.

Another interesting event happened just south of Kitchens Ranch. One winter Ira Hatch of Panguitch, Utah, had his sheep camp in the high country close to Mollies Nipple. One afternoon it began to storm, and it snowed all night. The next morning the sheep bunched up beneath cedar trees, unwilling to brave the deep, newly fallen snow. Still the storm continued. For three days it snowed and when the storm finally broke, Hatch and his sheep were virtually prisoners in four or five feet [about one and a half meters] of snow.

Hatch left his freezing, starving sheep and made his way to the Nipple Ranch for help. Kitchen took one team, Ned and Colonel, cut down a tree, and dragged it around to make trails for the sheep to follow into lower country where the snow wasn't so deep.

During the summer of 1895, Kitchen let Ebbin Brown dairy at the Meadows Ranch and paid him $1.00 per head for all the three and four year old steers he could gather. He gathered 500 head. Then Kitchen and other cowboys gathered another 500 head and drove them to the railhead at Milford. Here they were loaded on cattle cars and shipped to Kansas City, Missouri, and to Omaha, Nebraska. Young John Jr. accompanied his father on this trip, traveling with and tending the cattle until they reached their destination. It was on this trip, and while in Salt Lake City on their return journey, that his father gave him the gold watch which he still carries(1947) and treasures so much, and a bicycle, which was the first one ever owned in Kanab.

At the lower end of the canyon there were clumps of squawberry bushes. Every fall Piute Indians would came to the Nipple country to hunt deer and to gather squawberry brush to make baskets. Kitchen made it a practice to buy two baskets, two tanned deer hides, and several deer hams from them each fall. The baskets were used to haul laundry and for storing dried fruits and vegetables. The deer hides were used to make belts, saddle strings, harness parts and shoe laces. The deer hams were cured in the smoke house

There are numerous old cowboyglyphs on the door frames of the Monkey House.

and eaten during the winter.

One interesting story is told about the "tally stick" method of keeping track of calves branded. Whenever Kitchen went out to brand calves, he would carry a short stick in his back pocket. When he branded a calf, he would whittle a notch in the stick. In the evenings after he had returned to the house, the notches were transferred to a much larger tally stick, which was 8 or 10 feet [2.5 or 3 meters] long and kept overhead on the rafters in the kitchen. Whenever he desired a count of the seasons branding, he would take down the tally stick and count the notches. One side represented the heifers; the other side the steers. It was when his branding count reached enormous figures that he became known as "The Cattle King of Southern Utah." It was estimated at one time that he owned about 5000 head of cattle, ranging from St. George on the west, Panguitch on the north, and to the Colorado River on the east and south. [When the late Dunk Findlay of Kanab heard about the 5000 head of cattle, he doubted very much the country could have sustained that many. Maybe 1000 could have been a closer figure?].

Kitchen was a great lover of knowledge, and so that the children might have an advantage of better schooling, and his family enjoy some of the finer things of life, he appointed George Adams foreman of his ranch, and moved the family to Kanab in the early 1890's. This move seemed to climax his career, and his star of success began waning. Liquor had always been his weakness, so while in Kanab and with plenty of leisure time and money, drinking got the upper hand. Trouble began brewing, which ended in the divorce courts.

The loss of his family was a great blow to Kitchen. Mollie ended up marrying Joe Honey, a man who once worked for Kitchen. Sorrowing, Kitchen made a liberal settlement both of alimony and for the education of his children, which Thomas Chamberlain faithfully administered. He sold his cattle to Scott Cutler and Hack Jolly, who moved them out of the country. The remnant of the box brand was sold to Johnny Findlay.

In 1898, Kitchen went to Lee's Ferry, where he lived only a short time. He died very suddenly, and under mysterious circumstances. A rider was dispatched to Kanab with the news. Young John rode in haste all night, but the body was already buried when he reached the Ferry.

Thus ended the career of a man with clouds of uncertainty hovering about the cause of his death as well as about the disposal of his property. In his will he bequeathed to each of his daughters $20,000, and to his sons $25,000, but through faulty administration, the fortune was dissipated. Although his family spent years in the inheritance courts, not a dollar was ever recovered.

In 1904, his children erected a monument to his memory at Lee's Ferry Cemetery. The monument which was there in 1991 read, "John G. Kitchen, Born in Canada, March 25, 1830, Died July 13, 1898."

After the death of Kitchen, there seems to be a gap in history of the Nipple Ranch. Evidently, it was in the courts for some time. Some of the old timers in the area thought it may have gotten into the hands of two men named Hunter and Clark, then after a time it may have been taken over by a Jim Henderson. However, the first recorded transfer of the property(Kane County Courthouse) was on July 2, 1908. The land, part of a grant of 100,000 acres, was given to the state of Utah by the Federal government, for the use of "Institution for the Blind".

The next transfer of ownership was on March 11, 1912, when the Cross Bar Land & Cattle Co. purchased the ranch land from the state of Utah. Later, on May 7, 1927, a John H. Johnson bought the land from Kane County, apparently for back taxes owed by the cattle company. The last time the land changed hands, was on January 16, 1956, when present owner Calvin C. Johnson, bought it from John H. Johnson.

At the ranch today, Calvin has a small headquarters located to the west of Nipple Lake, along with several corrals. Hikers are asked to stay away from this part of the ranch. Downcanyon and a couple of kms to the west or above the Kitchen Falls, are the ruins of the old Kitchen or Nipple Ranch. The author has seen the ruins of an old chimney in one location, and a rock wall just to the west of the chimney, as shown on the map. Just to the west of these ruined cabins, is the Kitchen house. It's in rather good condition, considering its age. The roof has collapsed, but the log walls and the two chimneys are still standing. When the author first saw the twin chimneys and rooms, he thought it was the home of an old Mormon polygamist. Instead the second room was for the school and teacher. Nearby is an old corral, made in the "stake and rider" fashion. The holes you'll see in the corral gate posts, are said to have been made by Kitchen who used a hot iron poker to run through the posts. Nearby, are the ruins of the smoke house and other structures.

From Kitchen's house, walk along an old seldom-used road to the northwest. After about a km, you'll see some of Calvin Johnson's work in erosion control. Crossing the valley is an earthen dam, and just to the north of it is a rock cabin, called the Monkey House.

The Monkey House and Nipple Lake

According to Calvin C. Johnson, the Monkey House was built in 1896 by Dick Woolsey, at the mouth of what the USGS maps call Wilsey Hollow(he also says it should be "Woolsey" Hollow). It's made of stones, and it sits up against a large boulder. When Woolsey and his wife first settled in at this location, they had with them a monkey. The monkey was kept in a box or cage on top of a pole near the cabin. When someone approached the homestead, the monkey would chatter loudly. This, plus in the eyes of some, can be seen a monkey shape in the rock, is how this dwelling got its name.

Inside the cabin and on the wooden doorway structure, are many names of early cowboys. A new roof has been added, and the ramada has been taken off from the original structure, evidently in the years John H. Johnson owned the land. The Monkey House is in good condition today. Behind the cabin is a small pen or corral in a small opening of the cliff.

About another km or two to the west of the Monkey House, is Nipple Lake. Evidently there has always been a small and shallow pond there in a swampy area, but today you'll see a low dam, maybe a meter high, which backs up the clear blue water to form the lake. However, the flash floods of 1997, filled in about half of this lake. All the while as you walk the valley bottom, you'll see to the south, the ever present Mollies Nipple, towering above the landscape.

If you're coming into the area to climb Mollies Nipple from the west, there are several things to see along the way. Leave Highway 89 right at mile post 37, and drive north on the Nipple Ranch Road. After about 6 kms you pass the old King Mine on the right. After about another 4 kms or so, you'll see on the right or east, a corral and stone house which is the old CCC camp at Kitchen Point. It's now used by Calvin C. Johnson of Kanab. To the west of this corral is the old Burch Ranch. Read about the history of that ranch in the part with *Map 11, Mollies Nipple and the Burch Ranch*, page 68.

Continue north from the CCC rock house & corral about 2 1/2 kms and at the mouth of the first canyon coming in from the east, is an old stockade-type corral(with the poles standing upright and stuck in the ground). This is called the Kitchen Corral, but he didn't build it.

For those who like to explore, drive about another km north of the Kitchen Corral and to the mouth of Box Elder Canyon coming down from the east(see the *Kanab* 1:100,000 metric map). You can walk up this canyon to reach Mollies Nipple. Somewhere at the head of this canyon and before you reach the Nipple, is an old *"stake and rider"* or *"rip gut"* fence, which runs from northeast to southwest from the Nipple area toward the head of Box Elder Canyon. The author looked for it, but found nothing. Calvin C. Johnson can perhaps give you a more accurate idea of just where it's located. This fence is of historic value because of the way it was constructed and when it was built. The corral next to the Kitchen Cabins is also made the *"stake and rider"* way.

This is the Monkey House sometime in the early 1900's. No one knows who took the picture or who the cowboys are. (Morris Shirts family foto)

Starlight Canyon

Location and Access Starlight Canyon is located not far north of Highway 89, about halfway between Kanab and Page. It's also just to the east of Mollies Nipple, a prominent landmark in southern Utah. To get there, leave Highway 89 between mile posts 30 and 31, at the sign stating *Paria Movie Set, 5 miles (8 kms)*. This dirt road is very good and maintained, but it can be slick in wet weather because of the presence of the Chinle and Moenkopi clay beds. It's about 8 kms to the old movie set, and another 2 kms to old Pahreah. Park somewhere along the river across from the old Pahreah townsite.

Trail or Route Conditions From where you'll be parking, simply walk north in the flood plain of the Paria River canyon bottom. You'll cross the creek many times on your way to Kitchen Canyon. Once inside Kitchen Canyon, you'll also be walking right along the small creek or beside it. Just before you arrive at Kitchen Falls, you'll see Starlight Canyon coming in from the south. Walk straight up this narrow canyon, which has a small stream. This canyon is lined with cottonwood trees up to where the water first begins to flow, then it's just a dry, sandy wash in the upper parts. Easy walking all the way, but you'll have a short steep section in the slot part. Near the base of the cattle trail in the upper canyon, is a large cave with pictographs on one side, plus some old cowboyglyphs. You can also get into Starlight via Mollies Nipple and the car-park at 1806 meters.

Elevations Old Pahreah townsite, 1440 meters; bottom of Starlight Canyon, about 1550; base of Mollies Nipple and head of the canyon, about 1900 meters.

Hike Length and Time Needed It's about 7 kms from old Pahreah to the mouth of Kitchen Canyon; another 1 1/2 kms to the bottom end of Starlight Canyon; and another 7-8 kms to the top of Mollies Nipple if you stay in Starlights' main channel. Consider it an all-day hike from old Pahreah to the upper end of the canyon and back. Strong hikers could climb Mollies Nipple on the same hike, but only if they're coming in from the west.

Water There's running water year-round in the bottom half of Starlight, plus several short stretches upcanyon. If there aren't any fresh signs of cattle around, and since it's a fast flowing stream, you should be able to drink Starlight water as-is. Kitchen Canyon also has a year-round stream, but don't drink that.

Maps USGS or BLM maps Kanab and Smoky Mountain(1:100,000), or Deer Range Point and Calico Peak(1:24,000).

Main Attractions A short but interesting narrows sections, a chance to climb the conspicuous Mollies Nipple, and total solitude in an unknown canyon. Also charcoal pictographs.

Ideal Time to Hike Spring or fall. Winter has ice water wading; summers are hot.

Hiking Boots Wading boots or shoes.

Author's Experience On one trip the author walked from old Pahreah, up to the Kitchen Cabins, up Starlight to where the water first begins to flow, then about halfway up Hogeye Canyon and back to the car, in about 9 1/2 hours. A 1997 hike was up Starlight to the cave, then up into lower Hogeye Canyon and back to Pahreah, all in 8 hours. A bit later, he parked at car-park 1806, and walked the sandy track to Mollies Nipple, then explored parts of upper Starlight. Round-trip was 8 1/4 hours.

The narrows of Starlight Canyon are short, but very interesting.

Map 13, Starlight Canyon

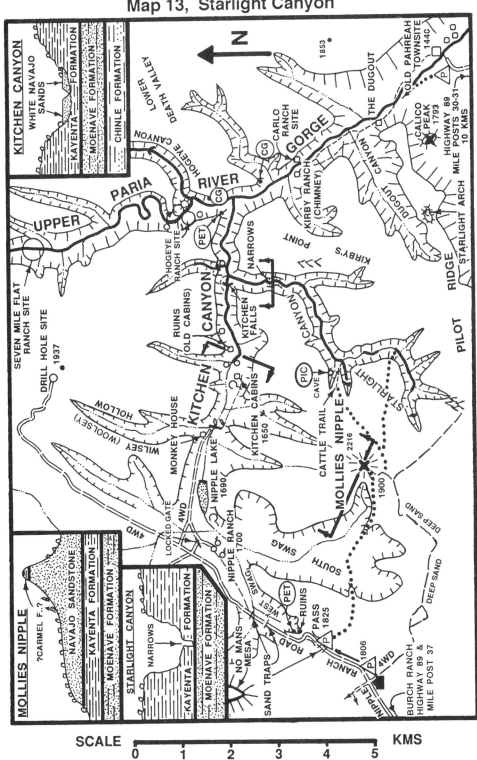

SCALE

KMS

0 1 2 3 4 5

Kodachrome Basin Trails

Location and Access This book covers areas which are mostly wilderness and with no foot trails, but it also includes places like Bryce Canyon National Park, which is heavily used and crowded. This map includes something in between those two extremes. It's Kodachrome Basin State Park. It's located only about 3 or 4 kms directly south of Henrieville, but you can't approach it from there, except by trail. Get there by driving south out of Cannonville and follow the signs. It's about 5 kms to the Skutumpah Road junction, then after another 7 or 8 kms on a paved road, turn left or north at the Kodachrome Turnoff. You must pay a small fee at the pay booth. The road is now paved all the way to Kodachrome Basin. Inside the park are two resident rangers, a camper's store(with camping supplies and horseback rides), a campground with showers and a dump station, a picnic site and several constructed trails. This park is open year-round and is a fee-use facility. There is a fee for each car, plus a per/person charge, and a fee for camping and/or a shower.

Trail or Route Conditions For the most part, the hiking trails are in the area of the park northwest of the rangers residence. Right next to the campground, is the beginning of the Eagles View Trail. It takes you up a steep trail to a pass, now known as Eagles View Pass, at 1935 meters. From this pass you have a fine view of the basin below, making it worth the walk. To the south of the campground is the Panorama Trail. It's a constructed path, which takes hikers into and through another section of the park. At its far end is Panorama Point, an overlook situated on a rock outcropping, with a good view of the rock monoliths in the park. This walk is along a sandy trail and is well-signposted. On the other side of the park is a short trail through some cliffs to the minor Shakespear Arch. Another site to see, but which you can drive to, is Chimney Rock. Get there by driving northeast from the ranger station on a road which could be slick in wet weather.

Elevations Rangers residence, 1765 meters; the campground about 1800 meters.

Hike Length and Time Needed The walk to Eagles View Pass is only about one km or less, and will take you only 10 or 15 minutes, one way. The Panorama Trail, which makes a loop-hike, is something like 3 or 4 kms, round-trip. You could do this one in about an hour, but you may want more time than that. The distance to Shakespear Arch is less than a km, and will take you less than 10 minutes for the one-way walk. While there are no trails around most sand pipe towers west of the rangers residence, it can make an interesting walking area for someone looking for good fotos.

Water At the camper's store, the picnic site, and at the campground.

Maps USGS maps Henrieville and Cannonville(1:24,000).

Main Attractions Red rock spires and cliffs, and a constructed campground, for those who enjoy that type

One of many Sand Pipes in Kodachrome Basin.

Map 14, Kodachrome Basin Trails

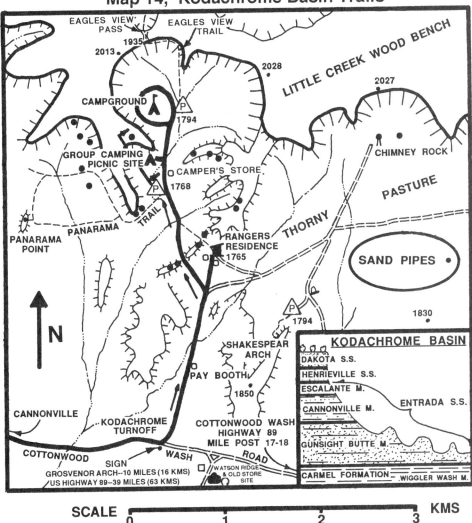

SCALE 0 1 2 3 **KMS**

of camping. Also, a rare geologic feature known as *Sand Pipes*. See explanation below.
Ideal Time to Hike Spring or fall, but the park is open and can be visited year-round.
Hiking Boots Any dry weather boots or shoes.
Author's Experience The author walked all the trails on this map in about half a day.

Sand Pipes of Kodachrome Basin

Within the park are some unusual geologic features called Sand Pipes. They occur almost no where else. In the park, they are found mostly in the red colored Gunsight Butte Member of the Entrada Formation. They seem to be concentrated in the areas to the west of the rangers residences. These pipes are lighter colored and more weather resistant than the surrounding rock, and average about 20 meters high and about 8 meters in diameter. The sand making up the pipes is normally much courser than the surrounding rock. It's been thought they came about by the injection of liquefied sand, perhaps triggered by an earthquake and possibly initiated by cold water springs. Later erosion left these pipes standing high and dry.

Round Valley Draw

Location and Access Round Valley Draw is one of the main tributaries to the much larger Hackberry Canyon. Use this map for access into the upper end of Hackberry. The location is about halfway between Kodachrome Basin State Park and Grosvenor Arch. If you're coming in from the Bryce Canyon area, drive south out of Cannonville and follow the signs to Kodachrome Basin. When you arrive at the Kodachrome Turnoff, continue straight east on the graded Cottonwood Wash Road. Drive another 10 kms or so. About one km before you go up a very steep dugway, you'll see a road heading south. Cars can be driven down this for 3 or 4 kms and parked. This could be one of your entry or exit points to Hackberry Canyon. Or better still, continue east on the Cottonwood Wash Road, climb a steep dugway, and go up to the pass marked 1984 meters. On top you'll see a fence and cattle guard. Turn right, or south, and drive down this never maintained, but good track, to either of the car-parks shown. The Slickrock Bench Car-park is a good one; it allows you easy access to the lower part of the narrows. The normal entry route however, is the one going down Round Valley Draw itself. From the pass of 1984 meters, continue down the hill and second dugway to the dry creek bed signposted *Round Valley Draw*. Just beyond is a turnoff to the south signposted, *Rushbed Road*. Drive south on this road about 3 kms, to where you cross the dry creek bed for the second time and park where you can. This is where most people park when hiking down Round Valley Draw. If you're coming from Highway 89, turn north between mile posts 17 and 18, and drive along the Cottonwood Wash Road for about 54 kms to the Rushbed Road.

Trail or Route Conditions From the Round Valley Draw Car-park, walk right down the creek bed about 1 1/2 kms. At that point you'll see the top layer of Navajo Sandstone exposed. This is where the slot canyon begins. You can get in where it first begins to cut down, but some will need a short rope, especially if you plan to come out that way. Or you can bench-walk on the north side of the slot for about 300 meters until you come to a juniper tree which marks another steep, but fairly easy route, down into the depths. To some this second route in looks fearsome at first, but it's easier than it first appears. Take 25 meters of rope or parachute cord to help those not accustomed to rock climbing. Take it slow and easy and most hikers can make it OK. In the bottom of the narrows, it's much like the Bull Valley Gorge or Buckskin Gulch. As you walk downcanyon you'll come to a large boulder which you pass on the left. Fifty meters beyond this first boulder, you'll come to another large chokestone. This has created a dryfall or dropoff. You could jump off, chimney down, or lower members of your group down with a rope; but you can also go down the crack between it and the wall to the left. If you're about 183 cms(about 6 ft.) tall or taller, you can easily *chimney* down this crack by placing your feet on the wall and your back against the chokestone, and wiggling your way down(and back up). This is just difficult enough to make it fun. After another 50 meters or so, you come to perhaps the deepest and darkest section of the hike. In the middle of this narrow part, there used to be a chokestone which had formed still another dryfall. However in 1991, that disappeared, but in 1997, there were a couple of mud hole in the same place. If it's dry, you practically walk right through this section. But with every flood, expect changes in the canyon bottom. Downcanyon there are still more narrows, but no more obstacles. After passing through the narrows, you could return the same way, or exit to the Slickrock Bench Car-park, then rim-walk back to your car.

Elevations The two main car-parks are both at 1850 meters altitude, while it's about 1775 meters elevation at the bottom of the Slickrock Bench entry route. That makes the lower part of the gorge about 75 meters deep.

Hike Length and Time Needed It's about 5 kms from the Round Valley Draw Car-park to the junction of the Draw and the main Hackberry Canyon. If you were to hike down the narrows, then exit at the Slickrock Bench Route(a walk-up), and rim-walk back to your car, it would take about half a day, depending on how long you want to enjoy the narrows.

Water If you continue up the Rushbed Road to the south, you'll come to a metal stock trough on the right. This is where water from the Round Valley Spring is piped, and it should have water in it year-round. However, the pipe is under water and you'd have to take water from the tank itself, which may be risky. Best to take your own water and have a good supply in your car at all times.

Maps USGS or BLM map Smoky Mountain(1:100,000), or Slickrock Bench(1:24,000).

Main Attractions Another deep, dark and narrow Navajo Sandstone slickrock canyon, more than one km of which is equal to the Buckskin Gulch.

Ideal Time to Hike Spring or fall are best, but it can be done year-round. There doesn't seem to be any water seeping into the bottom to make icy walking conditions during winter, and it's very cool in the narrows during summer. June is the very best time, because it's the driest month in this region.

Hiking Boots If you're there right after rains, take wading shoes. Otherwise, you can get by with dry weather footwear.

Author's Experience On one trip the author went down in late March and found half a meter of snow on the narrows floor. There was no water in any of the potholes then. He went down again in June, a week after heavy rains, and found some mud in the low places, but no pools of water. He has entered or exited all four routes into the Draw. His last trip was in 1997.

Map 15, Round Valley Draw

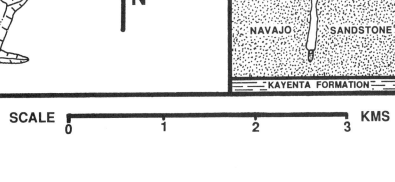

• 1923

KODACHROME BASIN
CANNONVILLE

PASS 1984
STEEP DUGWAY

CATTLE
GUARD

COTTONWOOD   WASH

ROUND VALLEY DRAW

LOWER SLICKROCK

UPPER SLICKROCK

BENCH

ROAD

FENCE

STEEP DUGWAY

SLICKROCK

FENCE LINE

UPPER

BUTLER VALLEY OR
GROSVENOR ARCH

COTTONWOOD WASH
HIGHWAY 89,
MILE POSTS 17 - 18

RUSHBED ROAD

△P
1840

△P
1854

E/E

ROUND VALLEY DRAW
CAR-PARK 1850

△P

1st ENTRY

2nd ENTRY

WATERING TROUGH

ROUND VALLEY SPRING

SLICKROCK
BENCH
CAR-PARK
1850

△P

CHOKESTONE
& DRYFALL

VALLEY DRAW

E/E

RUSH BEDS

E/E

1775

ROUND

CANYON

HACKBERRY

N

• 2021

ROUND VALLEY DRAW

CARMEL   FORMATION

NAVAJO SANDSTONE

ROUND VALLEY
DRAW

CARMEL   FORMATION

NAVAJO   SANDSTONE

KAYENTA FORMATION

SCALE
0   1   2   3   KMS

83

This is the big boulder in Round Valley Draw you'll have to jump off, or chimney up or down, on the right side.

The upper-most part of Round Valley Draw from above. This is where the narrows begin.

This is the deepest and darkest part of Round Valley Draw.

Winter snows stay long, as the sun doesn't reach the bottom of Round Valley Draw.

Hackberry Canyon and Frank Watson's Cabin

Location and Access Hackberry Canyon is one of three long canyon hikes in this book, and it's one of the best around when considering availability of water, good scenery, pleasant campsites and interesting things to see. This canyon lies just east and runs south parallel to the Upper Paria River Gorge. The road you'll be using, whether you go in at the head of the canyon or enter from the bottom, is the Cottonwood Wash Road. For a better look at the lower end of the canyon, see *Maps 18, 19 & 20.*

From the Bryce Canyon area, drive east, then south through Tropic and Cannonville, and first follow the signs to Kodachrome Basin State Park on a paved road. At the Kodachrome Turnoff, continue east on the Cottonwood Wash Road about 10 kms. There you'll see a side road heading south into Hackberry Canyon. There's no way to describe the location of this road except to say that it begins about one km west of a steep dugway. See the previous map on Round Valley Draw. Most cars can be driven into upper Hackberry for about 3 kms.

Another possibility is to drive further along the Cottonwood Wash Road, up a steep dugway, and over a pass marked 1984 meters on the map. Just beyond this is a fence and cattle guard. From there, turn right or south, and drive this never-maintained and seldom-used, but rather good track to its end on the Slickrock Bench. See *Map 16, Round Valley Draw,* for a better look at the entry routes.

You can reach this same area from Highway 89. Between mile posts 17 and 18, turn north onto the southern end of the Cottonwood Wash Road. From the highway, it's about 20 kms to the mouth of Hackberry, and about 55 to 60 kms to the side roads mentioned above.

Trail or Route Conditions You'll be walking right down the creek bed of Hackberry all the way. The upper half is dry; while the lower end has a small stream. The easiest entry point is to come right down the main Hackberry Canyon, but it's also the least interesting. For the adventurous sort, it's possible to walk right down the narrows of Round Valley Draw, but take a short rope to lower your pack over one or two minor dryfalls in the upper part.

The author didn't see, but has heard good things about Booker Canyon. It has some minor dryfalls, and Ponderosa pines grow out of slickrock in its upper reaches.

About 8 to 10 kms below Booker Canyon, you may see the first spring or seep. A little further along, and as you see the huge Navajo Sandstone wall in front of you on the left, and as water is starting to flow, look to your right(west), and you'll see a fence on a bench. At that point is a constructed cow trail out of the canyon. This is called the *Upper Trail.* See Maps 18 & 19.

The late Herm Pollock of Tropic, believed this Upper Trail was first made by a group of Panguitch cattlemen in the last century. It was on this very narrow trail, as it runs along the rim of the canyon, that a cow once laid down right on the trail and died. Because it was so narrow, the other cows wouldn't step over her body to get to water. The end result was the choking death of many cows in the area which is now called Death Valley. Since this first disaster, the trail has been improved many times and by different

The upper part of Hackberry, just below the Upper Trail.

Map 16, Hackberry Canyon and Frank Watson's Cabin

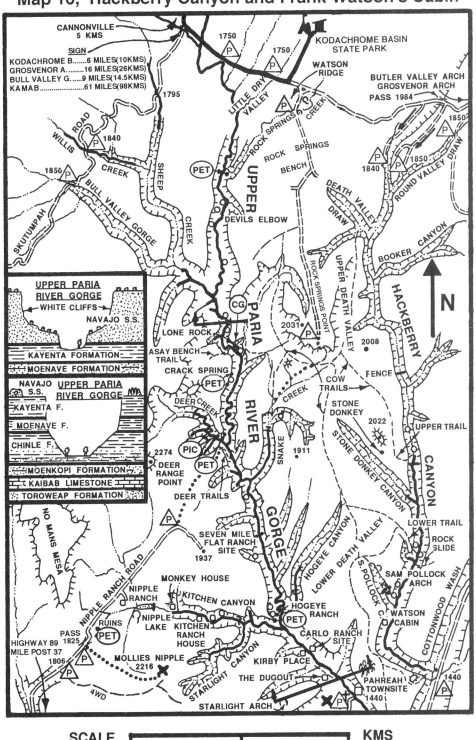

cattlemen who ran stock in the Upper Death Valley. One of these men was Sampson Chynoweth. Members of the Ott family may have also improved it some too. Today it's a rather good trail.

A bit further along is Stone Donkey Canyon, which has an excellent spring less than half a km from the mouth. Stone Donkey Canyon divides Upper from Lower Death Valley. The upper part of this drainage has some fine narrows and is a box canyon.

About a km downcanyon from where the lower red beds of the Navajo Sandstone first begin to show, is another cow trail out of the canyon to the west. At that point, high on the east wall, are several Navajo Sandstone alcoves, and right at a place where the creek turns abruptly west is a cowboyglyph, *W. M. Chynoweth, 1892*, about 5 meters above the creek. To the right of this is the constructed trail. This is mostly a natural break in the cliffs, but minor work has been done in the very lowest part. Just above the cliffs is a long sand slide which the cows walk on going to or from the creek. This is called the *Lower Trail*, and is used today by cattle in the Lower Death Valley area.

Just below the Lower Trail is a new feature in the canyon. Where there was once a minor one-meter high ledge indicating the top of the Kayenta Formation being exposed for the first time, there's now a huge rock slide blocking the canyon. Sometime in early fall 1987, part of the Navajo Sandstone wall on the west side broke away creating a dam across Hackberry Creek. The dam is 8 or 10 meters high and at first created a sizable lake above the dam perhaps 100 or more meters upstream. However, the waters finally seeped through the dam and there's no lake there today (except perhaps right after a big flood in the upper canyon).

Not far below the rock slide dam, is supposed to be another trail heading up to the east between Hackberry and Cottonwood Wash. For lack of a better name, let's call this the *Rockslide Trail*. This is one the author didn't see. In this same area there's another little side canyon entering from the west which has a small stream flow. A km below that are two goosenecks bends in the canyon. Just below this is a nice spring on the right or west side.

Further along is Sam Pollock Canyon. Three kms up this drainage is an arch with Sam's name on it. At one point in this side canyon, you'll have to route-find to the right or north side, to get around a dryfall which otherwise blocks the way. It's an easy climb up.

Half a km downstream from the mouth of Sam Pollock Canyon, and on a bench on the west side of the creek, is the old Watson Cabin. Read the full story about this old cabin below. As the canyon turns to the east, it cuts dramatically through the Navajo Sandstone part of The Cockscomb, before reaching Cottonwood Wash. This is the deepest and narrowest part of Hackberry Canyon.

Elevations Trailheads, about 1850 meters; bottom of canyon, 1440 meters.

Hike Length and Time Needed This hike is around 28 to 30 kms long. It could be done in one long day but normally it takes 2 or 3 days, depending on how many side canyons you visit along the way. If you're going all the way through the canyon, consider leaving a mtn. bike at one end to substitute as a car shuttle.

This rockfall occurred in the fall of 1987 and blocked the small stream in Hackberry Canyon for a while. You can now climb over this obstacle easily.

But riding back to one's car on a bike would take 3 or 4 hours. Hitch hiking is another option. In October, 1997 there was 200-300 cars a day using the Cottonwood Wash Road.

Water It begins to flow in the creek bed about 12-13 kms below where Round Valley Draw enters. It then flows all the way, or very near, to Cottonwood Wash. There's a good spring up Stone Donkey Canyon a ways, and there are several seeps or springs just below the new rock slide, including a side canyon.

At times, usually from the end of October or first part of November through about mid-May, there are cattle in the canyon, so try to take water directly from a spring, or purify it first. In summer when there are no cattle around, it's probably good as-is, if you can take it at or near a spring source.

Maps USGS or BLM map Smoky Mountain(1:100,000), or Slickrock Bench and Calico Peak(1:24,000).

Main Attractions Good water, shady campsites, narrow side canyons, old historic cattle trails, an old homesteader's cabin, and solitude.

Ideal Time to Hike Spring or fall. In late spring and early summer, you'll be plagued by deer flies(from late May into July) in the more open parts of this canyon. To avoid these pests, wear long pants.

Hiking Boots Wading boots or shoes.

Author's Experience He has made 7 or 8 trips into the canyon, but only once did he walk all the way through. On that occasion, he left late in the evening and rim-walked above Round Valley Draw to about its confluence of Hackberry, and camped. Next day he hurried all the way through and hitched a ride back to his car along the Cottonwood Wash Road. In the spring, summer and fall, you might now see as many as 200 to 300 cars a day on this road. Other trips were to see Round Valley Draw, Sam Pollock Arch and the cattle trails.

Frank Watson and the Watson Cabin

There's a rather well-built and well-preserved cabin in the lower end of Hackberry Canyon, and an interesting story behind it. It's called the Watson Cabin, after a man known locally as Frank Watson.

The man's real name was Richard Welburn Thomas, who came from Wisconsin. As the story goes, Thomas apparently had a quarrel with his wife one night, but early the next morning, he got up, left the house and walked to the railway station where he boarded a train for the wild west. This is the story that's told, but he could have been a fugitive from the law? No one will ever know for sure.

After some wandering, it seems he ended up at Lee's Ferry under the employment of Charles H. Spencer. Spencer was the big-time promoter who got lots of money from investors and tried to find a way to separate gold from the Chinle clay beds at Lee's Ferry. Spencer worked at Lee's Ferry between 1910 and 1912. It was at this time, Thomas changed his name to Frank Watson. Evidently Watson was a good all-around handy man and mechanic. It's been said by several men in Bryce Valley, that Watson was involved in the running of the paddlewheel steamer *Charles H. Spencer* up the Colorado River to Warm Creek, where they were to load coal and carry it down to the gold diggings at Lee's Ferry. This whole

Very near the beginning of the Lower Trail to Death Valley, is this cowboy signature,
W.M. [Will] Chynoweth, 1892.

89

operation failed in the end, and the miners left in 1912.

From Lee's Ferry, Spencer and his men went up the Paria River to the old town of Pahreah, and were involved in mining the Chinle clay beds for gold from 1912 to about the end of World War I. Watson was also there at that time, and it appears it was sometime during the war, that he went over Carlo Ridge and into lower Hackberry Canyon and built this cabin. It's been said that he had a rough trail from the cabin, over the ridge, and down to Pahreah, but no one knows of it's whereabouts today.

The late Herm Pollock, and rock hound from Tropic, remembered the Watson Cabin as being well built. Watson made the wooden hinges on the door with only a pocket knife. About 150 to 200 meters south of the cabin, Watson had made a flume and a sluice box, both of which were painted bright yellow when Herm saw the place in 1922. Apparently, Watson had tried to do the same thing in lower Hackberry, as Spencer was trying to do over the ridge at Pahreah, and evidently without success.

George Thompson of Cannonville, and Herm Pollock, both remembered a little about the cabin and the time when George's father, Jodi Thompson, tried to homestead the bench land where the cabin was located. Jodi and some of his brothers went to the area sometime in about the mid-1920's, and tried for two seasons to grow crops and plant peach trees. They dug a ditch with shovels only, and had successfully brought water from the creek above the cabin down to the bench where they grew vegetables. But in the second year they had a flash flood, which lowered the creek bed to the point where water couldn't be diverted to the bench, and that ended the garden scheme at the Watson Cabin.

There's an interesting story about one dark night in the cabin, as told by several old timers in Bryce Valley. Jodi and one of his brothers either got to the cabin late at night, or were sleeping there, when they heard rattlesnakes in the darkened room. With only a candle for light and a pitch fork with five prongs, they managed to spear one rattler with each prong. In the morning they stood the pitch fork up against the cabin wall with the five snakes on it, which nearly reached the ground.

According to the late Ken Goulding of Henrieville, Watson was employed by the Goulding family off and on for several years herding sheep, apparently during the mid to late 1910's. At one time Watson lived in a tent, which was pitched behind the Goulding house in Henrieville. Ken recalled one winter, Watson tore down an old Model A Ford, and put it back together again the next spring.

At about the end of World War I, and after the time when Watson had built his Hackberry Cabin and had worked for the Gouldings, he built a small store on what is now known locally as Watson Ridge. Watson Ridge is south of Henrieville, and due south of Chimney Rock, which is in Kodachrome Basin State Park. The store was small, and catered to the sheep men who were numerous in the area at that time. He sold all kinds of supplies but Ken Goulding remembered him selling candy, Bull Durham tobacco, and a bootleg whisky everyone called *Jamaica Ginger*.

The well-preserved Frank Watson Cabin in the lower end of Hackberry Canyon.

This was in the early days of prohibition, and selling this rot-gut whisky was forbidden. The lady who owned and operated the only store in Henrieville, bought it from someone, then it was transported out to Watson's store, where they used to have some wild parties. It was sold and drank at Watson's place, because it was so far away from the law.

To get to Watson's old store site, drive east from the Kodachrome Turnoff on the Cottonwood Wash Road about one km. At the first road running south, turn right, and drive about 100-200 meters. It's near the crest of the hill, but on the west side. Today there's only some scattered tin cans, etc., marking the spot.

The last time Goulding saw Watson was in about 1921. Herm Pollock and the Otts pick up the story from there. After leaving the store on Watson Ridge, he likely went to the bottom end Heward Canyon, a tributary of Sheep Creek, which is just east of Bryce Canyon, and to the southwest of Cannonville and Tropic. About 2 kms to the west of the old Johnson Ranch on Sheep Creek, is a very well-built stone house along the road running up Heward Creek. This may have been built by Watson, since it was well-built and is still in very good condition except for the wooden roof, which has collapsed under its own weight. Watson lived there, or perhaps just downcanyon at the Johnson Ranch. While there, he apparently tried to develop a coal mine just west of the cabin for one or two winters(See the map, *"Bryce Valley & Skutumpah Road Ranches"*, in the back of this book on page 221).

To get to the Heward Canyon rock house, drive south out of Cannonville for about 4 or 5 kms, and turn west toward the old town site of Georgetown. From the Yellow Creek Road just west of Georgetown, turn south and head for Sheep Creek and the sites of the old Henderson and Johnson Ranches and Heward Creek. About 2 kms west of the old Johnson Ranch, which is now owned by Colorado City(Short Creek) people named Binion and Stubbs, is the rock house on the right side of the road.

Later, Watson landed at the old W. J. Henderson Ranch, which is about 1 1/2 or 2 kms southwest of the Georgetown site, and just up the hill from where the James R. Ott Ranch was located. At this ranch, Watson lived with an old man named Hyrum "Hite" Elmer. Wallace Ott remembers when old Hite died, because Watson came down to their ranch to get a wagon to haul him off.

From the Henderson Ranch, Watson went back to Wisconsin to see his aging mother sometime in the mid-1920's. She was apparently very happy and surprised to see him, according to Ken Goulding. Since he had been gone for so long, and had lost touch with the family, his mother thought he surely must have been killed by Indians.

The old fireplace inside the Frank Watson Cabin.

Upper Cottonwood Wash Narrows

Location and Access Featured here is a short narrows section in the upper end of Cottonwood Wash. These narrows aren't very long, but they are nearly as deep and narrow as parts of the Buckskin Gulch, against which most slot canyons are judged. The location is about 7 kms south of the Butler Valley Arch(this was the name of the arch before the National Geographic Society came into the area in about 1948, and changed the name to Grosvenor Arch after their NGS President). To get there, drive south from Bryce Canyon on Highway 12, and through the towns of Tropic and Cannonville. From Cannonville head south and first follow the signs to Kodachrome Basin, then continue straight east on the Cottonwood Wash Road instead. Where you see the sign pointing out the direction to Grosvenor Arch, continue south(rather than turn east), for about 7 kms. The only land marks to look for are two passes with steep descents and some very colorful red & white rocks, as shown on the map. If you're coming upcanyon from the south, turn north from Highway 89 between mile posts 17 and 18. From the highway to the above mentioned passes and red & white rocks is about 41 kms. When this Cottonwood Wash Road is wet, stay away--**it's impassable!** However, it tends to dry quickly in summer after it rains.

Trail or Route Conditions Park near the bridge and scramble down into the drainage. After just a few meters, you'll have a choice of going up the short section of Butler Valley Draw, or down the Cottonwood Wash Creek bed. Go up first, as that part is perhaps the best, then head downcanyon. There are several very short side canyons and some high dryfalls to see as well. After about 2 kms, you'll come out the bottom end and back to the road. These narrows are formed by a strange twist of the dry stream channel, which has cut into the ever present Navajo Sandstone.

Elevations Entry point, 1735 meters; bottom of narrows, 1675; campsite at the arch, 1900 meters.

Hike Length and Time Needed You have only about 200 meters or so of interesting narrows up Butler Valley Draw, then about 2 kms of narrows where the main wash is back away from the road and where it cuts deep into the Navajo Sandstone. You can do the whole hike in one or two hours.

Water Carry water in your car, as the well shown on the map doesn't always produce. There's no water at the little undeveloped campsite at Grosvenor Arch.

Maps USGS or BLM map Smoky Mountain(1:100,000), or Butler Valley(1:24,000).

Main Attractions A very short, but interesting and easily accessible narrow canyon, and Grosvenor Arch.

Ideal Time to Hike About anytime, but summers are a little warm, and cold winter weather prevents the road from drying quickly after storms. Spring or fall are the ideal times.

Hiking Boots Dry weather boots or shoes.

Author's Experience Once in early April, and again in mid-October, the author did this entire hike in about one hour each, round-trip.

Inside the Navajo Sandstone narrows of the Upper Cottonwood Wash.

Map 17, Upper Cottonwood Wash Narrows

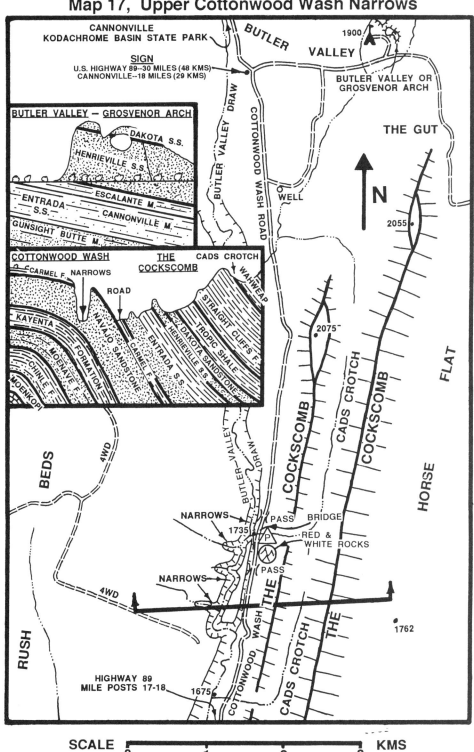

SCALE

0   1   2   3   KMS

Sam Pollock and Hogeye Canyons

Location and Access This loop-hike involves a couple of side drainages in the lower parts of the Upper Paria River Gorge and Hackberry Canyon. It takes in some historic sites and a traverse of some high mesa country between two major canyons. You have two starting points to choose from. One is at the mouth of Hackberry Canyon, where it drains into the lower Cottonwood Wash. Reach this car-park by leaving Highway 89 between mile posts 17 and 18, which is about 5 kms east of the Paria Ranger Station & Visitor Center. This is the Cottonwood Wash Road. Drive northwest about 20 kms to the mouth of Hackberry Canyon. The other starting point is at old Pahreah. Get there by exiting Highway 89 between mile posts 30 and 31, where the sign points to *Paria Movie Set, 5 miles(8 kms)*. Drive north about 10 kms to the river and park. Both of these access roads are maintained and heavily used in the warmer months, but both are slick and impassable during wet weather. However, during the warmer months, these clay-based roads dry quickly after rains.

Trail or Route Conditions Here's the recommended route. Park at the mouth of Hackberry and walk upcanyon where it cuts through the Navajo Sandstone narrows. Further up you pass the Watson Cabin on a bench above the creek; then less than a km away, enter the lower end of Sam Pollock Canyon. About a km up this canyon is a dryfall which can be skirted on the north side. Further up on the right, is Sam Pollock Arch, named after a Tropic cattleman. From the arch, head in a northwest direction over a divide and toward a Navajo Sandstone rock which looks like a beehive. Walk around this rock on the right or east, and enter the upper part of Hogeye Canyon. Walk down Hogeye to the lower part where there's year-round water and many good campsites. Then finish the hike by walking down the Paria, past the site of old Pahreah, and through what is called The Box. This is the part of the Paria which cuts through The Cockscomb. Just beyond The Box, turn north and walk the lower Cottonwood Wash back to your car. Also, consider some kind of alternate route involving some of the old cattle trails discussed with the next map

Elevations Both car-parks 1440 meters; the high point along the divide, about 1775 meters.

Hike Length and Time Needed This loop-hike is about 36 to 38 kms, and should be considered a two day walk. For a good water supply, camp somewhere near the springs north of Sam Pollock Canyon(in Hackberry) or in Hogeye Canyon.

Water There's year-round water in Hackberry, Hogeye(very good) and the Paria. There are also some good springs coming out of the west wall just north and south of the old Hogeye Ranch site.

Maps USGS or BLM map Smoky Mountain(1:100,0000), or Calico Peak(1:24,000).

Main Attractions Deep canyons, several historic ranch sites, good water and campsites.

Ideal Time to Hike Spring or fall.

Hiking Boots Wading boots or shoes.

Author's Experience The author made it into upper Hogeye from the mouth of Hackberry, but returned the same way to get fotos of the arch. Round-trip, about 7 hours. He has also been into Hogeye from old Pahreah twice, as well as hiking all the cow trails shown.

One of several minor waterfalls in the lower end of Hogeye Canyon.

Map 18, Sam Pollock and Hogeye Canyons

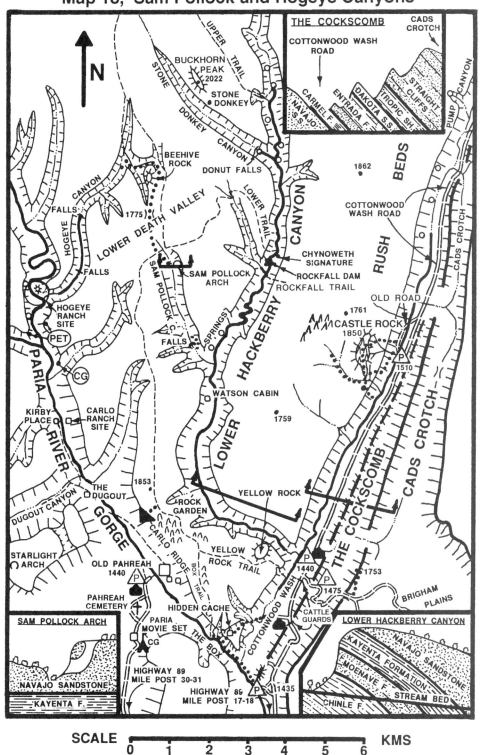

SCALE ┣━━━━━━━━━━━┫ KMS
0   1   2   3   4   5   6

Lower Death Valley Cow Trails

Location and Access Featured here are some of the trails and routes used by early day sheep and cattlemen in the high country lying between the lower Hackberry and the Paria River. For over a century, sheep and cattle have been grazed in the area now called Lower Death Valley, and in areas south around the Rock Garden and a Navajo Sandstone dome, called Yellow Rock. In recent years the BLM has sent crews out to relocate and mark these fading historic trails. There are three trailheads or car-parks to choose from, but two are more commonly used. About 5 kms east of the Paria Ranger Station & Visitor Center on Highway 89, and between mile posts 17 and 18, turn north onto the Cottonwood Wash Road. Drive about 16 kms and pull off the road to the left, where it comes closest to the confluence of the Paria and Cottonwood Wash. Or drive another 4 kms, and park at the confluence of Hackberry Canyon and Cottonwood Wash. The third and perhaps least feasible access point would be to leave Highway 89 from between mile posts 30 and 31, and drive 10 kms northeast to old Pahreah townsite.

Trail or Route Conditions The best-marked and easiest trail to follow is the one running north from the middle of The Box. This is where the Paria River cuts through The Cockscomb. From the trailhead near the Cottonwood Wash Road, walk into The Box. About halfway through, and at the contact point of the red Kayenta and white Navajo Sandstone Formations, look for a trail running northwest, and up at a steep angle. In its beginning, the Box Trail was constructed and easy to follow.

From the Hackberry Trailhead, cross the creek and walk about 300 meters south from where Hackberry meets Cottonwood Wash. This is the first drainage south of Hackberry. There you'll find a small canyon coming down from the west. Walk up the gully less than 75 meters, and look for the beginning of the Yellow Rock Trail running up a slide area to the northwest. It's very steep at first. Follow it up, then go west, and along the south side of a huge bald Navajo Sandstone dome, called Yellow Rock. Finally head northwest to meet The Box Trail at the Rock Garden Junction. This trail junction is probably lost in the sand, but it's just south of several white Navajo Sandstone pinnacles.

From this junction the trail used to be well-marked to where it passes north of the Rock Garden, then fades in the sand. The trail circles around to the north of Sam Pollock Arch heading east, then zig zags northeast. Finally it drops down a sandslide and crosses a shallow drainage, before turning southeast following a ridge. Near the bottom of Hackberry Canyon, it follows another sandslide to the lip of the canyon, where the constructed part of the Lower Trail can be found.

If you're planning to *leave* Hackberry Canyon by the Lower Trail, it may be difficult to locate. If you're looking for this trail from inside the canyon, remember it's found somewhere just above the new rockfall & dam shown on the map. As the canyon makes a hard right turn to the east(going upcanyon) just above the rockfall and about 5 meters above the present creek bed, is a cowboyglyph, with the name *W. M.*

The Box of the Paria River, and the beginning of The Box Trail.

Map 19, Lower Death Valley Cow Trails

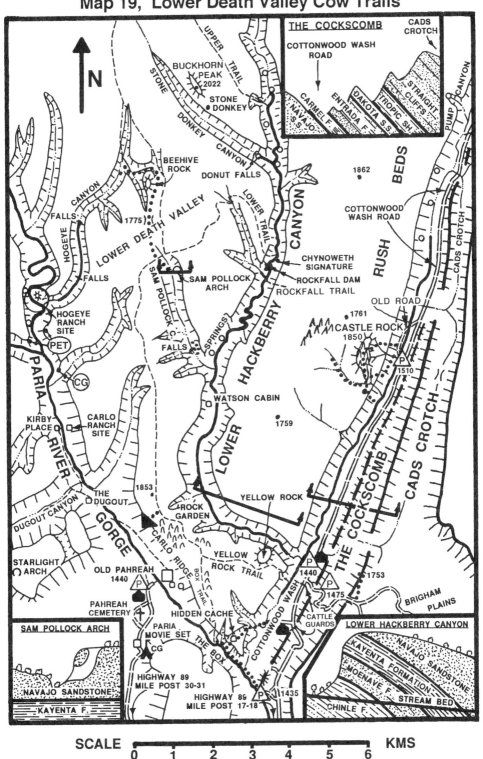

Chynoweth--1892, written. At that corner and to the west is the beginning of the Lower Trail.

There's still another cow trail further north which you can use to get out of Hackberry. Just downstream from the upper-most spring in the canyon, and where there is a very high Navajo Sandstone wall on the east side, is a bench on the west side of the creek. On it is a short fence, and above the fence is the Upper Trail, so called because it allows passage to Upper Death Valley. It heads northwest in a shallow drainage to join the main north-south cattle route.

It was because of an incident on this trail that we have the name Death Valley, both Upper and Lower. About a century ago, Panguitch cattlemen ran cows in the area. They were the ones who first built a trail down to Hackberry Creek. But in those days it wasn't as good a trail as you see there today. Since that time a better route has been blasted out of the cliff. It was very narrow, and cows had to step from one foothold to the next. Once a cow laid down right on the trail and died. The rest of the herd was too spooked to pass by her on the very narrow path. Since they couldn't get to water, they all choked to death, thus the name Death Valley.

You could use this Upper Death Valley Trail to skirt around Stone Donkey Canyon, and head south towards The Box, or down Hogeye or Sam Pollock Canyons. In the northern part of the area, the trails fade into *cow routes* only. Those who want to hike into the northern parts of this area, such as Upper Death Valley, should have some good topo maps and a compass, and expect to use their route-finding skills and their heads. Read the information on Snake Creek with *Map 8A,* on the Upper Paria River Gorge.

Elevations The trailheads are about 1440 meters; the highest point on the mesa top, about 1900 meters.

Hike Length and Time Needed From The Box Trailhead to the Rock Garden Junction is about 5 kms. From the Hackberry Trailhead up the Yellow Rock Trail to the same junction, is about 3 or 3 1/2 kms. From the Rock Garden Junction to the bottom of the Lower Trail in Hackberry, is about 11-12 kms. From the bottom of the Lower Trail to the mouth of Hackberry is about another 10 or so kms. A nice half-day hike, would be to begin at either of the trailheads on Cottonwood Wash, walk to the Rock Garden Junction, and return by the Yellow Rock Trail, thus making a loop-hike, and maybe 4 or 5 hours walking. Fast hikers could begin at the Hackberry Trailhead, walk up the Yellow Rock Trail, enter Hackberry via the Lower Trail, then return down Hackberry to the trailhead. This would be an all-day hike. Keep in mind, for all of these hikes you'll find evidence of constructed trail at their beginnings, but once on top of the plateau, little if any evidence exists of any trail.

Water There is no water on the mesa, only in the canyons. There are several good springs in the vicinity of Stone Donkey Canyon and in the area north of Sam Pollock Canyon. There's also good water in Hogeye Canyon, and a couple of springs near the old Hogeye Ranch site. Water from springs is usually drinkable as-is. Always carry plenty of water in your car.

Maps USGS or BLM map Smoky Mountain(1:100,000); or Fivemile Valley and Calico Peak(1:24,000).

Main Attractions A higher and cooler hike, strange rock formations, an overlook of old Pahreah, and some route-finding in a little known country. Here's a fotographer's alert. Check out Yellow Rock, and points south southwest around the Hidden Cache. Some of the coloring in the white Navajo Sandstone there is similar to what is found in Coyote Buttes. See the next map for more routes to fotographic sites.

Ideal Time to Hike Spring or fall are best, but it could be hiked in summer or in mild winter weather.

Hiking Boots Waders to reach The Box Trail and to use Hackberry Canyon; otherwise dry weather boots or shoes.

Author's Experience Once the author left late in the afternoon and entered The Box from lower Cottonwood Wash. He found the trail and went as far as the Rock Garden Junction, then returned, in 3 hours. The next morning, he found the Yellow Rock Trail going up from the Hackberry Canyon side, hiked it all the way to Sam Pollock Arch, then entered Hackberry via the Lower Trail. He then hurried upcanyon and found the Upper Trail, before returning to his car via the canyon bottom. All in 9 1/2 hours. A very long day, but if the hike to the Upper Trail had been eliminated, it would have been a pleasant day-hike.

These are some of the white rocks which are part of the Rock Garden.

This is the constructed part of the Upper Trail running from Hackberry
Canyon to Upper Death Valley.

The Hidden Cache Trail, and The Cockscomb, Castle Rock, and Yellow Rock Valley

Location and Access One of the most striking land forms of southern Utah is the feature known as The Cockscomb. The Cockscomb is a fold in the earth's crust, more properly called a monocline, which has created a rather sharp erosional ridge. This ridgeline runs in a north-south direction; it begins just south of Canaan Peak in the north, and continues past Highway 89 in the south. The part shown on this map stands the highest, has the sharpest ridges and is the most fotogenic.

This same feature continues south to Coyote Buttes and into Arizona. There it goes by the name of the East Kaibab Monocline. From Highway 89, you can follow it south along the House Rock Valley Road. In the area of Highway 89A, in the House Rock Valley, you see it running further south to Saddle Mountain and into the Grand Canyon. However, this northern section is the most rugged and the most interesting part to see.

Cottonwood Wash, and the road by the same name, run right down the middle of The Cockscomb Valley, from Grosvenor Arch to the Paria River. While the highest and most rugged part of The Cockscomb is east of this road, there is also a less-dramatic ridgeline on the west side formed mostly by the Navajo Sandstone. The most prominent feature on the west side of The Cockscomb is Castle Rock, at 1850 meters. It stands up like a sore thumb above all its neighbors. Another prominent feature is Yellow Rock. It's located just south of the mouth of Hackberry Canyon. It's made of the Navajo Sandstone, but it's bright yellow in color. Between Yellow Rock and The Box of the Paria, is a small valley right on top of the western ridge. Most of the rocks there are also yellow, but some are capped with bright red. The author is calling this place Yellow Rock Valley, for lack of a better name.

Besides all this scenic stuff, there's one last interesting place to visit. The author is calling it the Hidden Cache. It's on top of the western side of The Cockscomb not far from where Cottonwood Wash and The Box of the Paria River meet. The story behind this is told below.

To get to this area, leave Highway 89 between mile post 17 and 18, and drive northwest about 16 kms to a point about 200 meters from the Paria River and just below where The Box and Cottonwood Wash meet. Drive along a side road about 200 meters to the river and stop. By parking, and perhaps camping there, you'll have access to the Hidden Cache and The Box Trail.

If you continue north about 3 or 4 kms, you'll come to the second of two cattle guards. You can park there which is near the Yellow Rock Trail. Or, continue up the road another 200 meters, turn right or east, and drive up to the base of the highest Cockscomb Ridge on the road to Brigham Plain. If you have a powerful 4WD, you can likely get up to the pass above, which would shorten any hike.

If getting into the lower end of Hackberry is your goal, then park just east of the mouth about 200 meters north of the Brigham Plain Road. Of if going to Castle Rock, continue north from Hackberry for about

Castle Rock to the left, Cottonwood Wash in the middle, and the highest part of
The Cockscomb Ridge to the right.

Map 20, The Hidden Cache Trail, and The Cockscomb, Castle Rock, and Yellow Rock Valley

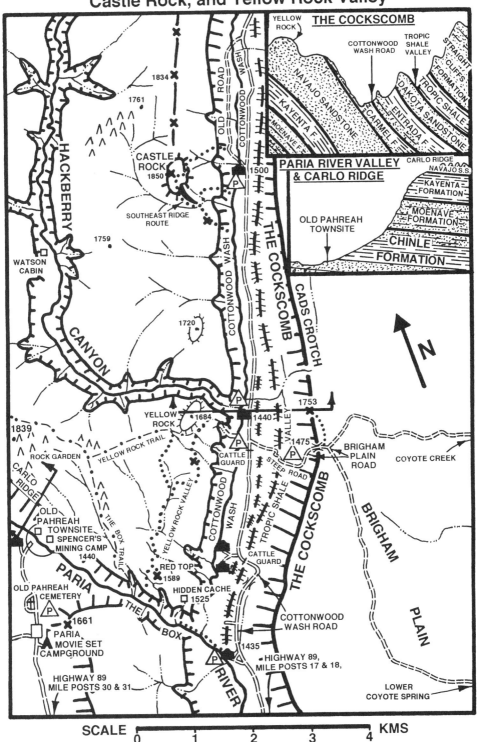

THE COCKSCOMB

YELLOW ROCK
COTTONWOOD WASH ROAD
TROPIC SHALE VALLEY
STRAIGHT CLIFFS FORMATION
NAVAJO SANDSTONE
DAKOTA SANDSTONE
TROPIC SHALE
KAYENTA F.
ENTRADA F.
CARMEL F.
MOENAVE F.

PARIA RIVER VALLEY & CARLO RIDGE

CARLO RIDGE
NAVAJO S.S.
KAYENTA FORMATION
MOENAVE FORMATION
OLD PAHREAH TOWNSITE
CHINLE FORMATION

HACKBERRY

CASTLE ROCK 1850

1834 ✕
1761
CASTLE ROCK
SOUTHEAST RIDGE ROUTE
1759
WATSON CABIN
CANYON
1720

OLD ROAD
COTTONWOOD WASH
COTTONWOOD WASH
1500
P

THE COCKSCOMB
CADS CROTCH
1753
P 1440
1684
YELLOW ROCK
1475
P
VALLEY
BRIGHAM PLAIN ROAD
COYOTE CREEK

1839
ROCK GARDEN
YELLOW ROCK TRAIL
CATTLE GUARD
STEEP ROAD
CARLO RIDGE
THE BOX TRAIL
YELLOW ROCK VALLEY
COTTONWOOD WASH
TROPIC SHALE
THE COCKSCOMB
BRIGHAM
OLD PAHREAH TOWNSITE
SPENCER'S MINING CAMP 1440
RED TOP ✕ 1589
CATTLE GUARD
OLD PAHREAH CEMETERY
P
HIDDEN CACHE 1525
PLAIN
PARIA
✕ 1661
PARIA MOVIE SET CAMPGROUND
THE BOX
COTTONWOOD WASH ROAD
1435
P
HIGHWAY 89, MILE POSTS 17 & 18,
HIGHWAY 89 MILE POSTS 30 & 31
RIVER
LOWER COYOTE SPRING

SCALE
0   1   2   3   4   KMS

another 4 or 5 kms. When you get to a point immediately east of Castle, you'll see part of the old original road veering left or west. Drive along this for 100 meters and park before going down to the creek bed.

Trail or Route Conditions To climb **The Cockscomb**, if you have parked at the base of the steep part of the road going up toward Brigham Plain, then you have only to walk about one km to the pass overlooking The Cockscomb Valley. At the pass, walk almost due north and angle up to the left as you climb to the highest part of the ridge marked 1753 meters.

From where you park just east of **Castle Rock**, cross Cottonwood Creek walking along the old road. From the creek, continue north for about 200 meters and look for an easy, but steep route, up the face of the western ridge, which will put you on the northeast side of the peak. You'll have to route-find to the base of Castle Rock, then scramble up a steep brush-filled gully to the summit which has a dozen or so pinnacles. The highest peak is on the west side and easy to climb.

Perhaps the easiest way up Castle Rock would be to walk south from the creek crossing for 200-300 meters and look for one of several routes up the steep face. Higher up look for ways to reach the smooth and prominent southeast ridge or buttress. Once on this buttress, head northwest to the summit area.

To reach the area between Hackberry and The Box, which is **Yellow Rock Valley**, leave your car parked near the most northern of the two cattle guards, and walk west across Cottonwood Wash. Enter the first little drainage about 300 meters south of the mouth of Hackberry. Once inside this little canyon, veer to the northwest and climb straight up an old horse trail. This is the Yellow Rock Trail. Once on top, the trail fades, but just head west toward the big dome which is **Yellow Rock**. From the top of Yellow Rock, you'll have some great views looking north. There's another yellowish dome-type rock just to the north at 1720 meters altitude, and of course Castle Rock is in the distance. Looking south, you'll see lots of mostly yellow dome rocks, with the highest place off to your left or east.

There are no trails down through Yellow Rock Valley, so pick the route that suits you best. Two possible routes are shown on the map. At the southern end just above The Box, is a another colorful sight. It's what this writer calls **Red Top**. The top is red, the lower parts yellow--all varicolored Navajo Sandstone. This one sours above everything else in the area as viewed from the Pahreah Cemetery. You can also get into this southern section from the Paria and The Box Trail, as shown on the map.

Now for the trail to the Hidden Cache. Read the story behind this mysterious place below. From the car-park near the confluence of the Paria and Cottonwood Wash, walk to the beginning of The Box. This is about 400 meters from the car-park. About 300 meters into The Box, and on your right or north, is a minor drainage. Head up and into this mini canyon. After just a short distance and on the left side, you'll begin to see a trail heading straight up the canyon bottom. Around 500 meters from the river, and just after you begin to level out, you'll see the first gray metal shelter, and just behind it, the remains of a second metal box and cave.

Looking north in the middle of Cottonwood Wash, or The Cockscomb Valley. Picture was taken looking north from just northeast of The Box of the Paria River. The monoliths in the middle are part of the Entrada Sandstone.

Elevations For The Cockscomb, from 1475 meters up to 1753, or higher further north. Climbing Castle Rock ranges from just over 1500 where you park, up to 1850 meters. For Yellow Rock, you'll walk from 1440 up to 1684 meters, and for the Hidden Cache, it's from about 1435 to 1525 meters.

Hike Length and Time Needed From the Cottonwood Wash Road to the pass in The Cockscomb, is less than 2 kms. From the pass to the high point is another half km. The round-trip hike can be done easily in a 2-3 hours--less if you can drive up to the pass. For Castle Rock, either way requires some route-finding for nearly 2 kms, and will take up to about 2 hours to climb, 3 or 4 hours round-trip, maybe more. To explore the country between Yellow Rock and Red Top, you'll need no less than half a day. If you're a color fotographer, you'll want all day. It's only about 1 1/2 km from the car-park to the Hidden Cache, and can be done in 20-25 minutes, one-way; a couple of hours round-trip.

Water Take your own, and always have extra water in your car. There's usually water in both Cottonwood Wash and the Paria which can be used for washing.

Maps USGS or BLM map Smoky Mountain(1:100,000), or Calico Peak and Fivemile Valley(1:24,000).

Main Attractions An interesting look at an unusual geologic feature fully exposed. Geology students shouldn't miss this one, as these are some of the most interesting hikes in this book. The view from the top of The Cockscomb, Yellow Rock or Castle Rock is geologically spectacular. It's also one of the most fotogenic places covered by this book. Also, a short hike to what has become a local legend at the Hidden Cache.

Ideal Time to Hike Spring or fall, but it can be climbed anytime.

Hiking Boots Any boots or shoes, but a rugged pair for climbing The Cockscomb Ridge. For the southeast buttress route up Castle Rock, and Yellow Rock Valley, use running-type shoes because of the slickrock. You'll have to wade the Paria several times on the way to the Hidden Cache, so go prepared.

Author's Experience The author parked at the bottom of the ridge, then walked up the road to The Cockscomb. Round-trip was about an hour and a half. He climbed Castle Rock twice, along both routes mentioned above. He did some exploring around the west side on the second hike, and that took about 3 hours round-trip. On one of his hikes up Yellow Rock, south through the Yellow Rock Valley to Red Top, and back the same way to his car, took about 3 1/3 hours. On two trips to the Hidden Cache via The Box route, it took about one hour each, round-trip.

The Story of the Hidden Cache

The last hike to be added to the 1st Edition of this book happened quite by accident. While interviewing one of the old timers in Tropic, the story about an old hermit or possibly a German spy(?), and a cache of food and equipment was told. Later the author tracked down the people who originally found the cache, and

The west side of Castle Rock as seen from the southwest side.

got the full story.

It began on February 8, 1953. Harvey Chynoweth, his four sons, Jack, Gene, Wade and Ralph, and Harvey's brother Will Chynoweth, were running cows in the lower Cottonwood Wash and out to the east of The Cockscomb on the flats called Brigham Plain. They had worked all day, and had arrived back at camp late. Camp was on the lower Cottonwood Wash, not far above where it flows into the Paria River, at the bottom end of The Box.

Since the bottom of the valley had been grazed-out by cows and there wasn't much feed for the horses, it was common practice for cowmen working in the area to run their riding horses up on top of the Carlo Ridge to the west where they could pasture at night. Up there they couldn't go far because of rough terrain and there was plenty of grass. Since Ralph was the youngest of the boys, he was chosen to take the riding stock up above the cliffs.

It was after dark, but there was a full moon and the sky was clear. Ralph recalls having trouble with one little sorrel pony which was trying to run away or something. At any rate, when the horses were left in the upper pasture, they were always hobbled, so they could be found and caught easy the next morning. When Ralph finally got a hold of the little sorrel, he began putting the hobbles on it. But then something caught his eye. The moonlight was so bright, it reflected off something made of metal. He went over to check it out and found a couple of small metal buildings, or sheds, or boxes. He could see inside one of them and saw that somebody had lived there. He returned to camp a little spooked and told the story. No one believed him. They thought he was dreaming or just telling stories.

The next morning they all went back up to get the horses and saw in full light what was there. It was some kind of camp but hadn't been lived in for some time. There were two galvanized metal boxes or shelters, measuring only about 1 1/4 x 2 x 2 1/2 meters each, and a cave which had the entrance cemented up with a little rock wall.

Inside one of the boxes was a bed with blankets on it, all tucked in neatly; a small metal wood burning stove which was new and apparently hadn't been used; and an old .22 rifle which hung above the door. The .22 was a hex-barreled single shot, which broke in the middle to load, like some single shot shotguns. There were also several new denim shirts, underwear, socks, pajamas, two pair of boots, tooth brush, tooth paste, and neatly folded napkins. The clothing items were neatly put together and folded, like what you'd find in the military. Besides these things, was some kind of a military uniform. One man swears it was from W.W.I.

In the other metal shelter, and all very neatly packed away, was a food cache of sizable proportions. The food cache included jars or buckets of peanut butter, canned milk, chocolate, sugar, rice, flour, raisins, canned fish, sardines, corned beef, and other canned goods. Most of the cans had rusted badly, from the inside out apparently, and had leaked, spoiling the contents. Indications were that it had been there for some time. One witness said they found one can of corned beef dated 1942.

The summit area of Castle Rock as seen from the upper part of the southeast buttress.

Just behind the two metal shelters, was a small cave. The front of this cave, measuring about one by two meters, had been sealed up with a rock and mortar wall. The job was so well done, that in 1997 when the author last saw it, it appeared as if it could have been made only a month or two before. The entrance passage was a small metal-framed window, like the kind you see in some homes or buildings of W.W.II vintage. The inside of the cave had been dug out a bit, and it measured about 1 1/2 x 2 meters at the front end, and it tapered back to the rear about 4 meters. Not much headroom, but cozy.

Inside the cave, the Chynoweths found an electric hot plate and several five gallon(19 liter) water storage jars full of water. The fact that they had not frozen and broken the jars, indicates how well insulated the cave was in winter. There were also a dozen batteries of various kinds, and some witnesses said there were radios too, but not everyone agreed on that point.

Right in the corner next to the window-entrance, are three wires which were built into the rock and mortar wall. These wires led outside to a wind mill contraption and a generator mounted on a rock behind the cave. The single blade propeller was 4 or 5 meters long, and mounted horizontally(instead of vertically as is usually the case). The cave had built-in wiring so electricity generated by the wind mill generator outside, could be used for lights, cooking, and the radio inside.

According to the newspaper report in the March 19, 1953, *Garfield County News* in Panguitch(a week later in the Kanab paper), all identifiable marks on the generator and other equipment found, had been scratched off. Even the numbers on a thermometer had been removed! Jack Chynoweth also stated that all labels from canned goods and from all clothes were also removed.

According to the Chynoweths, as soon as they got back home, they immediately called the Sheriff of Kane County, Mason Meeks, and told him the story. Shortly thereafter, the Sheriff and Highway Patrolman Merrill Johnson, Merle(Peaches) Beard, and others, went to the cache and removed what items were left. There are two conflicting stories--the Chynoweths and the Sheriffs--as to what items were originally discovered, and what the Sheriff took out. Merrill Johnson said nothing was removed?

Sheriff Meeks sent a report to the FBI. Later they contacted Meeks and it was their speculation that whoever set up the place had likely been a spy of some kind from the W.W.II era.

There were several different theories advanced as to who built the cache: 1. He was a deserter from the army and on the run; 2. That he was a draft dodger; 3. He was just an old hermit, who happened to have been in W.W.I; 4. He had worked for Charles H. Spencer in the gold diggings at old Pahreah, and had returned to hide out; 5. And because some of the clothing items had foreign labels(French), some thought he may have been a spy of some kind. The radio and generator equipment prompted this idea.

There was also endless speculation as to how this person may have gotten all the equipment and food there without detection. At that time, which must have been in the early to mid-1940's, there were no roads in the area except the one to old Pahreah. When this story finally came to light, there was all kinds of talk about it, and then people started remembering events that had happened in the previous years, which may have had a connection with the cache.

The one which seems to hold the most credibility is the story told by Calvin C. Johnson of Kanab, the man who now owns the Nipple Ranch. He remembered the time as being in 1944 or 1945. On several occasions he and other cattlemen in the area of old Pahreah, had seen a Willeys Jeep parked inside The Box, and at the bottom of the cliffs where the cache was later found. Calvin also remembers that he and others had talked to the owner of the Jeep on several occasions as they met on the deserted road between The Box, just below old Pahreah, and Kanab. The man was in his 30's, had a trimmed beard, was always dressed up in an old army uniform, and spoke with some kind of a foreign accent. He never did say much, and the conversations were always short; like howdy and good-by. Calvin recalls the boys he rode with on the range used to call this fellow, *our little German spy!* Apparently this had more meaning in 1953 after the cache was discovered, than it did earlier.

Another event happened in 1963, which may have had a connection with this place. At that time, the Sheriff of Kane County was Leonard Johnson. His people lived in the polygamist community of Short Creek, now called Colorado City, Arizona, and Hildale, Utah. He had a pilot's license and once, while flying in the area between Hurricane Mesa and Short Creek, spotted something from the air. Later, they went to it on the ground, and found another small cabin full of food similar to the cache near old Pahreah. Nothing else was found in that cache, but everyone familiar with the two sites, seemed to think there was a connection.

Looking at the southeast side of Yellow Rock a few days after a rainstorm.

This is the metal box at the Hidden Cache which held the bed, clothes, and a .22 rifle.

At the Hidden Cache. This is the remains of a second old metal storage box, and behind it, the little cave with a rock & cement wall across the front.

Inside the cave at the Hidden Cache is Mason Meeks looking at one of the batteries. Merle Beard is at the window behind.
(Merril Johnson foto, 1953)

The Hattie Green Mine Trail & Fivemile Ranch

Location and Access Perhaps the easiest hike featured in this book, and the one with the best access, is the trail and hike to the Hattie Green Mine. The Hattie Green is an old copper mine which sits right on top of The Cockscomb, sometimes known as the East Kaibab Monocline. This mine consists of two tunnels, and three other pits, prospects or adits. The claim on the site was first filed in 1893. Get more information on this mine under *Mines and Mining History* in the back of this book. The location of this hike is about halfway between Kanab and Page. It's also about 11 kms northwest of the Paria Ranger Station & Visitor Center. Access is very easy. Park right on Highway 89, about 300 meters or so south of mile post 28. Or with a high clearance vehicle(HCV), and if the gate near the highway is not locked, then you can drive into the short canyon near the mine. It's perhaps best just to park on the highway, because you'll have to cross a narrow piece of private land, and it's better you walk across than take a vehicle in.

Trail or Route Conditions From the highway, walk due east. Cross a fence, then a shallow drainage. In the middle of a meadow surrounded by sagebrush, look for a HCV track running east. Follow this as it curves to the south and around the southern end of a low and minor sub-ridge of The Cockscomb. Once around this, the road enters a short little valley within The Cockscomb. At about the point where the campsite is shown on the map, the track then follows the dry creek bed north, which is very rough and sandy. Walk north from the campsite about one km, and notice on the left or west, a small man-made stone structure (a pile of rocks). About 40 meters or so north of the stone pile, look uphill to the east, and search for some stone cairns marking the lower part of the trail. Further up, you'll see the trail, which is an old wagon road. This first trail takes you to the top of The Cockscomb, where some of the mining activity took place. A second trail, this one running to the western tunnel, is located about another 30-40 meters north of where the first trail runs up the slope. The bottom of the trail is marked by cairns, but a bit further up, it turns into an old wagon road. Both of these trails can be seen as you walk up the canyon, but only if you know where to look.

If exploring old mines is your thing, take a flashlight. Twenty meters into the east side tunnel is an old door, and there are still wooden rails inside the western tunnel. Could be interesting.

Elevations The highway trailhead, 1500 meters; end of HCV road, 1550; the ridge-top adit, about 1675 meters.

Hike Length and Time Needed The one-way distance is about 3 kms. The hike can be made in as little as 2-3 hours, round-trip; or it could take half a day.

Water There's none on the hike, so take your own.

Maps USGS or BLM map Smoky Mountain(1:100,000); or Paria(1:62,500); or Fivemile Valley(1:24,000).

The east side tunnel at the Hattie Green Mine.

Map 21, The Hattie Green Mine Trail & Fivemile Ranch

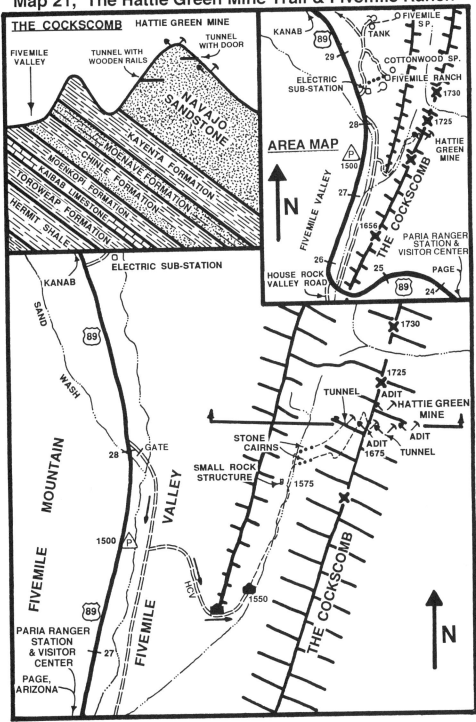

THE COCKSCOMB

HATTIE GREEN MINE

TUNNEL WITH DOOR

TUNNEL WITH WOODEN RAILS

FIVEMILE VALLEY

NAVAJO SANDSTONE

KAYENTA FORMATION

MOENAVE FORMATION

CHINLE FORMATION

MOENKOPI FORMATION

KAIBAB LIMESTONE

TOROWEAP FORMATION

HERMIT SHALE

AREA MAP

KANAB

89

29

28

27

26

25

24

FIVEMILE SP.

TANK

COTTONWOOD SP.

FIVEMILE RANCH

1730

1725

HATTIE GREEN MINE

ELECTRIC SUB-STATION

P 1500

1656

THE COCKSCOMB

FIVEMILE VALLEY

PARIA RANGER STATION & VISITOR CENTER

PAGE

HOUSE ROCK VALLEY ROAD

89

N

ELECTRIC SUB-STATION

KANAB

SAND WASH

89

28

GATE

FIVEMILE MOUNTAIN

1500 P

89

27

PARIA RANGER STATION & VISITOR CENTER

PAGE, ARIZONA

FIVEMILE VALLEY

HCV

1550

SMALL ROCK STRUCTURE

B 1575

STONE CAIRNS

TUNNEL

ADIT

HATTIE GREEN MINE

ADIT 1675

ADIT

TUNNEL

1725

1730

THE COCKSCOMB

N

SCALE

0 .5 1

KMS

Main Attractions A good look at The Cockscomb, some interesting tunnels and one copper ore heap. Old mine enthusiasts should take along a flashlight for exploring the tunnels--which will be done at one's own risk.

Ideal Time to Hike Spring or fall, but can be done anytime.

Hiking Boots Any dry weather boots or shoes.

Author's Experience The author has been there three times, the last trip was in November, 1997.

The Fivemile Ranch

Added to the Hattie Green Mine hike is a little history on one of the nearby ranches. The Fivemile Ranch is one of the least known outposts mentioned in this book. It's also one of the very last places to have been homesteaded in the entire region. The ranch is located in what is called Fivemile Valley, about 8 kms(5 miles) due south of old Pahreah, thus the name Fivemile. At least one old timer from Tropic says the name of the place was the Cottonwood Ranch, as it's near Cottonwood Spring. It's just west of The Cockscomb and east of Highway 89. To get there, turn off Highway 89, between mile posts 28 and 29, and park at or near the gate where the road enters the electric sub-station.

The earliest written record the Kane County courthouse has on the Fivemile Ranch is dated May 11, 1913. That's when William J. Henderson filed a claim on the water rights to one or both of the springs involved with the Fivemile Ranch spread. To the north is the Fivemile Spring; to the south about one km is Cottonwood Spring. The old ranch house is at Cottonwood Spring.

The next recorded information about Fivemile was on June 17, 1937. This was when Herman Mangum got a patent deed on it from the government under the Homestead Act. To have gotten it under the Homestead Act, he would have had to live there, or make improvements to the place for 5 years, before getting title to the land, which apparently came in 1937. Herman Mangum was the son of John Mangum.

The John Mangum family lived in or around Pahreah after it was mostly abandoned in the early 1900's. Later on Herm Pollock, Wallace Ott, and Kay Clark remembered the family when they lived in The Dugout, two or three kms north of old Pahreah. That time period was the late 1920's and early 1930's.

In about 1930 an oil company outfit was drilling test holes in the northern end of the Rush Beds, in the area south and west of Grosvenor Arch. That outfit pumped water to their camp from what has been called ever since, Pump House Spring and Canyon. This is located in upper Cottonwood Wash where the water begins to flow. When their hole came up dry, they sold parts and equipment to various local people. One of those people was John Mangum, who bought a wagon load of used lumber.

John and son Herman, along with Jim Ed Smith and his son Layton, hauled the lumber down Cottonwood Wash to Cottonwood Spring in the Fivemile Valley, before a road was built. That was sometime between 1932 and 1935. Just southwest of the Cottonwood Spring, they built a small house out of the used lumber. It's a two-room house, not too fancy, and without insulation. The back room wall was papered; not with wallpaper, but with pages from the latest magazines. This homemade wallpaper job is gone today, but before you could read up on events from the 1930's. The author once saw an advertisement for new Dodge cars selling for $640.

Throughout the years, the area around the Fivemile Homestead has been owned by two individuals. Apparently the Fivemile Spring was held by Henderson through 1945, but before that, Delmar G. Robinson of Kanab, bought out the Fivemile Ranch from the Mangums in May, 1942. The Mangums then headed for Idaho.

Later on, in September 1959, it was deeded over to Delmar's son, Don R. Robinson. Finally in 1963, the Litchfield Company obtained a Quit Claim Deed on at least part of the property around the spring and ranch house. In the late 1980's, Jeff Johnson of Kanab leased the place and runs cows there. If you park at the sub-station, and walk in, no one should care. Just don't go in hunting for some kind of souvenirs because it is on private land.

The copper ore heap on top of the ridge at the Hattie Green Mine.

The Fivemile Ranch house and corrals just beyond.

The Buckskin Gulch & Paria River Loop-Hike

Location and Access Map 22 and Part 1, includes the upper part of what is traditionally known as the Paria River hike and its best known tributary, the Buckskin Gulch. This map covers all the upper part of the Lower Paria River Gorge and includes the Paria down to as far as The Confluence; that's where the Buckskin Gulch enters from the west.

Map 23 and Part 2, includes that part of the Paria from The Confluence down to Wrather Canyon & Arch. This is the best part of the Paria, because it has many springs, good narrows, excellent campsites, an old historic trail to the rim, and at least one good panel of petroglyphs.

Map 24 and Part 3, shows the Paria River from Wrather Canyon down to about Bush Head Canyon. This is the part of the gorge where it begins to open up and becomes wider. This is where it begins to look more like the Grand Canyon. This section has one of the best arches in the world, four routes to the rim for fine views of the canyon country, more good springs and water, campsites, and more petroglyphs.

The last part of the Paria is shown on Map 25 and Part 4. It begins just below Bush Head Canyon and ends at Lee's Ferry on the Colorado River. The canyon in this section opens up wide, and it has old ranches, some abandoned uranium prospects or adits, and some of the best petroglyphs on boulders the author has seen. Each of these segments could be a one day hike, but to see all the side canyons, and do side trips, it may take 5 or 6 days. Most people do the whole thing in 3 or 4 days however.

In 1984, all of this Lower Paria River Canyon and the Vermilion Cliffs, was put aside as a wilderness area. Now this one large crescent-shaped region is officially called the Paria Canyon--Vermilion Cliffs Wilderness Area. It includes all of the Paria Canyon from the power lines below the White House Trailhead, and the Buckskin Gulch, down to near Lee's Ferry.

There are four ways to get into this gorge, all of which are from Highway 89, which runs between Kanab and Page. The normal entry point for the Paria is the **White House Trailhead**. It's easiest of access and can be used regardless of the weather conditions, as it's at the end of a graveled road. The other three entry points are via the Buckskin Gulch. They are; the **Middle Trail** on top of West Clark Bench, the **Buckskin Trailhead**, and the most-used, the **Wire Pass Trailhead**. All these are discussed later.

The beginning point for all hikes in the Paria River--Buckskin Gulch is at the new Paria Ranger Station & Visitor Center. It's located about 200 meters south of Highway 89, about halfway between Kanab and Page, and between mile posts 20 and 21. Be sure to stop there before entering the canyons and talk to a BLM employee or volunteer. They now sell books, maps and post cards, etc. It's open from 8:30 am to 5 pm daily. In the future, and because of the new Grand Staircase-Escalante National Monument, it may now remain open year-round(?). Usually someone lives behind the office in a trailer house, and they keep the latest information on weather and hiking conditions posted outside on an information-bulletin board which is well-lit at night. That information comes from the Kanab BLM office, Tele. 435-644-2672. The visitor center has some kind of radio telefone which is used for emergencies only.

The upper part of the Buckskin Gulch. It's like this for nearly 20 kms.

Map 22, Lower Paria River Gorge--Part 1
The Buckskin Gulch and Paria River Loop-Hike

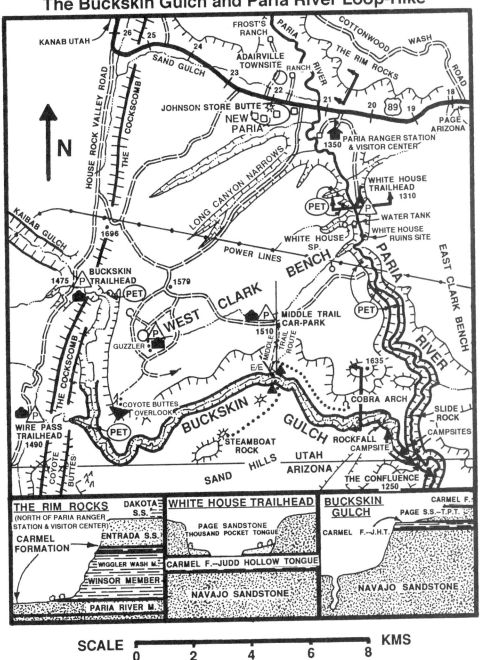

If a ranger is not at the visitor center, you can pickup & fill out the Recreation Fee Permit Envelope at the self-service pay station or information-bulletin board. After filling it out, drop it in the metal box provided. As of 1997, day-hikes down the Paria and/or Buckskin cost $5 per day, with the second day free; as well as $5 a night for camping in the canyons. See more details of the latest regulations in the introduction to this book. Also, after leaving the visitor center, you are requested to sign in at any of the four trailheads. All hikers are urged to sign in at the trail registers, whether they're going on an overnight trip, or day-hiking. **Because of the heavy visitor use around The Confluence of the Paria and Buckskin area, everyone is urged to day-hike only, rather than camp in that area.**

If you need to fill water jugs, do that at the tap about 75 meters west of the visitor center, as all the trailheads are dry. To reach the normal trailhead for entry to the Paria River, turn left or east right at the Paria Ranger Station, and drive south about 3 kms on a good gravel road to the White House Trailhead.

The White House Trailhead has picnic tables, fire pits, toilets, and can be used as a campsite. Beginning in 1997, the charge for camping was $5 a night. If you get there without water, go back to the ranger station; or walk across the river and downstream about 300 meters and up a small side canyon to the west, where the White House Spring is located. This water is very good if taken directly from the spring. If you have time, you can visit some petroglyphs just across the river to the west and up two minor draws. The white sandstone seen at this trailhead is the Thousand Pockets Tongue of the Page Sandstone(although some geologists still call it the upper part of the Navajo Sandstone).

The White House or Clark Cabin ruins

The story behind the name of this trailhead, and the White House Cabin and White House Spring was told to the author by Kay Clark, who used to live in Henrieville. The story begins in the Luna Valley of New Mexico. In February, 1887, Wilford Clark(Kay Clark's father) was born to the wife of Owen Washington Clark. Right after this child was born and the mother strong enough to travel, the small family moved from Luna Valley to southern Utah and set up a homestead on the Paria River just downstream from where the White House Trailhead is today.

They arrived in June, 1887, and immediately built a small cabin. The family lived in the Clark Cabin only about one year, then in 1888, moved upriver a ways to the Adairville site(Adairville existed only from 1873 until 1878, and was abandoned because of lack of summertime water). Largely because of water problems, that place didn't work out either, so in 1889 the family moved upstream to Pahreah, which at that time was in the process of losing population. The first big floods to come down the Paria River, which caused many people to have second thoughts about living at Pahreah, roared down the canyon in 1883 and 1884. Another big flood came in 1896.

In 1892, Kay Clark's grandfather, Owen W. Clark, then moved the whole family once again, this time to a safer and more promising land around the town of Cannonville. The family has been in Bryce Valley ever since.

Back now to the name of White House. After the Clarks left their original cabin, sheepherders used the place as a camp and a supply depot when they had their flocks to the southeast on top of East Clark Bench(both the East Clark and West Clark Benches are named after Owen W. Clark). Sometime in the 1890's, the cabin burned down, apparently due to carelessness on the part of a sheepman.

One of many pools you'll have to wade through on the Buckskin Gulch hike.

It was the sheepmen who gave the place the name, White House Cabin and White House Spring. When they were out on the range for a long time, and had to drink any water they could get, they always enjoyed going back to the Clark Cabin because of the good tasting water they could get out of the little year-round spring located just upstream and up a little draw to the west. As the story goes, someone commented that this water was so good, it could have come direct from the White House(in Washington DC). Thus the name stuck, on both the cabin and the spring.

To find the White House Ruins today, walk south from the parking lot along a bench trail on the east side of the river; or perhaps in the stream channel. After about 300 meters you'll see to the west, the mouth of the drainage with White House Spring, and a large metal storage tank. From there the ruins are about 200 meters southeast. Get on the east side bench as soon as you can. One in that area, you may see a hiker's sign pointing downcanyon. About 10 meters meters east of the sign is a pile of stones. This is said to be the remains of the cabin's fireplace. There were at one time some corrals just north of the ruins, but they've been washed away by floods. About 40 meters east of the pile of stones, and at the base of the cliffs, is a cowboyglyph or etching. It looks old and could be someones brand.

Buckskin Gulch Trailheads

The other three trailheads are for entry into one of the best slot canyon hikes on the Colorado Plateau, the Buckskin Gulch. To reach the Buckskin Trailhead, drive west from the Paria Ranger Station & Visitor Center on Highway 89 and through The Cockscomb. Just west of where the highway cuts through the monocline, and between mile posts 25 and 26, turn south on the House Rock Valley Road. This road is rather well-maintained. If you drive this road south, you'll end up on Highway 89A between mile posts 565 and 566 in the House Rock Valley, at the western end of the Vermilion Cliffs. This House Rock Valley Road is fairly well-traveled in the warmer months and by all kinds of vehicles. From the highway to the first car-park, called the **Buckskin Trailhead**, is about 7 kms. This is where the Kaibab Gulch cuts through The Cockscomb.

From the Buckskin Trailhead, continue south for about another 6 or 7 kms and you'll come to the **Wire Pass Trailhead**. This is the more popular starting point of the two entries at the head of the Buckskin Gulch, because it shortens the walk by a couple of hours. You can camp at either trailhead but both are dry, so take plenty of water with you. The BLM has installed a pit toilet at each of these trailheads. The Wire Pass Trailhead is located on the lower end of Coyote Wash, but for some reason, that part of the drainage below the trailhead is not called Coyote Wash. Instead it's the Wire Pass. At the bottom end of this drainage just before the Buckskin, is the narrowest part of this hike.

The fourth and last entry possibility into the Buckskin, is from the West Clark Bench and the **Middle Trail.** Until recently it was really more of a route than a trail. Get there by driving south from Highway 89 between mile posts 21 & 22, on the first road running south on the west side of the Paria

In the lower part of this picture is the bottom of the Buckskin Gulch where the
Middle Trail or Route enters the narrows.

River Bridge. That road is immediately east of the Paria River Guest Ranch. This gives everyone public access, but you pass through some private land and two gates. Leave the gates as you find them; either open or closed. Then drive up Long Canyon, on a maintained road which can be slick and muddy in wet weather. At the head of the canyon, stay on the most-used road, the one which veers left at two junctions, and continue south, then southeast. The last part will be down a shallow drainage towards the Middle Trail Car-park near a fence, as shown. When you first see the fence, stop quick, because there's a big sand trap right there. There are several sandy places in the last km or so before the fence, but the author made it several times in his VW Rabbit. Near the trailhead are several good places to camp.

In June, the driest month, sandy roads tend to be their worst, so a shovel in the trunk should be standard equipment, just in case. Park just before the north-south running fence. This latter car-park and the Middle Trail or Route is the least used of the entries to the Buckskin, but it affords a different view of the country you'll be walking through, and the access road is generally good for all vehicles.

Trail or Route Conditions Most people just going to the lower Buckskin, usually begin at the **White House Trailhead** and walk down to The Confluence and up the Gulch a ways, then return the same way to their car. This part of the hike down the Paria is very easy, and normally there are no obstacles. However, in September, 1980, a flood came down and scoured out a deep hole just above The Confluence in the Paria. For much of one season, and until the river gradually filled it in, hikers had to ferry packs across on air mattresses or inner tubes. Be sure you inquire at the Paria Ranger Station or see the bulletin board in front, about this possibility before you start hiking, then go prepared for any kind of difficult situation.

If you walk slowly and watch carefully along some of the canyon walls on the west side not far below the White House Trailhead, you may find several panels of petroglyphs. Just upcanyon from the power lines(which mark the wilderness boundary) is one panel, and not far below the lines is a second. The third petroglyph panel shown on the map is near the one that's whiteman-made, perhaps a survey marker, high on the west wall. About 15 meters upstream from that obvious marker is another hard-to-see panel. Further down and about one km above The Confluence, is Slide Rock. This is a section of the Navajo Sandstone wall which has broken off and slid down into the river. Presently, the river flows underneath it, making a short tunnel.

If you begin at the **Buckskin Trailhead,** you also have an unobstructed walk into the Gulch. Just after you begin the walk, after maybe a km, and just after you walk through a gate-like narrow place, turn to the left, or north, and look for a good panel of big horn sheep petroglyphs on a wall on the bench above the creek bed. After the petroglyphs, the canyon is open for the first part, but then begins to narrow as you near the confluence of the Buckskin and Wire Pass drainages.

From **Wire Pass Trailhead,** you'll first pass through open country, then the wash narrows quickly. Soon you'll come to the place where there used to be a minor obstacle, a chokestone which created a dropoff of about 3 meters. But in the early summer of 1991, that was gone and you simply walk down the

About 3 kms from the Middle Trail is the unusual Cobra Arch.

canyon now. In the lower end of the Wire Pass drainage and just before you arrive at the Buckskin Gulch is a very narrow slot that may be difficult to take a big pack through--but everybody makes it! Right at the Wire Pass--Buckskin Confluence, there are several big horn sheep petroglyph panels.

From the Wire Pass--Buckskin Confluence, the real Buckskin Gulch begins, and doesn't end until The Confluence of the Paria. This part of the canyon is nearly 20 kms long, and averages 4-5 meters in width for its entire length. At times the gorge may open to 8 or 10 meters in width, then narrow down to no more than a meter wide. The author recalls something like 40 to 50 places in the Buckskin where logs were seen wedged into the walls high above--mute evidence of nature on the rampage, and a grim reminder of the danger of walking this gorge. *One last reminder, have a good weather forecast before entering this canyon!* Normally this slot's depth is somewhere between 30 and 50 meters, but downcanyon near the Paria, the walls are maybe 100 meters in height. This is the longest slot canyon in the world.

For the most part, walking down the Buckskin is uneventful, but normally there are several small pools of water or mud you must wade through. These pools are concentrated in the 3 or 4 kms upcanyon from where the Middle Trail enters. There is no running water in this upper part of the Gulch, except of course in times of flood, and the bottom is so hidden from the sun, and the temperatures so cool, there is little evaporation, even in the heat of the summer. Therefore muddy pools are usually there all the time. One such pool is called the Cesspool. It's about one km upcanyon from the Middle Trail entry/exit point. The chances are good you'll have to float your pack across this pool. Once again, be sure to bring an inner tube or air mattress with you to this area, then check at the Paria Ranger Station bulletin board for the latest word concerning the depth of this pool and others. Then at the last minute make the decision as to take this added equipment or not.

If using the **Middle Trail,** follow the fence line due south right over the minor cliffs. A trail is slowly developing along a drainage veering a little southwest from the trailhead. This takes you right to the rim of the Buckskin. From there turn east for 200-300 meters for the route into the bottom of the slot. From the lip of the narrows it's a slow and careful scramble down the slickrock to the bottom. **A Warning:** *Short people, inexperienced hikers and anyone carrying a large pack may find it difficult getting up or down this last 30 meters. Take a rope for safety and to lower your pack down some down-sloping slickrock which is often covered with sand.*

For those taking this hike in two days, this is a good place to camp, as it allows you to take another look at the weather situation halfway through the gorge. This is obviously a hike you don't want to do in a monsoon weather pattern. It also allows one to exit and take a 3 km side-trip to Cobra Arch. From this entry/exit point, you can also scramble up a steep slope to the south rim for a possible hike to fotogenic Steamboat Rock(don't walk on the delicate erosional features) and other landmarks atop the Sand Hills, sometimes known as the Paria Plateau.

Downcanyon from the Middle Trail entry/exit point, is what is normally the only obstacle in the Buckskin. This is **The Rockfall**, created by some large boulders which have broken off the canyon walls

This is The Rockfall in the lower Buckskin Gulch. You'll need a rope, even though there are steps cut into one boulder.

about 2 1/2 kms up from The Confluence. The worst part is a 4 meter-high climb or descent, over one of these boulders. In recent years, someone cut out several steps and handholds into one of the boulders, and you'll sometimes find a rope over the dryfall. The BLM rangers normally cut out ropes that appear to be unsafe. To insure you have no problems, **take along a 10 meter-long rope** to lower your packs over this dropoff. Without packs, hikers can sometimes slide, jump or wiggle down through this dryfall but it's a little risky without a rope.

In 1991, there was another unusual obstacle in the lower Buckskin between The Rockfall and the campsites in the lower end. This was several very deep swimming-type pools. Apparently a bigger-than-normal flood came down the Buckskin in the fall or winter of 1990-91 and scoured out deep holes where the walls constrict. At the deepest pool, the author had to hold onto a log with one hand, while he held his day-pack up with the other hand to keep it dry. People taking big packs down had to float them across, while others were just swimming. Later floods filled these hole in and by 1997, everything was normal, with ankle-deep water. **Expect big changes with every flood!**

About one km above The Confluence of the Paria River, there are several campsites in the lower Buckskin on some sandy benches high above the creek bed. This is a heavily-used area, and at times in the past has been closed to camping. The reason for closing it, is that it simply becomes overused and by closing it down, allows the vegetation to recover. If you're camping there, please tread lightly and stay on existing paths and tent sites. Because this area is heavily used, and because one element of the BLM doesn't want to improve the sites or install a toilet, they may in the future, require a permit and reservation to camp there. Read the author's view on this in the Introduction, and on Coyote Buttes, Map 28.

One campsite that's seldom used is one that's about halfway between The Rockfall and the beginning of running water in the Buckskin. You'll have to carry water back up from downcanyon, but it will lessen the impact on The Confluence campsites.

Elevations The White House Trailhead, 1310 meters; Buckskin Trailhead, 1475; Wire Pass Trailhead, 1490 meters; and the Middle Trail Car-park, about 1510 meters. The Confluence of the Buckskin and Paria, is near 1250 meters.

Hike Length and Time Needed The distance from the Buckskin Trailhead to the confluence of Wire Pass is about 7 kms. From the Wire Pass Trailhead to this same confluence is about 3 kms. From that point to The Confluence with the Paria is another 19 kms. From The Confluence back up to the White House Trailhead is another 11 kms or so. This makes the total distance from the Buckskin to the White House Trailhead about 38 kms. From Wire Pass to White House it's about 33 kms. This can be done in one long day, but it's not recommended for everyone. You'll also have to have two cars, or a mtn. bike and car, for a shuttle.

The author once left a mtn. bike at White House, then drove to Wire Pass. He walked down the Buckskin and up the Paria to White House in 8 hours. 13 min. This wasn't too bad, but the bike ride back to Wire Pass was--being at the end of an otherwise long day and peddling against the wind. It turned out to be a 10 hour-day. Despite its length, it's recommended you do this in one day to cut down on the number of campers near The Confluence.

The major problem with doing this hike in two days and a camp at the Middle Trail entry/exit point, would be that you'd have to carry at least a one gallon(3.75 liters) jug full of water; perhaps more in hot weather, less in cooler conditions. Most people however, make it all the way through the Buckskin in one day, and end up camping near The Confluence where there's a permanent water supply.

Water The Buckskin is normally a bone-dry wash, but with an occasional pool of water or mud to wade through. Since most people don't have the courage to drink this, count on it being a dry hike. Carry all the water you'll need. About two kms up the Buckskin from The Confluence, you'll begin to see pools of water, and about one km from the Paria, and just above the campsites, it begins to flow pretty good. This seep is a year-round water supply. But since this campsite area and the lower part of the Buckskin is so heavily used, and with people walking in the water all the time, especially in the spring and fall months, *you'd better plan to filter or purify it first.*

Another option for those camping near The Confluence, is to take empty jugs(always have plenty of empty jugs, as they weigh almost nothing) down the Paria a ways, and fill them up at Wall Spring or at the spring just above it(see the next map of the Paria, Part 2). This is about 3 1/2 kms below The Confluence. Still another alternative, is to purify or filter the water in the Paria River. Since most of this water seeps out of the bottom layers of the Navajo Sandstone in the Upper Paria River Gorge and below the town of Cannonville, it's not really that bad; it's just a little muddy looking at times, especially if there's any storm activity upcanyon. The author hasn't used filters, but it seems they would clog-up badly if used in muddy water. So a bottle of Iodine tablets might be necessary.

The part of the Paria below The Confluence flows year-round, but between the White House Trailhead and the Buckskin it's often dry in the early summer. The stockman who leases a ranch just north of Highway 89 near the site of old Adairville, uses a bulldozer to make a small temporary dam across the creek during part of the year, and uses the Paria water for irrigation. This is usually in May and June. However, in the heat of the summer, water in the Paria doesn't even reach old Adairville. In July, and after

Young hikers enjoying the narrows of Buckskin Gulch.

the first storm or flood of the season, the Paria River then flows again, usually until the next spring or summer. To check on the Paria water, just glance at the creek bed as you drive across the bridge on Highway 89. Also, it's important to check on the water situation at the ranger station, or ask other hikers of its whereabouts.

Maps USGS or BLM maps Kanab and especially Smoky Mountain(for the Buckskin Gulch only), and to these two add Glen Canyon Dam, which shows the Paria River from the state line, or The Confluence, on down to Lee's Ferry(all at 1:100,000 scale). The map Glen Canyon Dam also shows the Vermilion Cliffs. Or you might try the 1:62,500 scale maps Paria, Paria Plateau, and Lee's Ferry. These are no longer printed, but there may be a few still around.

The BLM has recently published a new map/guide called Hiker's Guide to Paria Canyon. It's in book form with 30 small maps covering the Paria and Buckskin down to Lee's Ferry. But it's not just one map showing the entire canyon. Their old map with the same title at 1:62,500 scale is a good one if you can find it. It may be republished.

Another excellent map is one of the series of four field study maps which were prepared by the BLM, USGS, and others, covering the Paria Plateau(the Sand Hills). These maps are in the series MF-1475, A, B, C, and D. Each map is at 1:62,500 scale, and very much the same, except each has a different emphasis; such as (A) geology, (B) geochemical data, (C) mines and prospects, and (D) mineral resource potential. Get these maps from any USGS outlet. Each of these covers the entire Lower Paria River Hike from White House to Lee's Ferry, and the Vermilion Cliffs and all of the House Rock Valley Road.

Main Attraction One of the best slot canyon hikes in the world. Also, with an exit at the Middle Trail, you can have a look at Cobra Arch, one of the most unique around. Be sure you read the part on *Fotography in Slot Canyons* in the Introduction, which will help you take home better fotos of this very dark chasm.

Ideal Time to Hike Because of the cold water in the pools of the Buckskin, June has become the popular time to visit this canyon. It's getting hot by June, but once inside the narrows, it's very cool. You'll seldom see the sun; and it's that way for nearly 20 kms! So the heat of the outside world(above the narrows) doesn't really matter, except for the walk back up the Paria to the White House Trailhead.

June is the driest month of the year, not only for this region, but for the entire state of Utah. Kanab receives about 31 cms(12 in.) of rainfall annually, part of it in winter. With the low temps and lack of sun in the gorge, the pools of water, especially the Cesspool, simply don't evaporate. Pools seem to stay in the Buckskin most of each winter, and often times until about June, then sometimes may be dry for a time. Each year is different. If you were to go down the Buckskin right after a summer storm, you'd likely have to float your pack across many pools on an air mattress or inner tube. See the ranger at the Paria Ranger Station for the latest word on the Cesspool situation and hiking conditions in the Buckskin.

You can hike the Buckskin throughout the summer, but you'd want a good weather forecast. If you're there in a dry spell, then fine. But if you're there in a wet period, with showers around, stay out of this canyon! Southern Utah has about two or three very wet monsoon periods each summer, each lasting a week or so. These periods usually occur from about mid-July to mid-September. This is the period you should be most cautious about the threat of flash floods.

Actually, as narrow as the place is, there are still many high places you could get up to and away from raging flood waters. But when the floods do come, they usually come in a surge, and you won't have much time to look for a hideout. Always listen to the local radio stations for the latest weather forecasts as you drive into the area. Remember, *the Buckskin Gulch is the worst place in the world to be in a flash flood!*

Hiking Boots If the latest information says the Gulch is bone dry, then you could use dry weather boots or shoes. But, you'll still have to wade in the lower Buckskin and usually the Paria as well, so best to take wading-type boots or shoes for the whole hike.

Author's Experience The author has been all the way through the Buckskin twice, and at least part way through on 4 other occasions, and from each trailhead. On one trip he made it from The Confluence campsite to the Wire Pass Trailhead, with large pack, in less than 6 1/2 hours. On his first, and last(1997) trip to the Paria, he walked from the White House Trailhead, down the Paria, up the Buckskin to the Rockfall, then back the same way, all in about 7 hours. Another time he left the Middle Trail Car-park, walked down to the bottom of the entry/exit point, then to Cobra Arch, and back to his car, all in 3 1/2 hours. His last hike was down the Middle Trail and up the other side to Steamboat Rock. Round-trip was about 4 hours. Most people will want more time than that taken by the author. Some may want to almost double the author's times.

A wide-angle view of The Rockfall in the lower Buckskin Gulch. Don't forget to take a rope for this one.

In 1991, this was the scene in the lower Buckskin Gulch. It was filled in soon after the picture was taken. Periodically, big floods scour out deep holes where the slot constricts, then they gradually fill in again with sand.

Lower Paria River Gorge--The Confluence to Lee's Ferry

Location and Access The Lower Paria River Gorge is so long and has so many interesting sites to see, it's been broken down into four parts, or at least four different maps. Part 1, covers mainly the Buckskin Gulch and the trailheads leading into it, and the upper part of the Lower Paria River Gorge or Canyon. The second, third and fourth maps, cover the canyon from The Confluence of the Buckskin Gulch and the Paria River all the way down to Lee's Ferry. This is where the Paria empties into the Colorado River.

If you plan to do this entire canyon hike from top to bottom, call the BLM office in Kanab, 435-644-2672, and ask if they have a list of people who perform shuttle service between Whitehouse Trailhead and Lee's Ferry. Or stop and ask someone at Marble Canyon, which is where you turnoff Highway 89A going in the direction of Lee's Ferry.

Normally, the people who do the whole Paria River hike, start at the White House Trailhead. Get to this entry point by leaving Highway 89 between mile posts 20 and 21, and by driving south about 3 kms on an all-weather gravel road. Read more about this and the three other entry points under Part 1, the Buckskin Gulch.

Elevations The White House Trailhead is about 1310 meters; The Confluence, 1250; the Paria River at the bottom of Wrather Canyon, 1165; the mouth of Bush Head Canyon, about 1100; and Lee's Ferry, 950 meters.

Hike Length and Time Needed Here are the latest BLM calculations for distances in the Paria River Canyon. From the White House Trailhead to Lee's Ferry, is about 39 miles--62 kms. From the Buckskin Trailhead to Lee's Ferry, about 48 miles--77 kms. From Wire Pass Trailhead to Lee's Ferry, around 45 miles--72 kms. A long hike anyway you look at it, but a fun one, and one which has several side canyons, or routes to the canyon rim to explore.

A marathon-type walker could get through the canyon in 2 days, but some people would have trouble doing it in 3 or 4 days. Most do it in about 3, but this book introduces some new hikes out of the canyon and up to the rim, so it could take 5 or 6 days. It you're the type who likes to take it easy, do a lot of exploring, and likes to set up nice camps and relax, then a week isn't too long. However, the longer you plan to stay, the heavier your pack will be!

Water From The Confluence to Lee's Ferry, you'll have year-round water all the way, but you can only drink this river water if you purify it with Iodine tablets or filter it first. During the irrigation season in the Bryce Valley(Tropic, Henrieville and Cannonville) which extends from about mid-April through the beginning of October, there is very little water flowing down the Paria below Cannonville. Most of the water you see entering this Lower Paria Gorge during this period of time, seeps out of the bottom layers of the Navajo Sandstone as the river cuts through the White Cliffs below Cannonville. So it's pretty good water, but of course there are cows in the canyon, usually in the cooler 7 or 8 months of the year, so therein lies the danger.

Slide Rock, with the Paria River flowing beneath it. It's not far above The Confluence of the Paria and Buckskin.

Map 23, Lower Paria River Gorge--Part 2
The Confluence to Wrather Canyon

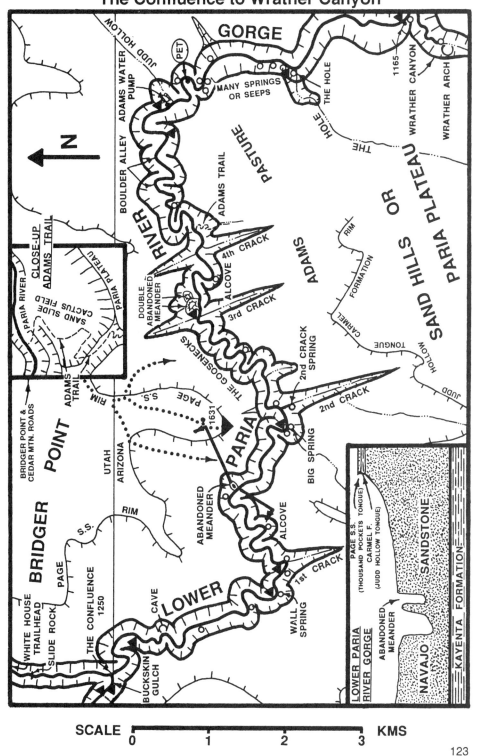

In the heat of the summer, or at least in June and July, the water in the upper gorge(between The Box, where the Paria cuts through The Cockscomb, and Highway 89) disappears in the sands. Then it begins flowing again in the lower canyon at the bottom end of the Buckskin Gulch near The Confluence. It then flows year-round to Lee's Ferry.

For those who prefer to drink good spring water without filtration or chemicals, take it from Wall, Big, and Shower Springs, and from springs inside Wrather and Bush Head Canyons. However, between The Confluence and Bush Head, are a number of minor seeps, which likely will have water flowing from them most of the time. The author always carries a small $3 bottle of Iodine tablets in his pack just for such situations.

The alternative to chemicals is filtration. The latest REI catalog lists filters designed for hikers for $55 to $130, but there are cheaper ones than that. Some manufactures are making a fist full of dollars on the scare tactics of some people, but the BLM and the NPS are required to tell hikers to boil or treat all water--even *spring water,* to stay away from possible law suits!. The author prefers spring water, and Iodine tablets as an emergency backup.

Another thing to remember, carry several empty water bottles or plastic jugs. They don't weigh much, and can be thrown away at the end of the trip. By having a couple of one gallon(3.75 liters) jugs, you can increase the number of potential campsites to you, which allows you to carry water from good springs to unoccupied sites.

Main Attractions A deep and narrow canyon, several places in which to climb or hike out to the rim, interesting side canyons, one of the best arches in the world, a chance to see desert big horn sheep, and many good campsites and petroglyphs. It's a great trip for those who have time off work in the spring or fall. More later under *Trail and Route Conditions.*

Ideal Time to Hike If you're doing this hike from the White House Trailhead straight down the Paria to Lee's Ferry, with just a quick look into the bottom of the Buckskin, then spring or fall is best. More specifically, the best time is from about the first of April through May; and again from about mid-September through mid or late October. If you go too early or late in the season, the icy water you'll be wading in all the time will make your feet fell like blocks of ice! The author prefers the spring months because the days are longer. Remember, March 21, has the same amount of daylight as does September 21.

By June 1st, the temperatures are getting up there to around 30°C(86°F) on average, and that's pretty warm when walking in the sun all day carrying a pack. You can count on temps of about 40°C(104°F) all through July and into August at Lee's Ferry. In the narrows parts, and when wading in the creek, the heat doesn't effect you so much; but in the lower end of the canyon near Lee's Ferry, the altitude is only about 950 meters, and you'll be walking in the sun constantly.

Another reason to stay out of the area in about June, is that there are big deer or horse flies which bite the back of bare legs. They seem to congregate in the more open areas in the bottom end of the canyon,

This is Wall Spring, located about 3 or 4 kms downstream from The Confluence.

The Confluence, of the Buckskin and the Paria.

with water and tamaracks around. You'll also be hindered by the very small gnats which get in your hair and bite. In the spring and fall, these two pests don't exist. Neither do they seem to exist in the narrow parts of the canyon at any time, just in the more open places.

Hiking Boots You'll be walking in or crossing the Paria River many times on your way to Lee's Ferry. In the narrower places you'll be hiking right in the stream continually. Your footwear will be wet all the time, so some kind of wading boots or shoes is a must.

In the last few years, a number of new hiking boots or shoes have been on the market, designed especially for this type of hike. What you'll want is the kind which aren't affected by water. In other words, a shoe which doesn't have leather. There aren't many like this around, but you can find them if you look. The Converse All Star basketball shoes, made of rubber and canvas, are good, except they have a thin sole and low heel. There are the plain ordinary running shoes too. They are very good, but they have leather parts, which will have to be oiled after the hike, or they'll shrink and crack.

Another tip, since this is such a long hike, take a pair of shoes in good condition. Or if you have an old pair, and are trying to put them out of their misery, it might pay to take along a newer and light weight pair as a back-up. This is an especially good suggestion, if you intend to use some of the trails or routes out of the canyon and up to the rim. It takes a lot out of footwear to be used under strenuous conditions when wet all the time.

Author's Experience The author has been down into the canyon from the White House Trailhead on four occasions, and up from Lee's Ferry on three other trips. On each trip, he went to somewhere in the middle of the canyon, and returned the same way to his car, thus avoiding a car shuttle or hitch hiking.

Trail and Route Conditions--from The Confluence to Lee's Ferry The first half of the way between The Confluence and Lee's Ferry is narrow, although it's not the slot-type canyon you find in the Buckskin Gulch. There are many springs, campsites, running water year-round, and no obstacles. If you were caught in this section by a flash flood, you would have very little trouble finding a high place out of the way of the torrent. There are many good campsites, and always one site near each of the good springs. Taking fotos is in some ways easier than in the darker Buckskin, because here you will see the sun part of the time. There are several abandoned meanders, or abandoned stream channels to explore, and there are some petroglyphs, an historic pumping site, and several trails or routes to the rim.

If you arrive at The Confluence, near mile P7 on the newest BLM log-type map, and find the campsites just inside the lower Buckskin too crowded or noisy, then you could walk downstream about a km to find another place, high and dry and safe--near mile P8. Some might prefer this campsite to the Buckskin sites anyway, as it's closer to the springs located another two or three kms down the canyon. Just a couple of bends downriver from this campsite is a large alcove-type cave, which might prove interesting.

About 3 1/2 or 4 kms below The Confluence, is a nice campsite and a usually good spring the author is calling Wall Spring--near mile P9. It has put out a lot of good water each time the author has

Hikers near The Confluence. The dog carries his own food.

been there, but Skip, the former Paria Ranger, recalled times where its flow was so low, it was hard to get a safe drink. But normally you can rely on this spring.

Just 300 meters below Wall Spring is a good campsite and yet another spring, which may in the long run be more reliable than its neighbor upstream. This spring, near mile P10, is at or near a side canyon this author calls the 1st Crack. It's the result of a minor fault, as are all four of the Crack Canyons shown on Map 23, page 123.

From the Wall Spring area, the canyon tends to the northeast a bit. Along this section you'll see a large alcove or overhang, which is one of the deepest in the Paria, and is similar to those found in the Coyote Gulch of the Escalante River. A km or so beyond this overhang or alcove, is another overhang where the river under-cuts the Navajo Sandstone wall, and just beyond, is a feature known as an abandoned meander, or an abandoned stream channel--near mile P11. A few thousand years ago, the Paria River ran through this channel, but it slowly undercut one of its' walls in the process of making a goose-neck curve. It finally abandoned the old loop for a new one. The former stream channel is 5 or 6 meters above the present level of the river bed. It'll be worth while to take a break from wading the river and check this one out. The access is easy and there are camping possibilities on the north side of the meander.

From the abandoned meander, the canyon tends to the southeast for about two kms. Just before you arrive at the 2nd Crack, you'll come to the best spring in the canyon. This one is called Big Spring. Across the river is another good and very popular campsite--near mile P12. If that site is full when you arrive, just go downstream a ways to find still more camping places and springs--near mile P13.

Right at the very bottom of what the author calls the 2nd Crack, is another seemingly good spring. It flows out of this little side canyon with a good discharge--at least when the author saw it. If you're a rock climber, it might be fun to look for a route out of the canyon to the south and up this 2nd Crack. Someone who is experienced with *chimneying* might be able to get out of or beyond the first set of ledges, and find a way up this crack canyon to the south rim. It looked promising, for a real tough guy or gal.

As you pass the 2nd Crack, the Paria then tends to the northeast again, and you enter a section of the canyon where there are few if any springs. Between 2nd Crack and the Adams Pump, there are no springs, just river water. The author has placed several springs on the map in this section, but they are mostly just minor seeps, and don't have much discharge. This part of the canyon has some very tight turns, very high walls and it's as narrow as any part of the Paria River below the area just above The Confluence. The author has labeled this section the *Goosenecks*. You'll be walking right in the stream throughout most of this part.

At or near the bottom of the Goosenecks is the 3rd Crack--mile P14. It, like the other two upstream, is a little inconspicuous. It's hard at times to follow the river channel on the map; that's part of the reason these crack canyons are not easily seen. It's also a little difficult to keep your orientation(north-south) as you walk down this narrow gorge. A compass is helpful.

Just beyond the 3rd Crack and on your left, is another abandoned stream channel. It's maybe 10-15 meters above the river level, and easy to get into. The author followed it for a ways, then returned the same

The first of several abandoned meanders.

127

way. But it appears on the Paria Plateau map(1:62,500), to be a kind of double abandoned meander--below mile P14. It might be worth while to take the time to check this one out. It could also make an interesting campsite.

Less than two kms below the 3rd Crack you'll come to the 4th Crack--near mile P15. This one is more obvious than the previous three, partly because the canyon is beginning to open up and become wider. From the rim above, it appeared that a good climber could possibly make it out of the canyon to the north, using this very narrow slit in the wall, but the author didn't take the time to give it a try. In the 4th Crack running south, there are some ledges to skirt and a little climbing, but from the top of the Adams Trail, where the author looked down on it, it appeared to be climbable, at least for an experienced person.

About half a km beyond the 4th Crack, and on the south side of the creek bed, is the beginning of the old Adams Trail. More interesting than the trail itself, is the hard-luck story behind it.

The Adams Trail and Water Pump

The area south of this middle part of the Lower Paria River Gorge is called the Sand Hills by all the local cattlemen; the Paria Plateau by others. The name Sand Hills is very fitting, as the top-most layer or rock formation is made up mostly of the Navajo Sandstone. When it weathers away, it forms very sandy conditions. Because of the sand, the only way one can get around the plateau, is to walk, ride a horse, drive a 4WD.

Despite the poor travel conditions, the area has been used for cattle, sheep and goat grazing since about the mid-1880's. It's fairly high, rising to 2043 meters on the southern edge at Powell's Monument. This means it has good pasturage, and it's surrounded on three sides by impassable cliffs or canyons. On the north is the Buckskin Gulch, the north and east by the Paria River Gorge, and on the south by the Vermilion Cliffs, which rise up 500 or 600 meters above the valley. The only easy way onto the plateau is from the west and the Coyote and House Rock Valleys.

Throughout the years, cattlemen slowly but surely began to develop water facilities, as there is no running water on the plateau, not one good reliable spring. They built small dams below exposed slickrock slopes to catch what rainwater there was. They blasted holes in the slickrock to make stock tanks, and of course there were already natural potholes or tanks in the slickrock. The number of cattle was always small and limited by the available water. Despite all the hardships, things went well for 50 years or so. Then a long drought began in the early 1930's, which coincided with the Great Depression.

During this drought period, there were several different cattlemen who had livestock on the Sand Hills range. The northeast quarter of the plateau was used by a man named Johnny Adams. As he began to see his cattle die of thirst, he started looking down into the Paria Canyon for water. He must have pondered long and hard as to how he might get his cattle down to the year-round flowing river, or how he might get some of that water up to his cows.

Finally he thought he had the problem solved. He had investigated pumping equipment and had come to

One of many gooseneck curves along the Lower Paria River Gorge.

Morning sun on the Navajo Sandstone wall streaked with desert varnish.

One of the best waterholes along the Paria is Big Spring.

The beginning of the Adams Trail.

the conclusion that with available technology and pumps, he could move water from the river to the rim, a vertical distance at one point of the canyon of about 215 meters. So in the winter of 1938-39 he made the decision to build a rough access trail to install pumping equipment. After searching the rim, he found a place, which with a little dynamite and work, could be used.

The Adams Trail was hacked out of the canyon wall in the spring of 1939, and the pump, gasoline engine, and 300 meters of 5 cm(2") pipe were trucked in over the Sand Hills access road. For the last part of the journey, pack animals were used to haul in the equipment.

According to P.T. Reilly, the man who researched the history of this pumping station(and which is written in the Utah Historical Quarterly), it was Dean Cutler who straw-bossed the job for Adams who was rather elderly at the time. The remaining crew members were Lorin Broadbent, Eugene McAllister, and Lynn Ford. The country was very rough, and getting the equipment to the rim was a major undertaking. Water and food were packed in, and the most luxurious comfort was ones bedroll spread out on the ground, although rattlesnakes were numerous after the weather began to warm up.

Their first job was to construct a rough trail to get the motor and pump down to the river. It was never intended to be a good trail, only good enough for men to scramble up and down. Horses were apparently never taken up or down the trail. The men lowered the pump and motor down the cliffs with ropes, one step at a time. Finally the pump and engine were in place, then pipe was carried down one section at a time, and attached.

It was well into summer when they installed the last section of pipe. They had intended to fill several potholes which were just above the rim. When the pipe was finally in place, they climbed down to the river to give it a try. But the river was very muddy, the result of storms upstream. They decided to abandon any pumping until the creek cleared. But that night it rained. It filled all the stock tanks and potholes. The drought was over, and the pump was never even tested. There it sat for two years.

In 1941, Adams sold the pump to another cattlemen, A. T. Spence. But Spence never used it. He ended up selling it to Merle Findlay in 1944. The pump continued to sit and gather dust and rust. Findlay owned the unused pump for four years, then sold it to Gerald Swapp in 1948.

Gerald Swapp's cattle range was the area north of the Paria, called the Flat Top and East Clark Bench. It was, and still is, a good grazing country, but lack of a good water supply has always restricted the potential of the range. After mulling over the idea of pumping water from the Paria up to the benchland for 10 years, Swapp finally bought the unused and untested pumping rig to give it a try. His intention was to pump water into the lower end of Judd Hollow, which is about 3 kms downstream from where the pump was originally set up at the bottom of the Adams Trail.

To do the job, Swapp hired Eugene McAllister, who was one of the original members of the crew who put the pipe and pump in place, and Tony Woolley. In December, 1948, the three men walked down into the canyon along the trail, got the engine running and got a good flow of water out the upper end of the pipe.

The upper part of the Adams Trail. It angles up to the left making a dugway.

Later, in January of 1949, under some rather cold conditions, Woolley rode a horse down the Paria Canyon, in similar fashion to the feat performed by John D. Lee in 1871. The pipe was all disconnected, and placed in bundles, then tied together at one end. A rope was tied to the cross-tree of the saddle, and the pipe was dragged down the partially frozen stream to Judd Hollow. The 4 cylinder, Fairbanks--Morris flathead engine and the pump, were carried by horseback downstream, one at a time.

To avoid damaging the pump by using it with muddy water, the crew dug a sump at the edge of the north bank of the stream. It was a hole, lined with rocks, which would allow water to filter in slowly, thus avoiding the muddy water when the stream was running high. Their intention was to run the pipe directly up to the bottom of Judd Hollow, a rise of 300 meters. Then they hoped to run it northeast for another 3 kms to a tank in the area where cattle were located. This would require much more pipe. So Woolley rode the horse downcanyon to Lee's Ferry, while Swapp and McAllister hiked back up the Adams Trail to the truck and drove back to Kanab, to get more pipe and a booster to the pump.

But things just didn't work out for Swapp. He had been ill throughout the ordeal of replacing the pump and pipe, so he decided to remain in Kanab until he felt better. However, he got worse instead. Finally he was taken to the hospital in Cedar City, where he died on March 28, 1949.

After this second effort to pump Paria River water upon the benchland surrounding the canyon, no one every tried the feat again. And there it sits today; the engine, pump and one length of pipe running into the ground where the sump was dug. You can still see it on the north side of the stream, on a low bench, at the mouth of Judd Hollow between miles P17 & P18 on the latest BLM map. More on this later.

Now back to hiking. To find the Adams Trail, walk downstream about 200 meters from where the south arm of 4th Crack drains into the canyon. On the south side of the creek, on a minor bench, and in an area which is rather broad, look for yet another rounded bench rising perhaps 10 to 15 meters above the embankment. You may first notice some hand or foot holds notched into the sandstone wall, which could be old Indian-made steps. They are very smooth and worn today. The author never did make it up the steep part using these steps. But just to the east or left(as you look at the rock face), is a broad vertical crack in the sandstone bench. You have to get down on all fours to make it up, but it seems easy climbing. For a closer look at this trail, see the little insert map on the Lower Paria River Gorge--Part 2.

Once you arrive on this first bench, walk east along the top, gradually turning to the right or south. Almost immediately you begin to walk up a steep sandslide covered with cactus. To avoid damaging this pristine cactus field and the cryptogamic soil, veer to the right and walk west a ways, then turn south up the minor drainage. Further up you'll come to the base of a talus slope on the right.

Head up this slope which comes down from where a minor drainage comes off the wall in front of you. Once you arrive near the top of this talus slope, you begin to see the old trail. Near the top of the slope, and almost next to the canyon wall, you'll turn right or to the northwest, and walk along near the base of the cliff. After about 100 meters, you come to more cliffs and at a kind of dead-end place. At that point, look to the left, or south along the cliff face, and you'll just be able to make out a faint line indicating the trail angling up

Typical campsite along the middle part of the Paria.

Another shaded campsite along the river.

The old and rusting Adams Pump, now located at the mouth of Judd Hollow.

along the cliff face. Walk up this ramp, which is a little steep in a place or two, but which is easy walking. An unloaded burro could surely make it up, and a big horn sheep or deer would have no trouble at all.

Further along you come to a level section, then less than 100 meters away, you'll again come to what is obviously a constructed trail. It zig zags up one last steep place to the southwest before running due south up the minor drainage you saw from below. At the top of this little draw, the trail vanishes on top of the plateau.

This is an easy walk, and it seems a pity no one took the time to finish the trail. Just a little more work, and it would be good enough for cattle to use. Once you get on the trail, anyone can make it to the top in about half an hour. From the top, you can walk along the rim in either direction for some fine views of the canyon below.

Now going downriver again. Between the Adams Trail and the mouth of Judd Hollow, the river makes some tight bends and is again enclosed in high walls. After about 1 1/2 kms, you'll come to a half km section where large boulders have fallen off the canyon wall and landed in the stream channel. In this part the river meanders back and forth between rocks. In times of flood and high water, deep holes are scoured out next to some of these boulders. If you're there not long after a flood, you may encounter the deepest water of the entire hike. A walking stick is helpful here.

An Episode of Military Explorations and Surveys--October, 1872

This place, with many tight bends, the author calls *Boulder Alley* and it may have been the place which inspired a story to be written about the Paria Canyon by a member of the October, 1872, military expedition to the region. The author found this story, *An Episode of Military Explorations and Surveys,* in the October, 1881 issue of The United Service. It was written nearly a decade after the event, and for obvious reasons. The author is identified only as T. V. B., and it goes like this(edited slightly for this book).

[I know that the hero of the following narrative would rather lose he tongue than speak of a noble deed performed by himself. Nevertheless, every noble action deserves to be known. I beg the Lieutenant's Pardon.]

In the month of October, 1872, the different field-parties composing "explorations and surveys west of the one hundredth meridian," rendezvoused near St. George, in Southern Utah, and after a week spent in preparations for the final work of the season again broke camp, the writer being assigned to the "party of the southeast," of which Lieutenant W. L. M., of the corps of engineers, had charge. The duty assigned to this "party" was the exploration of the "rim of the Great Basin" of Southern Utah, thence to go to the Colorado River, ascend and explore the Canyon of the Paria, and return.

After a couple of days' march the greater number of packers and escort were left in camp, as it was thought that a smaller party could do more effective work, and the number of explorers was reduced to ten,- -Lieutenant M., Mr. W., topographer, a cook, two packers, two soldiers, a Mormon, a Pah-Ute, and myself.

Another spring along the river, with a hanging garden above.

The Indian was to be our guide, but as he only knew enough of English to ask for whisky, the Mormon was taken along as interpreter.

In those high regions the nights were already disagreeably cold, so that after making camp we would pile up half a dozen dead pine-trees and start a fire that lit up the pine woods for miles, and sometimes even compelled us to shift camp, much to the disgust of our Pah-Ute, who was fearful of a visit from his dreaded foes, the Navajos, and did his best to convince us that one could warm himself better over a small fire than a large one, generally finishing the pantomime by telling us that "whitey man big fool!"

In due time we struck the "Great Navajo Trail," used by the Navajo Indians in their annual trading expeditions to the settlements of Southern Utah, and here our Indian became quite frantic with anxiety to go back to his own hunting-grounds, pleading that "his father never went farther;" but he had to stay with us, and every morning, without fail, he mysteriously showed us the footprints of savage enemies who had been lurking about the camp through the night,--though we failed to see an Indian during the entire trip, or had even a mule stolen.

The party derived considerable amusement from the repugnance of the mule ridden by Lieutenant M. for the Pah-Ute: neither did time do much towards reconciling the two. Whenever the Indian made his appearance unexpectedly before the lieutenant's charger, off came the lieutenant and away went the mule, a maneuver to which our chief at last became so accustomed that rather than be violently ejected from the saddle he would gracefully slide off when he saw "coming events cast their shadows before," and he owned, good-naturedly, that when that mule wanted him off he might as well come. So that the Indian was quite as much a trial to the lieutenant as to the mule.

We encamped on the Paria River two miles from its junction with the Colorado. I speak of the Paria as a river because it is honored with that rank on the maps, but feel as though I owed the reader an apology for deceiving him, for in a less arid country it would scarcely be dignified with the name of creek. But in this respect the pilgrim of the great trans-Rocky Southwest cannot afford to be fastidious. In those water-scarce regions everything having the appearance of running water is at least a creek, and the imagination delights in exalting a creek into a river. So on all the maps of New Mexico and Arizona the Rio Colorado Chiquito figures prominently, and would readily impose itself upon the unwary as a second Mississippi, yet memory vividly and lugubriously recalls the times when, not in one particular locality but in many, I boldly straddled it with my legs, and in that position washed my soiled undergarments; and worse, for too often it contained no water to wash with at all.

Two miles from our camp, at the junction of the Colorado and Paria, amid that weird scenery, isolated from all the world, was the ranch of John D. Lee, late bishop and major in the Mormon Church. The martial bishop was not often at home, and Mrs. Lee No. 17, with her nine children, garrisoned the ranch and battled with the elements for a livelihood.

In the mean time we had lost our Indian and his adjutant, the Mormon, much to the relief of Lieutenant M.'s charger. The two worthies had, from the beginning, overloaded their stomachs with ham and bacon, articles of diet to which the Indian and Mormon stomach is not accustomed, and had brought upon themselves severe bilious attacks.

The canyon of the Paria, which we were now to explore, was estimated to be about thirty two miles in length, and it was said that no human being had ever succeeded in getting through it. A flock of geese, the Mormons told us, had swam through the canyon, from the Mormon settlement of Paria to the Colorado River, and though we did not succeed in getting through it ourselves, our very failure, me-thinks proves that we were not geese.

Early on the morning of November 20 we started on the performance of what we all knew would be a difficult and dangerous task. At first the gorge was several hundred yards wide, the walls of the canyon sloping and not more than seven hundred feet in height; but with every mile the canyon narrowed and its walls became higher and more vertical, until at the end of five miles it did not average more than thirty yards in width, while the walls had attained a vertical height of fifteen hundred feet. The creek occupied the middle of the chasm, and often the entire space, from wall to wall, so that we were obliged continually to cross and recross it, as well as ride against the stream, a task which was rendered more difficult by oft-recurring patches of quicksand in which our animals became mired, obliging us to make frequent halts to dig them out. In this way we accomplished ten miles the first day, camping in a cotton-wood grove where the canyon had widened, and where enough grass grew to feed our animals.

The next day the difficulties increased. Occasionally the walls met overhead forming caverns dark as night, through which we waded and half swam, often compelled to bend over the saddle, so low was the rocky ceiling. Nor was the labor of urging the bewildered mules through these dark passages an easy one. That night we encamped, wet and chilled, on a peninsula of rocks large enough to accommodate ourselves and our animals.

The third day was bitter cold. Soon after starting the mule, ridden by the cook, Kittelman, a middle-aged German, whose duty on the march it was to lead the burdenless bell-horse, sank, belly-deep, in quicksand, and stuck fast, keeling over on his side and lying on Kittelman. We were occupied half an hour digging out the mule, during which time it required the strength of two men to keep the mule's head above water, and of one to perform a similar office for the poor cook. The mule, in his struggles, frequently struck Kittelman in the face, so that the latter, when extricated, was badly bruised and stupid from cold and excitement. No time was to be lost, however, and in his half-frozen condition the man had to mount the bell-horse and follow the party.

We now found ice formed in localities where the water was deeper and less rapid. This increased in thickness from one-eighth to one-half inch, when our mules refused to take to it farther, and we found ourselves compelled to dismount, wade up the icy stream, often to our armpits in water, and here and there break the crust of ice by means of our carbines, rocks, etc. This task was performed by Lieutenant M. and myself, for which purpose we kept a few hundred yards ahead of the party, leading our mules.

About 3 P.M. we came to a sharp bend in the canyon, where the water had cut into and undermined a portion of the wall, forming a large and deep pool, about fifty feet wide and forty long, which was also covered with a crust of ice, half an inch thick. This pool we must needs cross. After breaking up the ice with large rocks, I attempted to wade through it, but when about ten feet from the edge sunk knee-deep in quicksand and was fain to scramble back. I then mounted my mule and attempted to ride him in, but no amount of either urging or coaxing would induce the otherwise tractable animal to take to the water. Lieutenant M. then made the attempt with his mule, with the same result; the animals instinctively shrank back. By this time the remainder of the party had come up. The bell-horse had been ridden by the cook since the accident of the morning, and was saddled. I was about to mount him to ride him through the pool, knowing that he would obey under all circumstances, when Kittelman, though shivering with cold and scarcely more than half conscious, anticipated the movement, saying that he was not afraid to ride his horse where any other man was willing to go. The animal entered the pool without hesitation, and had gotten nearly half-way across when, as if sucked down, man and horse disappeared. In about twenty seconds the man's head again came to the surface, as well as that of the horse, Kittelman no longer on the horse but evidently still clutching the bridle,--his gaze vacant. After a few seconds, to our horror, man and horse again disappeared, and now it was that we began to realize that a human being, our companion and servitor during months of exploring, was about to perish before our eyes--almost within reach of our hands--and we utterly powerless for help, for who would plunge into that ice-covered pool, occupied as it was by a horse struggling for life?

Among the party was a packer by name of Evans, a large, powerful man. He had passed most of his life in Oregon, and his swimming-feats on the Columbia River, as related by himself, surpassed those performed by Leander and Byron. To him all eyes were now turned and there he stood, the picture of sickening fear and cowardice. Lieutenant M. now called out in agonized tones, "My God! will nobody save that man?" and hearing no response, without waiting to disencumber himself of overcoat or boots, he plunged, head foremost, into the awful hole. After fifteen seconds of terrible suspense, during which the horse had regained the surface and crawled to the rocks on which we were assembled, Lieutenant M. reappeared, holding the body of Kittelman in his arms. The latter was still alive, but only drew breath four or five times after leaving the water. We at once placed him on a pile of blankets, and four of the party chafed him vigorously for an hour and used other means of resuscitation, but in vain--he was dead.

In the mean time one of our packers had scaled a crevice in the rocks, to a point where a lot of stunted cedars could be seen, of which he threw down a sufficient quantity to keep up a fire during the night. Though not unused to hardships and stirring scenes, I shall never forget that night's camp. We were upon a peninsula of rocks, just large enough to accommodate the party; beside us flowed the dark stream; over us rose to a vertical height of over three thousand feet the rocky walls of the chasm, but a few stars being visible. The body of Kittelman lay a few feet from the fire, covered by a blanket. The glare of the fire served only to intensify the weirdness of the scene. Added to this was the knowledge that should to-morrow be an unusually warm day the snow would melt in the mountains, the stream would rise, and we should be drowned like rats in a cage before the end of the canyon could again be reached.

So we waited anxiously for morning. The body of Kittelman was sewed up, sailor-fashion, in a piece of canvas and packed on a mule, the frozen bones cracking horribly during the process. We carried the body with us for about two hours, when we came upon a crevice in the rocks, some twelve feet above low water, and into that we laid the remains and covered them with rocks, assured that no human hands would ever disturb them.

And though we returned to the mouth of the canyon unsuccessful, and with a life less, we had gained a hero more.

T. V. B.

Portions of this military episode in the Paria Gorge are obviously exaggerated and were written to entertain. Very seldom is there quicksand in the canyon, but horses could easily get quagmired. Their feet cover less area than do humans, but they might have 10 times more body weight. John D. Lee however did take a herd of cows down this same canyon, almost exactly one year before this military expedition, and it took him 8 days to get from about Rock House to the Colorado River. For cattle, horses or mules, it's apparently a different set of circumstances than for hikers.

Going downstream again. Not far below *Boulder Alley*, where the big rocks are in the stream channel, you'll come to the Adams Water Pump on the left, about 5 meters above the creek. Just behind the pump is another of many abandoned meanders in the canyon. About a km below the pump and on a sharp bend in the river, are several good campsites and one panel of petroglyphs--between miles P18 & P19.

Just below the petroglyphs, you'll normally begin to see seeps along the river's edge. In the river section between the petroglyphs and The Hole, there are many places where you can camp and get water-- just above mile P19. Each time the author visited this part of the canyon they were flowing.

The next attraction is The Hole, which is near mile P19 on the new BLM map. The Hole perhaps refers to two places; first, the canyon which comes down from the Sand Hills and flows into the Paria; and second, the very bottom end of this same canyon, right next to the river. All you'll ever see is this lower end. Because of the high vertical cliffs, it's impossible to reach the upper part of the drainage from the river. At the very bottom, and right next to the river, the seeping waters have eroded away the sandstone, making an alcove or cave-like feature shaped like an inverted key hole; thus the name The Hole.

You can walk into this dark recess about 40 meters, where you'll find a seep at the very back end, right where the water falls when it rains and water comes off the slickrock areas above. Near the front end or entrance to The Hole, you can set up camp on a little bench, which is completely under a big overhang. This would be a good place to camp for those hardy souls who prefer to travel without a tent. The seep will likely have water when you arrive, although this seep isn't on anybody's "best springs list". Upstream about 50 meters or so, is another seep, which had a good flow upon each of the author's visits.

It's in the area below where the Adams Pump is situated that the canyon begins to widen, and from The Hole down, it continues to open up. Between The Hole and Wrather Canyon there isn't anything special to see, except there are many places with scattered cottonwood trees which could make good campsites. Only problem is, the author doesn't recall seeing many good seeps.

Wrather Canyon

This canyon is one of the real gems of the Lower Paria River Gorge. It's a short side canyon, only about one km long, but it has one of the most interesting and impressive arches in the world called Wrather Arch. It also has a spring not far below the arch, which provides water for a small year-round flowing stream in parts of the canyon. This is between mile P20 & P21 on the new BLM map.

As you approach this canyon from upstream, you'll be looking right into it. But as the stream inside Wrather comes near the Paria, it turns abruptly east and parallels the Paria for maybe 150 meters. You'll have to reach the very mouth of Wrather Creek before you can enter the canyon. Inside the canyon is a hiker-made trail right up to and underneath the arch. Along the way is a good example of riparian vegetation. There are cottonwood and box elder trees, water cress, mosses, cat tails, and other plants this

This is what is known as The Hole. It's actually the bottom of a dryfall, and at the end of a dry creek on top of the Paria Plateau.

author can't describe. It's a little green paradise in the middle of the desert.

Because the bottom of Wrather Canyon is so narrow and fragile, the BLM asks that hikers not camp in the canyon. There's not much space anyway. Instead, camp at the canyon mouth across the river to the north, and in one of several groves of cottonwood trees. When you go up to the arch, take your empty water jugs to be filled. By not camping inside the canyon, you can also help preserve the good quality of water for those who follow in your footsteps.

Wrather Canyon Overlook Hike

For those with a little time who like climbing and want a break from trudging along in this seemingly endless gorge, here's a diversion. Take a hike to the canyon rim right above Wrather Arch.

From the camp sites at the mouth of Wrather, head downcanyon 700-800 meters. At about that point you'll be passing through an area of tall grasses, sort of like bullrushes. On the right will be a low bench which you can breech easily. Above this low bench, is a triangle-shaped sandslide coming down from the southeast. Walk straight up the sandslide toward its apex. At the top is a steep gully coming down to the top of the sandslide. Climb right up this mini canyon or gully, sometimes right in the bottom, or to the left side. This may be too steep for some.

At the very top of the gully is the most challenging part of the entire hike. There are two short cliffs or dropoffs you must scale. The height is only about three meters each, and there are plenty of hand and foot holds, but the sandstone is a little crumbly. Just take your time, and test each handhold. The author had no major problem, but some may want a short rope, perhaps just a piece of parachute cord, to add a touch of security, or to lower packs down on the return trip. If only one member of a group can get up, then all others should be able to make it.

From the top of the gully, make a hard right turn and head due west, contouring around the corner. You'll be just below some massive Navajo Sandstone cliffs. Shortly, you'll turn south, still bench-walking or contouring towards another minor, but steep drainage. It comes down from the pass to your upper left. There are several routes up this final slope, so pick the one which suits you best.

Upon arriving at the top, rim-walk to the west and towards the edge of Wrather Canyon. You should reach the rim directly above the arch. It looks a lot smaller from above than from below, indicating the great height of the wall you're on. When the author got to this rim, he spotted three desert big horn rams, but had the wrong lens on his camera to get a good foto. This hike may be one of the best side trips in the whole canyon. Take fotos of the arch from about mid-morning through mid-day.

North Rim Overlook Hike

If you're a natural bridge watcher, here's a hike that will place you high on the north rim of the Paria,

Looking down on the river from the North Rim Overlook.

Map 24, Lower Paria River Gorge--Part 3
Wrather Canyon to Bush Head Canyon

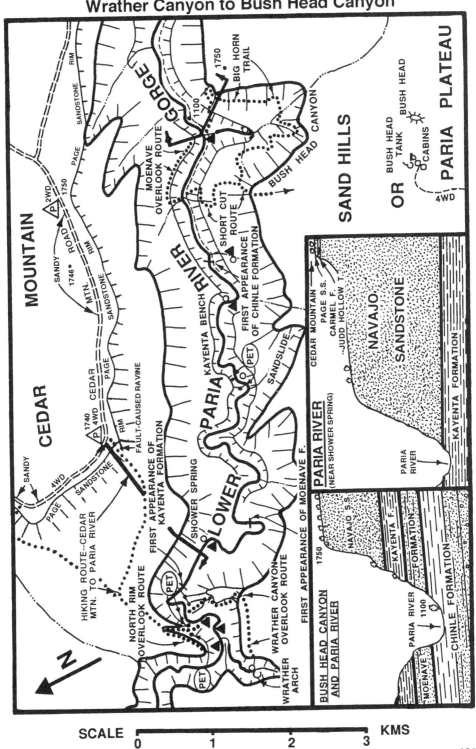

SCALE   KMS

0   1   2   3

Inside Wrather Canyon is a small spring and stream, with cattails and water cress.

The narrow bottom of Wrather Canyon.

From the North Rim Overlook. Looking southeast at the sandslide and route up to the overlook of Wrather Arch.

Wrather Arch as viewed from underneath.

and directly across from the mouth of Wrather Canyon. From this overlook, you can see right up the middle of Wrather and have perhaps the best view of all of the arch itself.

Begin at the campsites at the mouth of Wrather, and walk downcanyon about 300 meters. As you pass the last corner, look straight ahead to the north and to the left a little, and you'll see a kind of crack canyon, similar to the fault-made cracks further upcanyon. It's shape and geologic origin become very clear when viewed from the south rim.

Head straight for the crack, passing where you can through the low cliff or bench made by one of the lower layers of Navajo Sandstone. Just as you're about to enter the bottom of the crack canyon, look to your right and at the corner, and you'll see a good panel of petroglyphs. In about the same area on your left, is still another small panel. To the author and others, this tells of an old Indian passage, as they normally put up etchings on well-traveled routes. This is perhaps the only place in the canyon where you can go from rim to rim, via the river in between. There's another panel of petroglyphs on the other side of the river, at about the place you begin the hike to the Wrather Canyon Overlook, lending more credibility to the idea that this is an old Indian trail or route across the canyon.

As you get into the narrow chasm, you'll be climbing due north. The way is easy at first, then it steepens and narrows. Near the top you may see the bones of a deer, which didn't quite make it to water, just below the steepest part of the hike. But don't worry, you're better equipped than the deer were. This last steep little pitch is almost vertical, but since it's right on the fault line, there's been a build-up of minerals in the crack, which is now exposed. This new rock, different from the Navajo Sandstone, is harder and has numerous good hand holds. So although it's nearly vertical, and somewhere between 12 and 14 meters high, it's quite easy climb. Just at the very bottom of the pitch is a chokestone you must pass on the right. With a little help, maybe with a push from a friend, most people should be able to chimney or wedge their way up this two-meter high obstacle. Take a short rope for less-experienced hikers.

After the steep pitch, it's just a scramble to the rim where you'll then make a hard left turn, and walk southwest to a point overlooking the river and the mouth of Wrather Canyon. Late morning to mid-day, and in late spring or early summer, would be the best time for taking fotos of the arch.

Going downcanyon again. Within about a km from Wrather, you'll find about 4 panels or sites with petroglyphs--mile P21. The next important stop is Shower Spring, about 2 full kms downcanyon from the mouth of Wrather. It's at mile P22 on the new BLM map. Throughout the years this one has proved to be a good reliable waterhole. This one drips off a ledge, thus the name. This important spring comes out of the rock right at the contact point between the Navajo Sandstone above, and the Kayenta Formation below. This indicates the permeability of the Navajo, and the impermeability of the Kayenta. Across the river is a fine campsite.

Below Shower Spring, the canyon widens still further, and the Kayenta Bench becomes more prominently exposed. Between Wrather and Bush Head Canyons, there are several minor seeps or

Wide angle look at Wrather Arch.

springs, including one which comes out of the rock on the south side of the river below a big sandslide. Skip, the late Paria Ranger, pointed out two locations of petroglyphs near this spring on the north side of the river, but the author didn't see them. About 1 1/2 kms below the sandslide is the last reliable spring in the main canyon, before reaching Lee's Ferry. There's also a place to camp--mile P25.

Bush Head Canyon and the Big Horn Trail

The next major stop is Bush Head Canyon, between miles P26 & P27 on the new BLM log map. Like Wrather, this one is very short, maybe only 1 1/2 kms from its mouth to its headwall. At the mouth of this canyon are several campsites, and best of all, water. It may or may not be flowing down to the very mouth of the canyon when you arrive, but even if it does, it might be best to walk 700-800 meters upcanyon to where a very good spring comes right out of the bottom of the Moenave Formation. The water in this little canyon is surely good to drink as-is, because cattle don't quite make it up this far into the lower Paria. However, the water has a kind of swampy taste to it lower down near the river. This is caused by the decaying cottonwood and box elder leaves lying in the creek bed. At the spring itself, it's *puro agua dulce!*

Right at, and just above the spring, is a dryfall and you can't go up any further in the bottom of the canyon. For the adventurous hiker who enjoys a little climbing, here's a fun side trip. The author calls it the **Big Horn Trail**. Actually there are no trails involved, just a couple of routes to the rim top which may be used by a herd of desert big horn sheep.

The story behind the desert big horns must first be told. As indicated by the hundreds of petroglyph panels in the region, almost all of which show etchings of big horn sheep, one can conclude this magnificent animal has long been a part of the scene in this canyon and mesa country. But in the period of a little more than a century since the whiteman first began exploring the region, their numbers have gradually shrunk. Local ranchers believe the big horns caught diseases from domestic sheep and were hunted to near extinction. It appears they virtually disappeared in the Paria Canyon, so it was decided to re-introduce desert big horn sheep to this canyon.

In July of 1984, the Arizona Game and Fish Department, in cooperation with the BLM, started to carry out their plan. Because of the over-grazed desert big horn sheep range on the south shore of Lake Mead, which is part of the Lake Mead National Recreation Area, it was decided to capture some of those sheep and place them in other areas suitable for their existence. The places chosen were the Lower Kanab Creek(between Kanab and the Colorado River), the Paria River Canyon and the Vermilion Cliffs.

Altogether, 53 sheep were captured in July of 1984, sixteen of which were taken to the Kanab Creek area. The remaining 37 were taken to Lee's Ferry. Nineteen were taken to and released at Fisher Springs, not far to the west of Lee's Ferry, and up against the Vermilion Cliffs. The remaining 18 sheep were transported by helicopter to the Bush Head Canyon area and released.

Wrather Arch, as seen from the North Rim Overlook.

In the Bush Head Canyon release, there were 11 females, and 7 males or rams. Of the 18, five females were equipped with radio-telemetry collars. These special radios have the ability to send out a signal, not only when the sheep is alive and well, but can also detect when the animal dies with a mortality sensor. The radio signals are then monitored periodically by aircraft.

In the weeks and months following the transplant, numerous flights were made over both release sites to monitor their movements. Very little movement was detected at first, but in the time since, the herd of sheep at Fisher Springs has moved out along the base of the Vermilion Cliffs, and several into the Marble Canyon region. Those at Bush Head, seemed to stay nearer the release site. About 8 months after the release, two sensors noted fatalities in the Bush Head area. In late February, 1985, with the help of a helicopter, the two sheep were found dead, apparently having fallen from icy cliffs.

After about a years time, it was observed that the Bush Head sheep had started migrating, perhaps on a seasonal basis, to other locations along the Paria River and to the mesa top, or the Paria Plateau. But each time the Game and Fish people fly over the region, it's been found that the sheep stay pretty close to the initial release site, indicating that location is a good one. In November, 1984, a volunteer group from Arizona State University helped to build a slickrock water catchment basin somewhere on the plateau above Bush Head Canyon.

The author made one special trip up from the bottom of the Paria, just to check out the ways these sheep were getting up and down the canyon wall from the river to the rim. On an earlier trip the author saw at close range, three big horns on the lip of Wrather Canyon, which sparked this curiosity. In the end, he found two routes from the river to the rim and to the Sand Hills rock feature called Bush Head.

Here's one of two routes to the canyon rim. From the very mouth of Bush Head Canyon, look southeast up the steep slope. You'll see a talus slope, then a green spot with tall grasses and bullrushes, indicating a wet spot or minor seep, just below the first bench. Head that way, straight up to the southeast. From the first little ledge, make your way up through several more benches and minor cliffs. Remember, you're heading for the big bench, just below the massive Navajo Sandstone wall. There's an easy way through each little bench, but you'll have to zig zag a bit, and route-find on your own to find the easier places to pass through. As you near the big terrace, bench-walk or contour to the left or east, and into a minor canyon. On the other side of this drainage is one last step or cliff to get through, which is again very easy. Once on top of this, bench-walk or contour around to the west, then south, heading toward the big south wall of the upper Bush Head Basin.

As you near the headwall, you'll have to walk down through a break in the top layer of the Kayenta, to the mini valley below, then route-find back up to and into the most western of the two alcoves at the headwall of the canyon. Go straight for some trees, which appear to be near a spring(but there is no spring or water there).

Looking downcanyon (southeast) from the top of the route up to the Wrather Arch Overlook.

From the head of this second draw, walk due north, still contouring or bench-walking along the top of the Kayenta. In one little mini canyon, you'll come to a cliff where it appears that'll be the end of your hike; but from there simply walk uphill to the west, then head down a little ramp to the bottom, thence again to the north.

As you near the place southwest of the mouth of Bush Head Canyon, you'll see in front of you another small canyon coming down from the left, or west, and a sandslide. Head up this canyon, but just into it, veer to the right or northwest, and route-find up through some minor cliffs. This part is nearly a walk-up all the way to the rim. See Map 24, Lower Paria River Gorge--Part 3.

From the rim, you might choose to walk due south about two kms to Bush Head, or the Bush Head Stock Tank. At that old stockman's camp, are two old cabins, a stockade-type corral, and a small concrete dam, located at the base of a little slickrock valley. If there's been rain in the region within the month or so, this stock tank will be full. But don't count on drinking this cow-pie water! Cattle graze this area during the winter months, making the water unfit for human consumption.

Back at the Big Horn Trail. The longer and more scenic route has been described. If you've come up this one, but want a shorter way down, take the Short-cut Route back down to the river. Begin this one at the very last part of the first route described. Walk straight down the cliffy slope, but when it becomes less steep, veer to the left or west, and make your way around some of the intertongued beds at the contact point of the Navajo and Kayenta. There is no way of describing the route, except to say you may have to zig zag a little to reach the river. At one place, the author *chimneyed down* a 10 meter-high crack in one of the ledges. If he had walked still further west, he may have found an easier way, and walked down through this bench.

As you work your way down this slope, you'll see a minor drainage below. Head for it. But just as you think you've got it made, you'll come to one last little dropoff. The author jumped down this one, but you can walk through it if you'll veer to the right and bench-walk to the east, until you come to a mini-dugway, where you walk down to the north and to the river and trail.

Which ever route you go up or down, it'll involve a little route-finding. There are no serious obstacles, but you may have to do some zig zagging on either of these routes to find the easy way up or down through the Kayenta and Moenave Formations. Take all the water you'll need for the day, as there's none above Bush Head Spring, and you can't get to the spring from either of the routes just described. Also, take a lunch, as you can spend a day on this one. The author lost time exploring around for the Big Horn Trail, then went all the way to Bush Head Tank, finally returning via the Short-cut Route, arriving back at camp in just under 9 hours. Without the side trip to Bush Head, it would have been an easy day-hike. Most people would be happy to just get to the rim and return directly to camp, taking most of a day.

While interviewing some of the old timers in the region about the early-day history of the canyon,

Another good year-round water supply is found at Shower Spring

the late Mel Schoppman of Greene Haven(northwest of Page), told the author about a scheme by his father John, and Rubin Broadbent. It seems they were looking for ways to either get water up to their cattle on top of the Sand Hills, or take cattle down to the river below. They searched, and finally found a way off the plateau and down to the river at Bush Head Canyon. The route they made on *horseback* was along what has just been described as the Short-cut Route. They considered constructing a cattle trail there, but it turned out to be too big a job. Years later Mel Schoppman also made it up through the cliffs on horseback. With a little scouting around, this is an easy walk-up route.

According to everyone the author talked to, there are no routes up through the Vermilion Cliffs to the Paria Plateau between Bush Head Canyon and the Sand Hill Crack, discussed under Map 29. Rock climbers could surely find a route, but it likely couldn't be climbed by ordinary hikers.

As you leave Bush Head Canyon on your way to Lee's Ferry, you'll be walking along the south side of the river. You'll walk on an old cattle trail, which over the years has gradually gotten better and more distinct with the increase of hikers. Actually, from 3 or 4 kms above Bush Head, you can get on the south side of the river and stay there until you're in the area of the three prominent boulders with petroglyphs, as shown on Map 25. In this section of about 10-12 kms, you won't have to cross the stream once.

The reason for the trail winding its way up and above the river, is that in this part of the canyon the softer beds of the Chinle Formation are beginning to be exposed. When this occurs, the canyon automatically widens, and the cliffs made of the Navajo, Kayenta and Moenave Formations, begin to pull apart. As this happens, occasionally large boulders break off the walls and roll down into the stream channel. In this section, the stream channel itself is choked with these house-sized rocks, therefore it's been naturally easier to walk along the bench above, than right along the river.

Farther downcanyon and just past the place where you come off the bench and begin walking along the river flood plain, look for some large boulders beside the trail. On one, at the right(west) side of the trail, are some good petroglyphs right on top--near mile P31. This the author calls Flat Top Rock on Map 25. From about that point, look up and to the east side of the river, and you can see a couple of boulders standing alone on the sandy hillside. One of these also has petroglyphs.

Another km or two below Flat Top Rock, and as you first cross over the river to the east side, are at least three more very good panels of petroglyphs, all on large boulders--between miles P31 & P32. One is called Scorpion Rock, because of a large scorpion-like figure on it. Another is Upside Down Rock, because half the glyphs are upside down. The rock must have rolled down the slope halfway through an etching party. Just around the corner and up the slope a ways to your left, is another good one. This might be called 10 Sheep Rock. It has, among other glyphs, 10 big horn sheep in a line. These *boulderglyphs* are some of the best the author has seen, and up to date, there's no whiteman graffiti on them. There's a good campsite just across the river from these boulderglyphs, but you'd have to purify and drink river water.

From the top of the Big Horn Trail, looking down into Bush Head Canyon.

The Wilson Ranch

About two kms downstream from the petroglyphs, you may see, at a point where the river turns east, some old fence posts, some minor seeps, and an old mine test hole called the Lehneer Prospect. Another 100 or maybe 200 meters further on the right, is an old road going up on a bench. This is part of the old Wilson Ranch. Still further, you'll come to some large cottonwood trees, where the old Wilson Ranch house once stood. It's between miles P33 & P34 on the new BLM log map. Its foundations can still be seen. At that point, and just behind you to the north, is a small wooden shack, built at the side of a large boulder.

The Wilson Ranch was first built by Owen Johnson and Sid Wilson in about 1918. They gathered lumber from a sawmill on the Kaibab near Jacob Lake and logs from Lee's Ferry, and hauled them in wagons about 8 kms upriver to the site. With this material, they built a rather large two room cabin, in the shape of an "L". According to George W. Fisher, each room measured about 6 x 8 meters.

It was Sid Wilson who lived there and claimed the rights to the place. Throughout the years, no one ever actually owned the ranch, but each person who lived there was able to claim and sell his squatters rights. While at the ranch, Wilson ran some cattle, but worked at other jobs too. At one time he was the one who measured the water levels of the Paria and Colorado Rivers at Lee's Ferry.

In 1927, Wilson left and sold his rights to Pete Nelson, but Nelson didn't actually live at the place until after about 1930. In 1933, George W. Fisher bought out Nelson, and lived there until he was drafted into the military in 1944. The BLM, which in the days before 1947 was called the Grazing Service, allowed Fisher to run about 200 head of cattle during his stay at the ranch.

It was the Fishers who installed a rough wooden floor to the house and covered it with Navajo rugs. They also built a windmill, and hooked it up to a small generator. The electricity first went to several batteries for storage, then was used for lights and a radio. They had a pump, which pumped water from the nearby spring to their house in a 10 cm(4") pipe. Water from the spring was also used to irrigate a small garden.

When the Fishers left in 1944, they sold it to a Navajo man by the name of Curly Tso, who lived mostly on the reservation. Curly had it for a number of years until his death, then his son sold it to the Graffs of Hurricane, Utah. Sometime while Curley owned the place, the house burned down. Then in 1974, the National Park Service bought out all the private holdings at Lee's Ferry, including the Lonely Dell Ranch. Since no one had any ownership papers on the Wilson Ranch, and it was part of the public domain, it just became part of the Paria Canyon--Vermilion Cliffs Wilderness Area.

Almost next to where the old ranch house stood is Wilson Spring. This spring has a good flow, but it seeps out of the hillside for about 30 meters, and hasn't been cared for in many years, so you can't expect to get a safe drink there. You'd do better to go to the river for water. At one time it was encased in pipe and fenced off so cattle couldn't pollute it, but now the spring is full of cow pies and its water undrinkable.

One of two old cowboy cabins at Bush Head Tank.

Map 25, Lower Paria River Gorge--Part 4
Bush Head Canyon to Lee's Ferry

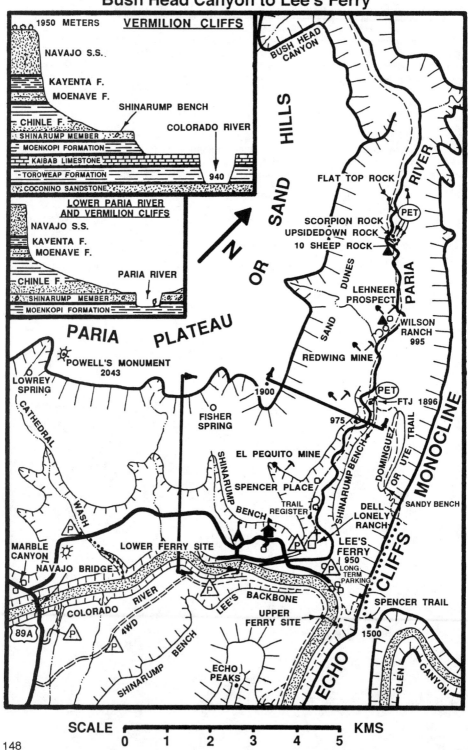

VERMILION CLIFFS

1950 METERS
NAVAJO S.S.
KAYENTA F.
MOENAVE F.
SHINARUMP BENCH
CHINLE F.
COLORADO RIVER
SHINARUMP MEMBER
MOENKOPI FORMATION
KAIBAB LIMESTONE
TOROWEAP FORMATION
COCONINO SANDSTONE
940

LOWER PARIA RIVER
AND VERMILION CLIFFS
NAVAJO S.S.
KAYENTA F.
MOENAVE F.
CHINLE F.
PARIA RIVER
SHINARUMP MEMBER
MOENKOPI FORMATION

BUSH HEAD CANYON
SAND HILLS OR SAND
PARIA RIVER

FLAT TOP ROCK
PET
SCORPION ROCK
UPSIDEDOWN ROCK
10 SHEEP ROCK
DUNES
SAND
LEHNEER PROSPECT
WILSON RANCH 995
REDWING MINE

N

PARIA PLATEAU

POWELL'S MONUMENT 2043
LOWREY SPRING
1900
PET
FTJ 1896
CATHEDRAL
FISHER SPRING
975
EL PEQUITO MINE
SHINARUMP BENCH
SPENCER PLACE
TRAIL REGISTER
DOMINGUEZ OR UTE TRAIL
DELL LONELY RANCH
SANDY BENCH
MONOCLINE
WASH
MARBLE CANYON
NAVAJO BRIDGE
P
LOWER FERRY SITE
BENCH
P
LEE'S FERRY 950
LONG TERM PARKING
P
COLORADO RIVER
4WD
LEE'S BACKBONE
SPENCER TRAIL
89A
P
SHINARUMP BENCH
UPPER FERRY SITE
1500
P
ECHO PEAKS
ECHO CLIFFS
GLEN CANYON

SCALE   KMS
0   1   2   3   4   5

148

From Wilson Spring look south, and on a hill just to the west of the creek bed, can be seen a couple of mine tunnels. This is known as the Red Wing Mine, which dates from the uranium boom days of the early 1950's.

A km or two below the Red Wing, you'll see on your left, a faint track running up the hill to the east. This hill is actually the Shinarump Bench, and the track is the beginning of the Dominguez or Ute Trail. Actually the thing you see there is another 1950's uranium prospecting track, but it's in the same place as the old trail. Right where the trail begins to climb, you may see on a 1 1/2 meter-high boulder, more petroglyphs, including a *"F.T.J. 1896"*. This glyph was etched by a member of the Johnson family who ran the ferry in the years after John D. Lee cashed in.

The Spencer Place

About 2 kms before you arrive at the Lonely Dell Ranch is another old building with the remains of a very old car(from the 1920's) lying there rusting away. This is what George W. Fisher calls the Spencer Place.

In the period between the two world wars, there were as many as 10 families living at Lee's Ferry, mostly in the vicinity of the old Lonely Dell Ranch. Most of them were polygamists; some of whom had been/or were to be, excommunicated from the Mormon Church. One of these families belonged to Carling Spencer(no relation to Charles H. Spencer). It was from Carling Spencer that Fisher bought this old house or cabin in about 1940. Fisher put this house on skids, and dragged it up to the place where it's seen today. In those days it was simply called the Spencer Place.

Fisher fixed the place up to live in part time when he wasn't up at the Wilson Ranch. Part of Fisher's time in those days was spent working on constructing roads in the area, because he couldn't make it on ranching alone.

Less than a km below the Spencer Place is another wooden shack and corral, which are part of some of the later development of the Lonely Dell Ranch. This corral is used periodically today by cattlemen who still retain grazing rights in the area.

Just beyond this corral, and in the middle of a big flat, is the trail register, where hikers are encouraged to sign in or out of the canyon(to get a count on visitor use). From this point continue straight ahead on the right or west side of the river. Soon you'll come to the Lonely Dell Ranch where you can see the old ranch houses, museum and cemetery. Beyond that is the day-parking place, then nearly a km past it is the long term parking lot. See map.

Lonely Dell Ranch

The Lonely Dell Ranch really started on December 23, 1871, when John D. Lee and wives Emma and Rachel arrived at the place late in the afternoon. Early the next morning, Emma looked around and made a

Scorpion Rock, with petroglyphs.

149

statement about how lonely the place was, thus the name. It was John D. Lee who was sent to the Paria to make and run a ferry for the Mormon Church. Read more of this man in *The Story of John D. Lee and Mountain Meadows Massacre,* in the back of this book.

After Lee was captured in November of 1874 in Panguitch, the church had to send help, because Emma Lee--wife No. 17, couldn't handle the job by herself. So they sent Warren M. Johnson in March, 1875, to take charge and run the ferry service. At first Johnson took his first wife, then about a year later, brought his younger second wife to the ferry. After he arrived, he built a large two level house, which stood until 1926.

At the time Johnson arrived, Emma owned the ferry and had squatters rights to the Lonely Dell Ranch. So she and the Johnsons both profited from the ferry service. But in 1879, the Mormon Church bought the ferry rights from Emma for a reported $3000. She then moved south into Arizona and eventually settled at Winslow, where she died in 1897.

Warren Johnson's family lived at the ranch and ran the ferry from 1875, until 1896. At that time the church decided he had completed his mission and released him. It had been a long struggle living at this desert outpost for so many years. Just one of the hardships he had to suffer through, was the loss of four of his younger children.

In May 1891, a family passing through the area traveling from Richfield, Utah, to Arizona, told Warren about a child of theirs which had gotten ill and died in Panguitch. No one thought about it then, but four days later, one of the Johnson children became ill and died. A few days later other children were struck with the same sickness. All together, four Johnson children died between May 19 and June 5, 1891. The disease was diphtheria, which three other children got, but recovered from. One large grave stone, with all their names on it, can be seen in the cemetery today just north of the Lonely Dell Ranch.

The church replaced Warren M. Johnson with a man named James Emett. Emett arrived in 1896, along with his two wives. While he ran the ferry he talked the church into building a cable across the river, to which the boat could be fastened. This made things much safer and easier. Before that time there had been a number of accidents and drownings associated with the crossing.

While running the ferry, Emett also did a little farming and ran cattle, part of which were in the House Rock Valley to the west. Even though that area was mostly public domain and open to all, he had troubles with the Grand Canyon Cattle Company, which was run by B.F. Saunders and Charles Dimmick. At one time in about 1907, Dimmick accused Emett of stealing cattle, and it went to court. Emett was found innocent.

But later, the GCCC got back at Emett, by buying the ferry service from the Mormon Church in August 1909. Shortly thereafter, Emett sold his land and property to this same company. At first the ferry was run by any GCCC cowboy who was staying at the Lonely Dell Ranch at the time. But things changed after less than a year, because the service was unreliable. In early 1910, the Grand Canyon Cattle Company hired the best men for the job, which were the sons of Warren M. Johnson.

Small shelter or chicken coop at the Wilson Ranch.

The Spencer Place, and the remains of a very old car.

Part of the Lonely Dell Ranch built by Leo Weaver in about 1940. This stone building was used as part of his dude ranch operation.

Jerry Johnson arrived at the ferry in February, 1910, and was joined by his brother Frank in July, and both ran the ferry. It was these men and their families who lived at the Lonely Dell Ranch and assumed responsibility for the ferry until the Navajo Bridge opened across Marble Canyon in January, 1929. Actually the last ferry crossing was on June 7, 1928. That's when the boat tipped over with two cars on board. All three men running the ferry were drowned, and the boat floated down into Marble Canyon. Because the bridge was so near completion, the ferry was never replaced.

Because of the way the ferry was handled in 1909-1910, the Coconino County became concerned about keeping this important link open. So the county bought the ferry service from the Grand Canyon Cattle Company in June 1910. They were the owners, but it was run by the Johnsons, until the bridge opened. In December of 1926, clothes drying near a stove caught on fire and burned down the two-story Johnson home at Lonely Dell. It had been built by Warren M Johnson in about 1877 and had stayed in the Johnson family until 1926.

After the bridge opened, there wasn't much traffic in or around Lee's Ferry, but several polygamist families lived there during the 1930's. The Church owned the ranch for a time, then the polygamist families of Lebaron, Spencer and Johnson bought it. At a later time the Church got it back, but then Leo and Hazel Weaver bought the Lonely Dell Ranch in the late 1930's and attempted, unsuccessfully, to run a dude ranch and raise Anglo-Arabian horses. While there, they constructed the long stone building which sits just to the northeast of the cabin refuted to have been built by John D. Lee himself, and which is now called Emma Lee's Cabin.

The Weavers stayed at Lonely Dell until the early 1940's, then moved out. Essy Bowers owned the ranch for a couple of years, then in 1943 sold it to a man name C. A. Griffin, a stockman from Flagstaff, who had a big herd of cattle on the Navajo Nation lands to the east. It was Griffin who first attempted to pump water out of the Paria onto farm land, rather than to build dams, which always washed out. In later years the LDS Church once again held title to the ranch.

In about 1963, Lee's Ferry was included into the Glen Canyon National Recreational Area, but the 65 hectares(160 acres) of private land remained private. In 1974, the private property of the Lonely Dell Ranch was bought by the U. S. Government and National Park Service. Lonely Dell Ranch was put on the National Register of Historic Places in 1978.

For a lot more detailed information about Lee's Ferry, read *Desert River Crossing,* by Rusho and Crampton; *Lee's Ferry,* by Measeles; and *John D. Lee, Zealot--Pioneer Builder--Scapegoat,* and *Mountain Meadows Massacre,* both by Juanita Brooks.

If you're hiking up the Paria for more than one day, or doing the entire Paria River trip from the Whitehouse Trailhead, be sure to park at the large paved parking lot southeast of Lonely Dell Ranch instead of at the small visitor parking place at Lonely Dell.

Lonely Dell Ranch, with Emma Lee's cabin on the right.

Looking down on Lee's Ferry from the top of the Spencer Trail. The Colorado River is on the left, the Paria River is coming down to the Lonely Dell Ranch from the far right.

JOHNSON

JONATHAN SMITH	LAURA ALICE	PERMELIA	MELINDA
OCT. 3, 1885	SEPT. 25, 1883	JULY 18, 1881	DEC. 3, 1875
MAY 19, 1891	JUNE 11, 1891	JUNE 15, 1891	JULY 5, 1891

The grave stone of four Johnson children in the Lonely Dell Cemetery.

The Upper Ferry Terminal at Lee's Ferry in the early 1900's. Beyond is the western or southern side of the Colorado River. You can still see some of the ruins at the ferry terminal today. (Arizona State Library)

Oxen pulling a wagon up the dugway to the Upper Ferry Terminal. (Arizona State Library)

The home Warren Johnson built at Lonely Dell in 1877. It burned down in 1926.
(New Mexico State Archives)

The muddy Paria River and it merges with the cold & clear Colorado at Lee's Ferry.
Downstream is to the left; ferry site is to the right out of sight.

Rusting hulks of old trucks at the Lonely Dell Ranch.

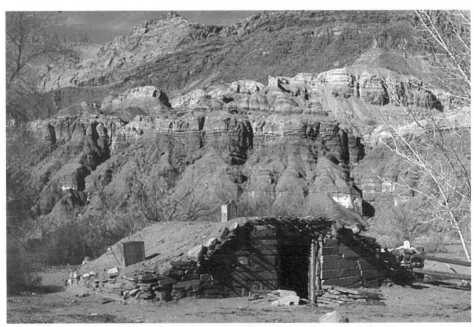

A cellar, the only cool place at Lonely Dell during the summer heat.

The dugway and road leading to the Upper Ferry Terminal. This place is on the south side of the Colorado just across from where the Paria River enters.

Ruins at the Upper Ferry Terminal.

North Rim Hikes--Lower Paria River Gorge

Location and Access Featured here are some hiking possibilities from the high country on the north side of the Lower Paria River Gorge. Three parts of this area are known as East Clark Bench, Flat Top and Cedar Mtn. While there are several 4WD-type roads running up to this region, the normal way up is to drive along Highway 89 about 5 kms east of the Paria Ranger Station & Visitor Center. Between mile posts 17 & 18, and directly across the highway from the start of the Cottonwood Wash Road, turn south. This is called the Cedar Mtn. Road. It's generally good for cars up to Cedar Mtn., but there is one little steep & rocky place with a short sandy section below. However, the author's VW Rabbit did fine(in October & November with a little moisture in the sand). The road is sometimes graded up to the communications facility, then it gets sandier and less-used. If you have a 2WD, it would be best to go there after a rain storm or in the spring, fall, or even winter, when the sand is firmer

In the Flat Top area are side roads out to the north side of Judd Hollow to some metal tanks & trough, and one going down toward Bridger Point. Both these are sandy in places, but with a little moisture, even cars can be driven there. Be sure to take a shovel!

Another possible way to reach the rim along the very bottom end of the Lower Paria River Gorge is from near Lake Powell. First head in the direction of Page. Near the entry roads to Greene Heaven, leave Highway 89 between mile posts 555 & 556, and drive southwest on some pretty good well-used roads in the direction of Ferry Swale. When you leave the main roads near the power lines, watch out for deep sand.

Trail or Route Conditions The best hike here, and one for an experienced outdoors person, would be make your way to the south side of Cedar Mountain. Drive past the communications facility to where the road begins to get real sandy and where the 2WD car-park is shown. From there, walk or drive a 4WD, along the road for another 2 or 3 kms. Along the way, watch carefully for a place on the rim jutting out to the south to form a point--near the 4WD parking place. On the west side of that point, along a minor fault line, is a walk-down route. At the bottom of the gully, contour west atop the Navajo Sandstone bench and to the north rim as shown on the map. There's also another way off the Page SS Rim as shown. Use Wrather Canyon as a landmark to find the steep gully route down from the rim. Also, see Map 24, page 139, and read the nearby description of how to climb up from the river under the heading, **North Rim Overlook Hike**.

If the environmental radicals in SUWA have their way and camping in the canyon in the future is by reservation only, you can avoid the camping problem by day-hiking down this route, and still see some of the best parts of the lower Paria River Canyon. Take a short rope for beginners and one of the more detailed maps for this hike.

Here are some other hikes. From the southeast side of Cedar Mtn., you can route-find down into a side canyon to a place called Water Pockets. However, you can't go too far as there are some big dropoffs halfway down. Also some good views from the rim. From the north side of Judd Hollow and the metal tanks & trough, route-find down over the rim via some old ladders and a pipeline. Once into Judd Hollow, it's an easily walk down to the edge of the canyon for look straight down at the old Adams water pump site on the river.

There are also some interesting rim-hiking possibilities from the end of the pretty good road down onto the south peninsula of Bridger Point. It's easy to get off the Page Sandstone Rim and to the very edge of the gorge. See Map 23, page 123. There might even be a route down into one of the Crack Canyons from along the north rim. If you find one, please write the author.

From the usually-dry stock pond in Ferry Swale, it's easy to walk to the rim along the lowest part of the canyon. The Thousand Pockets area isn't so interesting, but the views from the area just southeast of Water Pockets is well worth while. Beware of sandy roads, and park before you get stuck.

Elevations Cedar Mtn. 1800 meters; bottom of gorge at Bushhead Canyon, 1100 meters.

Hike Length and Time Needed Depending on where you park, it's about 3 or 4 kms down, but finding the North Rim Overlook Route to the canyon bottom, may take some time. Plan on staying all day, depending on how far you go once you get to the river. The other hikes to the rim would likely take about half a day, or less.

Water Take plenty in your car, but there should be some at the Bunting Well, Trough & Corral on top of Flat Top. Be prepared to purify it first, unless you can get to the water before it reaches the cow trough.

Maps USGS or BLM maps Smoky Mountain and Glen Canyon Dam(1:100,000); or USGS maps MF-1475, A,B,C or D(1:62,500); or Bridger Point, Glen Canyon City, Wrather Arch and Water Pockets, all at 1:24,000 scale.

Main Attractions Hopefully, an unregulated way to reach the middle part of the Paria Canyon from the rim, without having to camp there. And different views of the gorge from the north rim.

Ideal Time to Hike Spring or fall soon after some rains, as all road are made of sand. You'll seldom, if ever, see any mud out there.

158

Map 26, North Rim Hikes--Lower Paria River Gorge

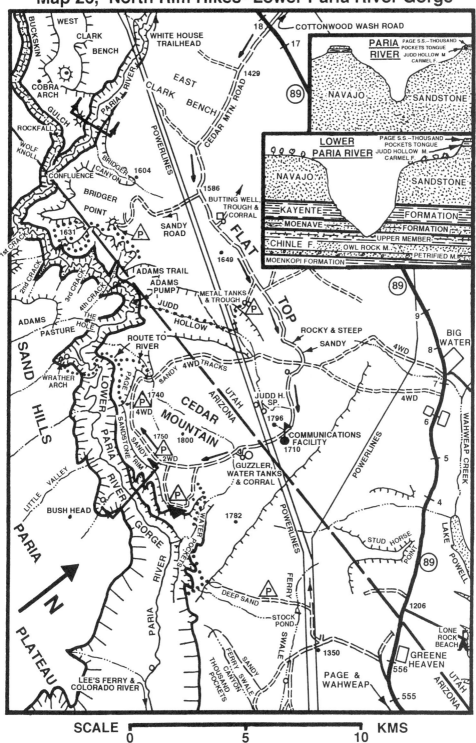

SCALE
0   5   10   KMS

Hiking Boots Any comfortable dry weather boots or shoes. If going to the canyon bottom, better take some wading shoes to cross the river.
Author's Experience Using the better parts of 3 days, he walked all the rim routes shown on the

From near the top of the Wrather Overlook Route, one can see the Paria River at the bottom, and the route to the North Rim Overlook in the center of the picture.

From high on the north rim and at the end of the upper Judd Hollow, one can look straight down on an abandoned meander and where the Adams Pump still sits today.

map. On one mid-November day, he parked at the 2WD car-park at 1750 meters on Cedar Mtn., and found the route off the rim. He went down to the river, climbed up to the overlook of Wrather Canyon, and returned using the second route back up through the Page SS Rim. That took 7 hours round-trip.

Looking northwest up the Lower Paria River Gorge, from the rim just to the southeast of the Water Pockets drainage.

This is a rock corral or holding pen near the top of the Dominguez or Ute Trail. Beyond, and looking northwest, is the Lower Paria River Canyon.

The Dominguez and Spencer Trails, and the Lee's Ferry Area

Location and Access Both trails featured on this map are at or near Lee's Ferry. The Dominguez Trail(sometimes called the Ute or Indian Trail), was used by Navajos and Utes in the early days, when they would cross the Colorado River to trade with the Mormons. In 1776, Spanish padres Dominguez & Escalante, used this same trail when looking for the Ute Ford(later called the Crossing of the Fathers) to cross the Colorado River on their historic journey. The Spencer Trail was built by the big-time promoter, Charles H. Spencer, partly as a short-cut from Lee's Ferry to coal fields to the north, and partly to impress investors who were given the grand tour of his mining operations at the Ferry. Park where they launch boats at the end of the road at Lee's Ferry.

Trail or Route Conditions To hike the Dominguez Trail, walk from the Lonely Dell Ranch parking lot upstream along the Paria River Trail for about 5 kms. On the right, you will see an old mining track running up a minor slope to the east and through a break in the Shinarump. It begins next to a boulder with some petroglyphs. Once on the bench, you can see the approximate route, *but not the trail*. From that point you could walk straight up the steep slope to the top of the sandy bench; or you could follow an old mining track south a ways, then scramble up to the sandy bench. Once on the sandy bench, contour southeast toward a low place on the rim. At the south end of the sandy bench, head straight upslope. When you reach the cliffs, you should pick up the constructed part of a trail as it zig zags up the slope, then turns south, at or near the ridge crest. There are two trails through the cliff near the pass. The Spencer Trail begins just east of Lee's Fort. The bottom of the trail veers left from the more-traveled route to the Upper Ferry Terminal. Once on the trail, you can follow it easily as it zig zags up the steep cliffs. If you'd like to do both trails together on the same hike, then walk up the Spencer, route-find north along the ridge crest, then head down the Dominguez. It's easier to locate the Dominguez Trail from the top, than from the bottom.

Elevations Lee's Ferry, 950 meters; top of Spencer, 1450; Dominguez Pass, 1500 meters.

Hike Length and Time Needed The Spencer Trail is about 2 1/2 kms, one way, and will take about 2-4 hours round-trip. Trailhead to Dominguez Pass is about 8 kms, one way. Most could do this in 5 or 6 hours round-trip, returning the same way. If a loop-hike is made using both trails, it's close to 16 kms. With the ruggedness of the ridge-top, it'll likely take the average person all of one day to make the trip.

Water Take it with you. There's water available at each trailhead.

Maps USGS or BLM map Glen Canyon Dam(1:100,000), or Lee's Ferry(1:62,500); or Ferry Swale and Lee's Ferry(1:24,000).

Main Attractions Historic trails in an historic region, with fine views from the rim of the canyon.

Ideal Time to Hike Spring or fall. Summers are hot as hell, winters not too bad.

Hiking Boots Dry weather boots, except waders for the walk up the Paria to reach the Dominguez Trail.

Author's Experience He first climbed both trails on separate trips, then in October, 1997, he parked a the boat launching site, and made the loop-hike suggested above in just over 5 hours.

On top of the big Sandy Bench looking southeast toward the Dominguez Pass. Off in the distance, and in front of the big peak beyond, the trail turns left and zig zags up the slope.

Map 27, Dominges and Spencer Trails, and the Lee's Ferry Area

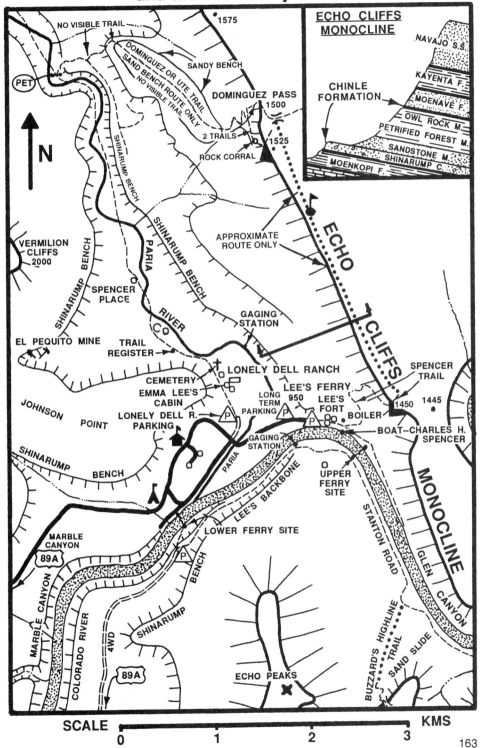

ECHO CLIFFS MONOCLINE

CHINLE FORMATION

Navajo S.S.
Kayenta F.
Moenave F.
Owl Rock M.
Petrified Forest M.
Sandstone M.
Shinarump C.
Moenkopi F.

NO VISIBLE TRAIL
1575
DOMINGUEZ OR UTE TRAIL
SAND BENCH ROUTE ONLY
NO VISIBLE TRAIL
SANDY BENCH
DOMINGUEZ PASS
1500
PET
N
2 TRAILS
1525
ROCK CORRAL
SHINARUMP BENCH
APPROXIMATE ROUTE ONLY
ECHO
VERMILION CLIFFS 2000
PARIA
SHINARUMP BENCH
SPENCER PLACE
RIVER
GAGING STATION
CLIFFS
EL PEQUITO MINE
TRAIL REGISTER
SHINARUMP BENCH
LONELY DELL RANCH
SPENCER TRAIL
CEMETERY
EMMA LEE'S CABIN
LEE'S FERRY
950
LEE'S FORT
1450 1445
JOHNSON POINT
LONELY DELL R. PARKING
P
LONG TERM PARKING
P
P
BOILER
BOAT--CHARLES H. SPENCER
SHINARUMP BENCH
PARIA
GAGING STATION
UPPER FERRY SITE
MONOCLINE
MARBLE CANYON
89A
LEE'S BACKBONE
LOWER FERRY SITE
STANTON ROAD
GLEN CANYON
BENCH
MARBLE CANYON
4WD
SHINARUMP
89A
BUZZARD'S HIGHLINE TRAIL
SAND SLIDE
COLORADO RIVER
ECHO PEAKS
X

SCALE   KMS
0   1   2   3

163

Coyote Buttes

Location and Access This map features what, until recently, was a relatively unknown corner of the Paria River drainage. The place is called Coyote Buttes, which is that part of the Cockscomb Ridge immediately south of Wire Pass Trailhead and entry point to the upper Buckskin Gulch. In the early 1990's, someone went there, made a motion picture, and showed it in Germany. Ever since, there's been a stampede of Europeans heading that way, along with American fotographers. The hike isn't necessarily that great, but the color, and the shape of some rocks, is something unique, making it high on the gotta-go list for foto hounds. This is the first time Coyote Buttes has appeared in this book, so it's clear some places get popular all by themselves, without the help of guidebooks.

To get there, you could come in from the south and the Arizona side. About halfway between Jacob Lake and Marble Canyon, and between mile posts 565 and 566 on Highway 89A, turn north and drive along on the House Rock Valley Road. When conditions are dry, this is a good road for any car; when wet it's impassable! See *Map 29A, The Sand Hills & Paria Plateau Ranches*.

But the more popular and most-used way there would be to drive along Highway 89 about halfway between Kanab and Page. Immediately west of The Cockscomb, and between mile posts 25 & 26, turn south on the same House Rock Valley Road. Drive about 13 or 14 kms until you reach the Wire Pass Trailhead, the most popular entry point to the Buckskin Gulch. Park, and/or camp on the west side of the road. Hiking from Wire Pass is the fastest, easiest and shortest way to the heart of Coyote Buttes.

Here are two other ways into the Buttes from the west and the House Rock Valley Road. With the help of the Fredonia 1:100,000 scale metric map, and Map 29A in this book, make your way along the main road, but turn off toward Coyote Spring, as shown. Park on top of the hill before going down the steep dugway to the locked gate below. That gate keeps people away from the Northcott Ranch house at the spring. By parking there, you can walk around the ranch on the way to Paw Hole at the south end of the Buttes.

Not far north of Coyote Spring is the beginning of a trail into the heart of the Buttes via The Notch. To know where to park, watch carefully for a big prominent notch, gap or pass in The Cockscomb to the east. When just west of that pass, park at one of several places on the east side of the main road, or near a large rusty metal tank about 250 meters to the west.

Here's one way into the Cottonwood Spring area. Using Map 29A, turn east from the House Rock Valley Road and head in the direction of the ranch house at Pine Tree Pockets, but turn northeast at the windmill & metal storage tank known as the Corral Valley Well. From there, **it's 4WD county only,** or walk. The name Sand Hills tells the tale! When you reach the old Poverty Flat Ranch house, you could turn west and reach Paw Hole, but the sand around that place is incredibly deep. Or head due north past the airstrip and up to a corral near the pass marked 1737 meters. The sand gets real deep on the north of the pass, so consider parking your 4WD about where the parking symbol is shown. Read the **permit requirements** for this area below.

Trail or Route Conditions The starting point for the normal route is the Wire Pass Trailhead. From your car, walk east across the road on an obvious trail. After 100 meters is a sign-in place for the

This is The Wave, perhaps the most-fotographed part of the Coyote Buttes.

Map 28, Coyote Buttes

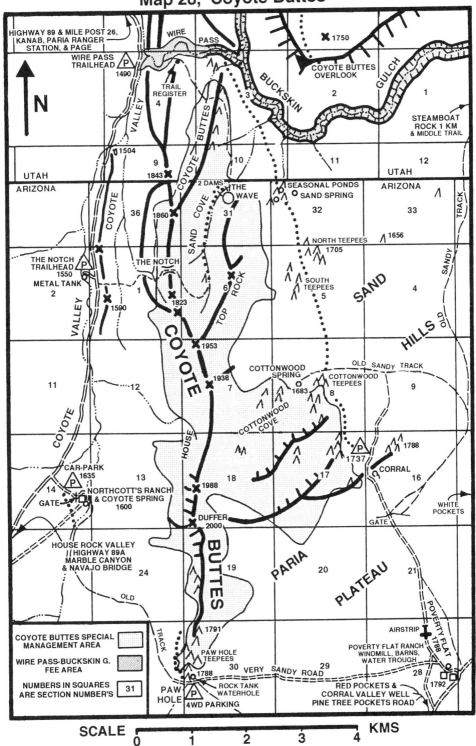

HIGHWAY 89 & MILE POST 26,
KANAB, PARIA RANGER
STATION, & PAGE

WIRE PASS
TRAILHEAD   Ⓟ
1490

N

TRAIL
REGISTER
4

WIRE   PASS

✖ 1750

COYOTE BUTTES
OVERLOOK

BUCKSKIN   GULCH

STEAMBOAT
ROCK 1 KM
& MIDDLE TRAIL

3

2

1

VALLEY

COYOTE BUTTES

Ⓘ 1504

9
✖ 1843

10

11

12

UTAH

UTAH

ARIZONA

ARIZONA

COYOTE

36
✖ 1860

2 DAMS
◯ THE
WAVE
31

SEASONAL PONDS
◯ SAND SPRING

32

33

∧

OLD SANDY TRACK

SAND COVE

∧ NORTH TEEPEES
1705

∧ 1656

THE NOTCH
TRAILHEAD   Ⓟ
1550
METAL TANK
2

THE NOTCH

∧ SOUTH
TEEPEES
5

SAND

4

1

✖
1590

TOP ROCK

6 ✖

∧

VALLEY

✖
1823

HILLS

✖ 1953

COTTONWOOD
SPRING

OLD   SANDY   TRACK

11

12

✖ 1938
7

◯
1683

COTTONWOOD
TEEPEES
8

9

COYOTE

HOUSE

COTTONWOOD
COVE

∧

CAR-PARK
1635
Ⓟ
14
GATE

13

18

∧

17

Ⓟ
1737

∧∧ 1788

CORRAL

16

✖
NORTHCOTT'S RANCH
& COYOTE SPRING
1600

✖ 1988

WHITE
POCKETS

DUFFER
2000

GATE

HOUSE ROCK VALLEY
// HIGHWAY 89A
MARBLE CANYON
& NAVAJO BRIDGE
24

BUTTES

19

PARIA

20

PLATEAU

21

OLD

TRACK

∧ 1791

POVERTY FLAT

AIRSTRIP ✈ 1788

COYOTE BUTTES SPECIAL
MANAGEMENT AREA

WIRE PASS-BUCKSKIN G.
FEE AREA

NUMBERS IN SQUARES
ARE SECTION NUMBER'S   31

PAW HOLE
TEEPEES

30

PAW
HOLE

Ⓟ
4WD PARKING

✖ 1788

ROCK TANK
WATERHOLE

VERY   SANDY   ROAD

29

POVERTY FLAT RANCH
WINDMILL, BARNS,
WATER TROUGH

28

1792

RED POCKETS &
CORRAL VALLEY WELL
PINE TREE POCKETS ROAD

SCALE

0   1   2   3   4   KMS

Buckskin Gulch. Continue on the trail, or right in the dry creek bed. About one km from the parking lot and as you're heading in a northerly direction, you should see a sign on the right stating Buckskin Gulch straight ahead. At that point, you'll also see an old road and many foot prints going up the steep hill to the right. Go up this hill. About 300-400 meters from the creek bed will be the trail register for Coyote Buttes. From there continue southeast on the old road to the bottom of the first drainage, then follow tracks east over a low divide in the ridge, thence south along the eastern side of the same ridge. Follow this map and other peoples tracks over sand & slickrock up to the most popular foto-op in the Buttes, a place called *The Wave*. It's located about 150 vertical meter up the north end of another ridge called Top Rock. Other good fotogenic sites are Sand Cove and the North & South Teepees, which this writer believes is the 2nd best place in Coyote Buttes for picture taking.

If you don't have a permit, you can still go to The Teepees which are outside of the Special Management Area. Instead of taking the trail to The Wave, continue down the Wire Pass drainage to the Buckskin Gulch, then retreat back up the same drainage about 200-300 meters and look for one of several routes out of the slot canyon to the south. If there are beginners in your group, take a short rope to help them upon the bench. This writer thought it was easy, but some may not. Once on top of any high point, look south, southeast and you can see the two groups of Teepees on the horizon in Section 5. Walk cross-country along the Lower Route in that direction.

Another trail-or-sorts into The Wave and Sand Cove, is via The Notch. From the main road or the rusty metal tank, head east over a low ridge. You should soon pick up a trail. Cross a fence and a sagebrush flat, then veer left to find a good trail running along an old road heading up the south side of a canyon. Above that is another flat area; veer left again and route-find up through several cliff bands and ledges until you're on top of The Notch. From there veer right to find a good sandy trail circling to the south, then east, then down into the slickrock valley called Sand Cove. Near the bottom are a couple of old historic rancher-made sand-filled cement dams and maybe some water(?). About 150 meters below the ruins of the 2nd dam, veer right with all the other tracks, and climb up the hill to The Wave.

To reach the southern end of Coyote Buttes and Paw Hole, start walking from the car-park west of Northcott's place at Coyote Spring. Walk cross-country to the southeast to avoid the ranch house and corrals. In Coyote Valley, stay left of the dry creek bed, to find the faded remains of an old road. Stay on this faint track all the way to Paw Hole, a sometimes-filled natural water pocket surrounded by teepee-shaped rocks. You can also walk north along the west side of these teepees, and if you stay down in the sand, you can legally do this without a permit. On the map, north of the road on either side of Paw Hole is designated wilderness, with the Special Management Area shaded. From the road north of Poverty Flat, walk northeast through the sand to the teepee-like rocks east of Cottonwood Spring. No permit needed if you stay to the east and north a little.

Elevations Wire Pass TH., 1490 meters; high point in the Buttes, 2000; The Wave, 1585 meters.

Hike Length and Time Needed It's about 4 kms from Wire Pass Trailhead to The Wave and if no stops are made will take just over an hour. From the car-park near Coyote Spring to Paw Hole is about 5-6 kms and will take about 1 1/2 hours each way. From Wire Pass Trailhead to The Teepees via the Lower Route is about 7 kms and will take 1 1/2 or 2 hours one-way. From the House Rock

The North Teepees, located southeast of The Wave.

Valley Road to The Wave via The Notch Trail is only 3-4 kms, but may take 1 1/2 hours or more one-way. Time and distance to the Cottonwood Spring area will depend on how far you can drive.

Water Always take plenty in your car and in your pack.

Maps USGS maps Pine Hollow Canyon, West Clark Bench, Poverty Flat and Coyote Buttes (1:24,000). Or USGS or BLM maps Kanab, Smoky Mountain, Glen Canyon Dam, Fredonia (1:100,000).

Main Attractions The Navajo Sandstone here comes in red, yellow, white and maroon colors, plus interesting shapes and erosional features. The Wave seems to get all the attention, but The Teepees and other similar sites are great too.

Tips for Fotographers Take plenty of film. Use film that's heavy on reds and yellows like Kodak Gold or 3M Company film such as K-Mart's Focal brand. Under exposing a little seems to bring out the colors better. A Polaroid filter might help(?). At The Wave you'll want no shadows, so be there between 10:30 am and 1:00 pm solar time--not daylight savings time--for best results. Be there on a day with 100% pure clear unfiltered & unadulterated sunshine--something that's difficult under the present booking & reservation system!

Ideal Time to Hike April, May and early June, and September & October. Summers are hot, plus there's desert haze. Winters can bring crystal clear skies, and it's easier to get reservations then.

Hiking Boots Running or athletic-type shoes that won't scuff or leave black marks on rocks.

Author's Experience He left his car at the Corral Valley Well and walked to Cottonwood Spring and back in 8 hours. He walked from the Wire Pass Trailhead to The Teepees via the Lower Route and returned, all in 4 hours. He walked from the car-park near Coyote Spring to Paw Hole and back in 3 1/2 hours. Using The Notch Trail, he made it to The Wave and back in 3 hours, but was hurrying fast. And he also hurried into The Wave via the normal route but missed the best time frame with the sun. Round-trip was 2 hours, but you'll want lots more time than that.

Permit Requirements for Coyote Buttes
Special Management Area--1997

Before going into the heart of the Coyote Buttes, the shaded area on the map, you're supposed to have a permit and reservation. As this book goes to press, here are the latest rules and regulations as outlined by **Coyote Buttes Information** handout sheet: 1997 Fee Schedule: $5/Person, Reservation/Permit Required, 2 Groups Maximum Per Day, 4 Person/Group Size Limit, No Refunds for Un-Used Permits.

But that's not all, there's more under **Regulations:** 1. Day use only. No overnight camping in the Special Management Area. 2. Maximum group size limit is four persons. 3. No more than two groups in the area per day. 4. No private or commercial recreational use of horse/pack animals in the Special Management Area. 5. The wilderness is closed to motorized or mechanized transport and equipment, including bicycles and hang gliders. 6. Campfires or burning of trash/toilet paper are prohibited. 7. Carry your trash and toilet paper out of the area. 8. Leave archaeological sites, such as petroglyphs, pot sherds and ruins, undisturbed. 9. Commercially guided trips require a Special Recreation Permit.

Pawhole, a natural waterhole, and teepee-shaped rocks, at the south end of the Coyote Buttes.

10. Use existing hiking routes. Do not create new ones. 11. Walk-in permits(no reservation) may be available at time [if slots haven't already been filled]. Reservations for available walk-ins may be made only at the Paria Information [Ranger] Station up to seven days prior to the available date.

At the bottom of the *Information* sheet mentioned above is an application form for a permit. Among other things it states, Each day of use requires a separate permit application. On the back of that form you must choose which Entry/Trailhead and Exit/Trailhead you plan to use. Evidently you can't change your mind once you commit yourself? Also, you must state the number of people that will be in your group and list 3 choices as to the days you'd like to be there. Quoting again, *Do not send any fees with this Application. Your fees will be due after confirmation of your hiking dates.*

Once you fill out the application form send it to: Paria/Coyote Permits, Northern Arizona University, Box 15018, Flagstaff, Arizona, USA, 86011. Or FAX to 520-523-1080.

It appears you've first got to get an application form. Call or write to the BLM Information/Visitor Center, 345 East Riverside Drive, St. George, Utah, USA, 84770, Tele. 435-688-3230. After that it'll take two more letters to Flagstaff. It looks like this reservation process could take one or two months, and you'll have to begin the process several months or up to a year in advance. In early November, 1997, about half the dates during December, January and February were open. Good Luck.

Comments and How to Change Public Policy on
Coyote Buttes Permit Reservation System

The above stated requirements for 1997 are being re-evaluated as this is being written and will surely be modified as of early 1998. One proposal is to allow more hikers in than the present figure of from 2 to 8 people per/day. That will surely be good news, but if this whole mess sounds too bad to be true, it probably is. In the opinion of this writer, that part of the BLM which sets the policy for Coyote Buttes is now being dominated by the *lunatic fringe* of the Southern Utah Wilderness Alliance--SUWA.

This policy of permits and especially **reservations**, has turned this into a first class *bureaucratic nightmare*. All because a few radicals in the environmental movement want everyone to have a "true wilderness experience". Another bunch out in California tried limiting the number of people going up Mt. Whitney on weekends too, but there was such public outrage they had to reverse themselves. For sure, those making the policy for Coyote Buttes have all been out to places like The Wave, maybe several times. All before this Soviet or Stalinist-type system was set up. And since they work for the BLM, they have the right to go there anytime they want without getting a reservation or permit. They don't have to jump through all the hoops the rest of us are required to. It seems some BLM employees want to keep this place a big secret, and part of their own little private sanctuary. Remember, it's out land, not theirs!

One of the legitimate issues BLM policy makers worry about in allowing more people to visit The Wave, is that everybody walks right on the places they want to fotograph. In time, some black soled shoes could leave scuff marks. Instead of asking hikers to just wear "soft soled shoes" into the area, this writer suggests everyone remove shoes entirely while at The Wave; that way 500 or 1000 people a day could visit the place and would do less harm than with the present policy. Beyond The Wave, there are few other place in Coyote Buttes where walking all over colorful rocks would have a detrimental effect, but some policy makers use this card to justify their actions. What this present policy seems to be doing is creating a type of "forbidden fruit", which everyone wants to taste, just to see if it really is poison. In the end, and with this type of bureaucracy in place, people will just go out there anyway, with or without a permit, and not pay the user-fee.

Here are some suggestions this writer is offering the BLM.

1. Have everyone pickup a one-day user-fee permit when they arrive at the Kanab BLM office, the Paria Ranger Station & Visitor Center; or with the increased fee collections, install a small trailer house at Wire Pass Trailhead and have a seasonal ranger sell permits there. That person could also inform hikers on proper ethics in the more sensitive areas, and recommend other places to get great pictures. That person could also make periodic hikes to The Wave to make sure everyone has a permit. This would eliminate the Soviet-style bureaucratic nightmare of getting reservations.

2. Charge $5 a day for a user-fee per person, and have no limitations on visitor numbers. If it turns cloudy, they can buy another permit and go out the next day with better light and sun.

3. Install a sign at the entrance to The Wave asking that all shoes be removed. A solar powered toilet could also be placed near The Wave, but out of sight, to eliminate that potential problem.

It's suggested trying this new policy with no limitations on numbers and see what happens. The only problem that could occur is that fotographers may have to direct traffic to get their shots. And the only thing that will be lost is "the true wilderness experience" as defined by SUWA. Please keep in mind, this world is getting smaller by the day, and the population getting larger. So we're all going to have to get used to the idea that some special places like Coyote Buttes is going to be a popular destination, even though it's in a wilderness area.

This writer has never heard of anyone trying to denying tourists the right to go to Delicate Arch in Arches N. M. when they wanted to, just so there wouldn't be so many people in their picture. There's never been anyone try to limit the number of tourists walking all around Bryce Canyon's hoodoos, just so some can have a wilderness experience. In most of our national parks, better facilities have been created to handle bigger crowds. I think that's what must be done in Coyote Buttes, and in the lower Buckskin and Paria River. This writer would much rather be at one of these places with a crowd, than to be required to make reservations 6 months or a year in advance. People still have to walk 4 kms to

The Wave, and the access road will remain dusty or muddy, so the herd heading that way will never be that large.

If you feel the same way about this nightmarish reservation system or limited numbers policy as this writer, please write a letter with your opinions to the BLM, 345 East Riverside Drive, St. George, Utah, USA, 84770, Tele. 435-688-3230. Or the Paria Team, Kanab BLM, 318 North First East, Kanab, Utah, USA, 84741, Tele. 435-644-2672. Members of that team are: Tom Folks, Janaye Byergo, Tim Duck, Mike Salamancha, Mary Dewitz and Mike Small. After these people come up with what they think is a workable policy, then Verlin Smith, head of the BLM office in Kanab; and Roger Taylor, Field Manager out of the St. George BLM office, sign it into policy.

These are the people who are creating public policy on your public land, so please write letters. If they don't hear from you, they think everyone approves of what they're doing. In the past, the BLM has been more responsive than some other government agencies when it comes to incorporating public comment into policy; hopefully that same trend will continue.

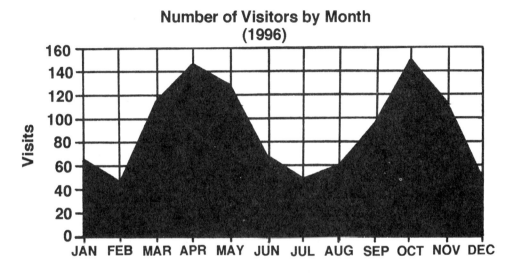

South Teepees, located just east of the Coyote Buttes Special Management Area.

169

Sand Hill Crack & History of the Sand Hills Ranches

Location and Access The Vermilion Cliffs is the wall of cliffs you'll see rising prominently to the north of Highway 89A as you drive from Jacob Lake to Lee's Ferry. Along this entire escarpment, there are only three routes up through the Navajo Sandstone wall--at least which are climbable to the average person. One of these routes is up through what is called the Sand Hill Crack, with a second one to the east and apparently having no name. For lack of a name let's call it the Eastern Crack. To get to these trails, turn north from Highway 89A between mile posts 557 and 558. Drive through the unlocked gate, closing it behind you. Then drive this fairly good road about 3 kms to the place called Jacob Pools(which is on a small piece of private land). Park at the old stone building or ranch house, which is on the old Honeymoon Trail. This is also the present southern boundary of the Paria Canyon--Vermilion Cliffs Wilderness Area.

Trail or Route Conditions There's an old track running north from Jacob Pools to the base of the cliffs not far below Hancock Spring. This is now closed to all wheeled vehicles. To reach the Sand Hill Crack, walk along this track toward Hancock Spring, but instead of turning to the left to reach the spring, turn right and look for stone cairns marking the lower part of the trail, which is on the far right-hand side of the canyon going up. While scrambling up a faint trail, look for a single pinnacle near the right-hand wall and near the top of the route. At the pinnacle, go around it to the left, where you'll find two petroglyph panels. After the pinnacle, head straight up the gully, which was originally formed by a minor fault. Near the top, you'll see on the right, a long panel of petroglyphs. Because of these petroglyphs, we can surmise this is an old Indian trail. At the top of the cliffs are what ranchers call the Sand Hills, others call it the Paria Plateau. You'll see an old sandy track on top, which you can use to walk to the Jarvis Ranch and Pinnacle Valley.

To reach a second old Indian route, called here the Eastern Crack, walk north from Jacob Pools on an old road in the direction of Rachel's Pools. As you approach Rachel's, be looking at the cliffs to the northeast. You will see an obvious break in the cliffs where the Eastern Crack is located. From Rachel's Pools, simply head up to the northeast in the direction of the crack. You won't see any trail at first, but when you get closer to the top, you will see one or two old stock routes. Immediately under the steepest part, you'll begin to see the beginnings of a constructed trail. As you head up through the narrow part, there are a dozen or so panels of Indian petroglyphs and cowboy etchings. One of these reads: G. M. Wright, 20 Apr. 1894. From the top, you could return the same way, or head northwest and return via the Sand Hill Crack.

Elevations Jacob Pools, 1589 meters; top of Sand Hill Crack, 2066; top of Eastern Crack, 2057; Jarvis Ranch, 2025 meters.

Hike Length and Time Needed From Jacob Pools to the top of the Sand Hill Crack is about 3 or 3 1/2 kms. Round-trip could be 3 or 4 hours, or about half a day for the average person. From the rim-top to the Jarvis Ranch is about 5 kms. From Jacob Pools to the ranch and back, about 17 kms, and will be an all-day hike. From Jacob Pools to the top of the Eastern Crack will take 3 or 4 hours round-trip.

Water There's good water at Hancock Spring, maybe some at Rachel's Pools, and maybe some at the

The stone house at Jacob Pools. The Sand Hill Crack is the canyon to the right in the cliffs beyond.

Map 29, Sand Hill Crack & History of Sand Hills Ranches

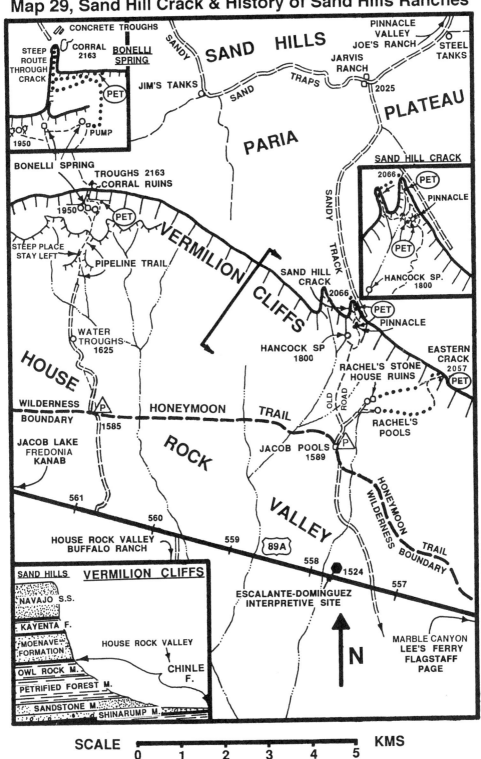

CONCRETE TROUGHS

SAND   HILLS

PINNACLE
VALLEY
JOE'S RANCH
STEEL
TANKS

STEEP
ROUTE
THROUGH
CRACK

CORRAL
2163

BONELLI
SPRING

JARVIS
RANCH

PET

JIM'S TANKS

SAND   TRAPS
2025

PLATEAU

PUMP

1950

PARIA

BONELLI SPRING

TROUGHS 2163
CORRAL RUINS

1950

PET

SAND HILL CRACK

2066

PET

PINNACLE

STEEP PLACE
STAY LEFT

PIPELINE TRAIL

VERMILION

SANDY

TRACK

CLIFFS

SAND HILL
CRACK

PET

HANCOCK SP.
1800

WATER
TROUGHS
1625

HOUSE

2066

SAND HILL
CRACK

PET

PINNACLE

HANCOCK SP
1800

RACHEL'S STONE
HOUSE RUINS

EASTERN
CRACK
2057

PET

WILDERNESS
BOUNDARY

P

HONEYMOON   TRAIL

OLD
ROAD

RACHEL'S
POOLS

1585

JACOB LAKE
FREDONIA
KANAB

ROCK

JACOB POOLS
1589

P

561

HONEYMOON

560

VALLEY

WILDERNESS

559

89A

HOUSE ROCK VALLEY
BUFFALO RANCH

BOUNDARY

558
1524

557

TRAIL

SAND HILLS   VERMILION   CLIFFS

NAVAJO S.S.

KAYENTA F.

MOENAVE
FORMATION

HOUSE ROCK VALLEY

OWL ROCK M.

CHINLE
F.

PETRIFIED FOREST M.

SANDSTONE M.

SHINARUMP M.

ESCALANTE-DOMINGUEZ
INTERPRETIVE SITE

N

MARBLE CANYON
LEE'S FERRY
FLAGSTAFF
PAGE

SCALE   0   1   2   3   4   5   KMS

Jarvis Ranch or at Jacob Pools. But don't bet your life on these last 3 sites having water.

Maps USGS or BLM maps Glen Canyon Dam(1:100,000); or Emmett Wash(1:62,500); or one of the four MF-1475 A, B, C or D(1:62,500).

Main Attractions Petroglyphs and cowboy etchings along two old Indian routes, great views from the rim, and historic Jacob & Rachel's Pools, which John D. Lee helped build.

Ideal Time to Hike Spring or fall, but you can hike almost year-round.

Hiking Boots Rugged hiking boots.

Author's Experience Two trips, last time 1997, were to the top of the Sand Hill Crack and back in 3 hours each. Another trip was to the steel tanks east of Jarvis Ranch, and back, in 6 1/2 hours. His hike to the Eastern Crack took less than 2 1/2 hours round-trip.

History of Jacob and Rachel's Pools, House Rock Spring and the Honeymoon Trail

In May, 1872, Rachel Woolsey, one of John D. Lee's wives, was moved into the area now called by various people as The Pools, Jacob Pools, or Rachel's Pools. Her first shelter was a mud and willow shack, not much better than what the Indians lived in. On June 2, a group of men from the Powell Survey came through the area, and fotographed the scene(see the foto below).

Later in the fall of the same year, John D. started building a better house. He hired a man named Elisha Everett to help, since the home was to be made of rock. It was mostly completed on Christmas Day of 1872. It measured 9 x 11 meters, and had two doors, two bedrooms, a kitchen, a parlor and covered with a wooden roof. Nearby was a cellar. The ruins of this rock house can still be seen just above the western-most spring called Rachel's Pools. In the same area, and just below the springs, are numerous rock walls, apparently used as fences to hold livestock.

This location was 32 kms from Lee's Ferry, and was set up to be a way-station for Mormons who were heading south to settle in Arizona. It was one day's travel between these two waterholes.

One day by wagon to the west, was another site of interest, which goes back to the spring and summer of 1873. This is the resting place or way-station along the Honeymoon Trail called *House Rock Spring*. This route got it's name later, after many Mormons had settled in Arizona, and after the St. George Temple had opened. After that, many young Mormon couples made the trip to southern Utah along this trail or road to be married in the temple. They usually returned home in a very dreamy state, thus the name, *Honeymoon Trail*. House Rock Spring is located in the upper west end of House Rock Valley. It was one day's journey from House Rock Spring to Rachel's or Jacob Pools. See *Map 29A, The Sand Hills & Paria Plateau Ranches*.

At, or just below House Rock Spring, are a number of interesting sites. There's a grave of a young

Rachel Lee's willow & mud shack on June 2, 1872. In the picture are John D. Lee, two small sons and a daughter. (Arizona Historical Society)

woman and a number of ruins of fences and old stone structures of some kind. If you walk up the drainage east about 400 meters from the grave site, and up against the cliffs and all along the lower cliffs themselves, you'll see dozens of *emigrantglyphs,* or signatures of some of the earliest Mormon settlers who were heading to Arizona in the very first year Lee's Ferry was in operation. Most of these signatures date from early June, 1873.

To get there, drive to House Rock located on Highway 89A between mile posts 565 and 566. From there, head north on the House Rock Valley Road in the direction of Highway 89. Using the *Fredonia* metric map, drive about 6 to 7 kms north from the highway until you come to the Signature Rocks Ranch on the right or east. This belongs to a John Rich and his brothers, who also own Jacob Lake Lodge. Presently at this ranch are people from The Peregrine Fund, who are watching both the ranch facilities and California Condor Release Site to the northeast. At the ranch, get permission to drive or walk through, if you can. People interested in the pioneer signatures are welcome, vandals are not! Head east about 1 1/2 kms to or near the end of the road. Those in cars can only drive part way, then they must walk the last little ways as the upper part of this road is very rutted. Remember, you'll have to do some climbing to reach most of the pioneer signatures.

Back at The Pools. At the end of the sandy road coming up from the highway, is what is called Jacob Pools. It's about 1 or 1 1/2 kms southwest of Rachel's Pools. At that location, are some corrals and a rather well-build stone building. Information as to when this structure was built is scarce, but most of the old timers around believe it was built in the early 1900's when the Grand Canyon Cattle Company ran cows throughout the entire House Rock Valley. In those days, B. F. Saunders was running things. It was likely built just after the turn of the century, and may have been both a way-station and a ranch house on the road running on to Lee's Ferry. Be aware that this place is privately owned, and is an active ranch, although no one lives there.

Release of California Condors

The December, 1996, release of six California condors at Vermilion Cliffs just north of House Rock Spring just outside the wilderness boundary, began a cooperative effort to reestablish a population of 150 condors in the Southwest. Nine additional condors were released in May, 1997.

Two of the birds have died (due to a golden eagle attack and a collision with a power structure), one was returned to captivity as a result of its frequent encounters with humans, one has been missing from radio contact since early August, 1997, and presumed dead, and another was captured and held for emergency medical treatment and recovery and then returned to the wild population.

On September 25, 1997, four more birds were taken to the cliff-top release enclosure site for a two month adjustment period and released to the wild in mid-November. These four joined the remaining 11 to make a total of 15 condors in northern Arizona through 1997.

The ruins of Rachel Lee's second stone house just above one of the springs at Rachel's Pools. This place is located about one km northeast of Jacob Pools.

Map 29A, The Sand Hills & Paria Plateau Ranches

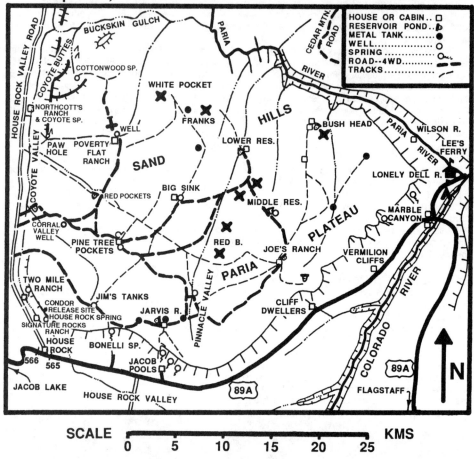

This release program is a cooperative effort between the US Fish & Wildlife Service, BLM, Arizona Game & Fish Department and The Peregrine Fund. The Peregrine Fund now monitors the release site from Marble Canyon and the Signature Rocks Ranch west of House Rock Spring. Just south of the ranch is a public viewing verandah next to House Rock Valley Road.

History of the Sand Hills Ranches

Sandwiched in between two hikes to the top of the Vermilion Cliffs, is a short history of some of the ranching activity which has taken place over the last century on top of the Paria Plateau. Local stockmen have always known the place as the Sand Hills.

In the region between the Buckskin Gulch, the Lower Paria River Gorge, the Vermilion Cliffs, and The Cockscomb(sometimes known as East Kaibab Monocline), is the Paria Plateau. For the most part, this is a moderately high and very isolated corner of the Colorado Plateau, which is extremely difficult to get to. The local name, the Sand Hills, tells the whole story.

The top layer of the Plateau, for the most part, is made up of sand, which has eroded away from the Navajo Sandstone Formation. This is primarily the reason it's almost a no man's land. It's not only difficult for a man to walk around on, but it's also difficult for horses; to say nothing of the problems people have in getting around in a 2WD car or pickup. This is 4WD county!

Actually, you can sometimes get around up there with a normal vehicle, but you have to do it when the sand is either wet or frozen, or both. Winter is the best time. Another method some of the old timers used, was to let about half the air out of their tires, which put more rubber to the road. As they left the sandy parts, they'd have to hand pump the tires back up again. For those without a 4WD vehicle, it's highly recommended you forego any visits to this little hideaway in the desert.

Joe's Ranch or The Ranch

Joe's Ranch was one of the first to be set up in the country, and because of the difficulty in travel, the isolation, and the total lack of any live running water or permanent springs, it has always been a kind of hardship post. The only real springs around are Two Mile and Coyote, located at the western edge of the Sand Hills, and in House Rock and Coyote Valleys.

The ranch got it's name from Joe Hamblin, one of three sons of Jacob Hamblin. Walt, Ben and Joe were their names. According to the late Dunk Findlay, Joe Hamblin had worked with John W. Powell on one or more of his surveying parties(but not the early river expeditions), had been in the area before, and returned later to build the ranch. The year he went there was 1884, and since it was the only ranch of any kind in the Sand Hills, it was always just called "The Ranch" or Joe's Ranch, by local cowboys and sheepmen. Joe Hamblin had cattle, as well as goats and sheep.

No one alive today knows how long the Hamblins had the ranch and the squatters rights, or in what year it was sold to Johnny Adams, the second owner. Dunk Findlay seemed to think it was in 1926 when Johnny Adams bought most of the squatters rights in the Sand Hills from Nephi, son of Joe Hamblin. Johnny Adam's herds grazed most of the Paria Plateau range for many years. He's the one who devised the scheme to pump Paria River water up onto the lower or northern end of the Sand Hills. It was in the winter, spring and summer of 1939, that he and his workers cut the trail, laid down the pipe and installed the pump. However, because the drought ended just at that time, he never used the pump. Read all about that scheme under Map 23, page 128, the **Adams Trail.**

It was during the time Johnny Adams was at The Ranch in 1934, that the Taylor Grazing Act was passed. In the years after this legislation, the Sand Hills was broken up into two or more different grazing areas, much to the consternation of the old timers. Other cattlemen got in on the western part of the Sand Hills range, and fences were erected. This changed the whole setup.

Quoting now from a letter written to the author by Dunk Findlay, *"The only water Adams had was at the Ranch, the Middle, and the Lower Reservoir. There was no other water on the Plateau. Other people had to graze when there was snow on the ground. That's when the sheep and goats were in there. Most times it served only as a winter range other than around the Ranch. That is why it was not over grazed".*

After many years of riding the Sand Hills range, and after having developed many of the stock tanks and ponds seen there today, Adams finally sold out. According to Dunk Findlay, Adams was somehow forced out, partly because of the Depression. The man in the middle was Jim Jennings, who foreclosed on Adams, but then A.T. Spence, a cattleman from Phoenix, ended up with much of the Sand Hills range in 1941. Spence built cement cores to some of the little stock ponds and brought in several metal tanks, although he only had it a short time. In 1944, Dunk's father, Merle Findlay bought out Spence.

Dunk remembered, *"The Ranch was a permanent ranch used year-round by Hamblin, Adams, Spence, and the Findlays. There were several times the cattle had to be moved away on account of lack of water,*

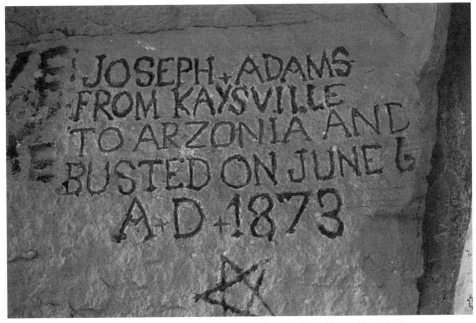

Signatures of early-day Mormon settlers on the cliff above House Rock Spring.

that's why we drilled a well. *After the Taylor Grazing Act, there was no place to move; before that cattle were moved any place there was water on the public domain. No one owned anything then."*

Once the Findlays had it, Dunk and his brother Lynn, did most of the work around the range. After Merle died in 1960, these two brothers split up the range; Dunk to the west, and Lynn to the east in the area around Joe's Ranch house. Actually, throughout the years each man or family who ran cattle or sheep on the range, did some work on it. One bit of work which had little to do with ranching was the building of an airstrip at Poverty Flat, located just east of the southern end of the Coyote Buttes. The man who built that and the only one to ever use it was Rowd Sanders.

Developing a water system was of primary concern. As stated before, there was never any live running water on the whole plateau. The range itself was excellent, due to the altitude, which ranged up to about 2200 meters. But because of the water problem, it was virtually impossible to take or have enough livestock there to overgraze the place.

In the early 1950's, the Findlays drilled a well in the lower northern end of Pinnacle Valley, with a drilling rig they had bought. A bit later they sold the drilling equipment to Fay Hamblin and Floyd Maddox, who drilled the second well at Poverty Flat. A third well was drilled by Roy Woolly at Pine Tree Pockets(locally it's just called *Pines*), which for many years was a kind of ranch headquarters for the western part of the Sand Hills range. Throughout the years, and since about 1950, eight wells in all have been drilled.

The Findlays were heavily involved with the development of a number of slickrock water basins or rainwater stock tanks, and they installed a number of metal tanks for water storage, etc. Dunk and a man named John Rich also installed 4 or 5 pipelines, which ran water from several of the wells, down hill to the north(by gravity) to other water storage tanks, so the cattle could be spread out on the range more evenly.

In 1962, just after the Findlay brothers had divided the range, Lynn sold his part of the range to John Rich, who called his outfit the Vermilion Cliffs Cattle Company. This was the part with the old Joe's Ranch house on it. Dunk held onto his part until March 1, 1980. That's when he sold his grazing rights to the Ramsay Cattle Company, along with about 500 head of cattle. Dunk recalls the times and said, *"We had 80 acres(about 30 hectares) of patented land at the Ranch. Adams got this after the survey; before that it was just a squatters claim. We had around 16 or 18 state sections leased, on the Ranch."*

Shortly thereafter and still in 1980, the Two Mile Corporation took over, and obtained all grazing rights to the entire Paria Plateau. Actually, the name Two Mile Corp. came about after they bought out Dunk Findlay and the Vermilion Cliffs Cattle Co. In 1998, the Two Mile Ranch was owned by Kay Sturdevant of Springville, with a BLM permit to run up to 1500 head of cattle, but they actually have closer to 1200-1300. They run cattle on the Sand Hills year-round, with their winter range being in the north, just south of the Buckskin Gulch and the Lower Paria River Canyon; their summer range in the higher and cooler south half of the Plateau. This is all BLM land, except for about 20 state sections; and quarter section(160 acres or 65

The ranch house at Pine Tree Pockets in the western part of the Sand Hills.

hectares) at Joe's Ranch, which is private.

The ranch headquarters is located at Two Mile Spring, at the head of House Rock Valley. In the late 1990's, the company had only three full-time employees. In 1998, the ranch foreman was still J. R. Jones of Kanab. The ranch also has one cowboy and the waterman who lives at Pine Tree Pockets most of the time, and makes frequent sorties out to the various wells to pump water to storage tanks, and keeps an eye on the range and the facilities. In the spring and fall Two Mile Ranch hires part-time help.

Jarvis Ranch

The Jarvis Ranch came about and had something to do with the grazing rights changes back in the mid to late 1930's as a result of the Taylor Grazing Act. Dunk Findlay said, *"Jarvis never got a permit to run cattle--he was not there in the priority period. Jarvis was working for Walt Hamblin(Fay's dad) when the BLM finally gave him a small allotment of three or four sections."* According to Dunk Findlay, they never had many cows, maybe 15 or so, but they built a rather fine ranch house there anyway, which is just north of the Sand Hill Crack. That was in 1935.

The Jarvis house isn't just a line cabin or a bunk house, but instead a nice home. It's still used today by cowhands when they're in the area working cattle. It's painted white, has five good sized rooms and a propane gas lighting and cooking system. There's even a refrigerator, which is run on propane gas. Water was collected by the use of roof rain gutters and down-pipes, which funneled rainwater into a cistern below the house. There's water in the tank today, but it won't be drinkable.

When A. T. Spence got a hold of the ranch in 1941, he(according to Dunk Findlay) used the *"house for his main headquarters. He had built the house at the lower reservoir, and it and the house at the Ranch were used as line cabins. Spence added two more rooms to the original Jarvis house. He said not to spoil a good thing he put hard wood floors in then too."*

After Dunk and his brother divided the range, Dunk made this house his headquarters. It was Dunk Findlay who put the propane lights and refrigerator in the house, in or around 1962. He installed the metal tank next to the barn, and pumped water to it from the Pinnacle Valley Well. This was done by a small portable gasoline engine.

The Jarvis place also has a good barn which is still used today. Behind the barn are a couple of other metal water tanks, and just to the west, a dam which could catch a lot of water, if and when big storms ever occur. Near the house is a fruit cellar for storage. The whole ranch site is situated in a part of the Sand Hills called the *Dark Forest*. It's a piñon & juniper covered region, with very healthy and rather large trees.

Joe's Ranch, a site used since about 1884. Slickrock tank left, ranch house to the right.

Bonelli Spring Indian Trail

Location and Access The hike featured here is one of three going up through the Vermilion Cliffs to the top of the Sand Hills, or if you prefer, the Paria Plateau. To get to Bonelli Spring and an old Indian trail, drive along Highway 89A, the road running between Kanab and Jacob Lake; and Lee's Ferry, Marble Canyon and the Navajo Bridge. Between mile posts 560 and 561, turn north. At first the road parallels the highway running along the fence line to the west, then you drive through a gate. The road then turns east for a ways, again paralleling the fence. Finally it turns north as indicated on the map. After nearly two kms, you come to a junction. This is the old Honeymoon Trail and the wilderness boundary. Park there. The rancher who owns the water troughs is allowed to drive into the area, but the public is not.

Trail or Route Conditions From the Honeymoon Trailhead, walk along the sandy track to and past some livestock watering troughs. Further along, this old road ends at the bottom of the Vermilion Cliffs, then you follow the plastic pipeline, which is upgraded periodically to bring water from Bonelli Spring down to the troughs. Use the pipeline as a trail guide. Veer left at the steep part to avoid cliffs. Remember, your target is Bonelli Spring straight ahead, about halfway up the cliffs, where you can see some greenery and three cottonwood trees(from a distance this appears only as brush). At the base of the Navajo Sandstone wall, you'll see the three parts to Bonelli Spring. From the eastern-most spring with the half-buried pump, climb due north up the steep talus slope to the Navajo wall, which has a panel of petroglyphs. Then turn west and make your way to the next wall, which is the bottom part of a steep crack. Scramble up using all fours along this narrow defile. At the rim are several stone corrals and three cement watering troughs.

Elevations From 1585 at the Honeymoon Trail, to 2163 meters on top.

Hike Length and Time Needed It's about 6 kms from the trailhead on the Honeymoon Trail to the rim-top, but in places it's steep and the going slow. It'll take about 4 or 5 hours for the average person to do the hike round-trip, or at least half a day.

Water Take some with you, it's always warm on the cliff face. There's good water in the open square box part of Bonelli Spring, but there may or may not be water in the troughs below.

Maps USGS or BLM map Glen Canyon Dam(1:100,000); or MF-1475 A, B, C, or D(1:62,500); or Emmett Hill and One Toe Ridge(1:24,000)

Main Attractions An invigorating climb, fine views from the top, an old pumping station by an early-day Basque sheepman, and a wall of petroglyphs, indicating this was an old Indian trail.

Ideal Time to Hike Spring or fall, but it can be hiked any time. Summers are extra hot.

Hiking Boots Rugged hiking boots.

Author's Experience The author climbed to the top twice in 3 and 3 1/2 hours each, round-trip.

History of the Bonelli Spring Development

The Bonelli Spring was unknown and unused until the early 1900's. Sometime after about 1916, Alex Cram, who owned a large ranch in House Rock Valley, began to develop this minor seep. He blasted a square hole in the bottom of the Navajo Sandstone cliff in order to increase the flow and to better capture the water. Sometime later, he traded his grazing rights to a man named W. J. Mackelprange for two horses.

Later, and in the early 1930's, a Basque sheepman named Bonelli from Flagstaff, Arizona, came into the country and bought the water rights to the spring. Prior to this time it may have been called Death Tanks, because there was never much water there(one source says the name Death Tanks referred to another little seep just downhill from Bonelli Spring?).

Bonelli brought sheep with him, but needed a better waterhole. After considering his options, he bought pumping equipment and pipe, then set to work to construct a pumping station, pipeline, and troughs, in order to pump the water from the spring up to the rim-top to several cement troughs. His operation was successful, and he had water on the rim for about four years. His sheep were on top of the Sand Hills during the summers; and down under the cliffs in House Rock Valley during the winters.

But in 1936, the newly established Grazing Service(forerunner to the BLM) ran him out. Bonelli had apparently not been in the area long enough before the Taylor Grazing Act was passed in 1934, and wasn't eligible for a permit to run livestock in that part of the country. So after four apparently successful years, he had to abandon the operation.

At the site today, you will see a half-buried pump, some hoses and an old rusty wheelbarrow at the most easterly of the three spring sites. The middle spring is the only one which has a flow large enough to get a drink out of today. It's shaped like a huge square tomb, which was blasted out of the lower Navajo. At the third seep or wet spot to the west, three cottonwood trees grow.

Just above the pump and next to the big wall, are odds and ends of the operation. On the rim top, are three cement troughs, still in very good condition. Also right on the rim, are several stone corrals--at least the author thought they were corrals. All the old timers said these were originally some kind of Indian ruins, but perhaps they had been modified to handle sheep or horses by Bonelli and others.

178

Map 30, Bonelli Spring Indian Trail

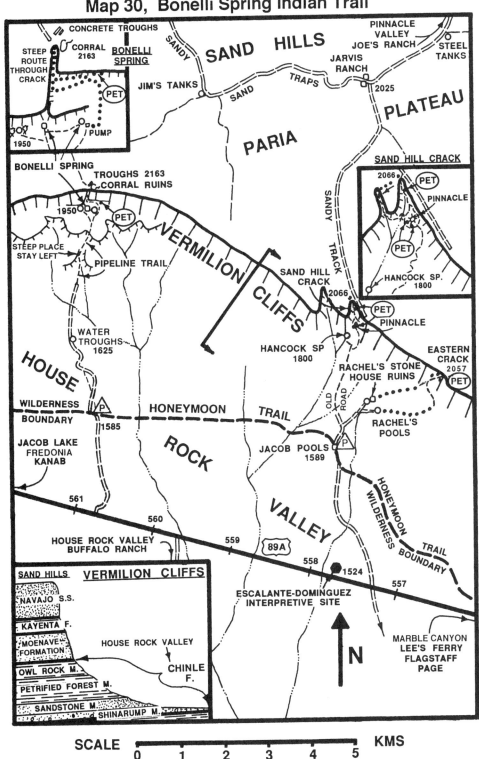

CONCRETE TROUGHS
SAND HILLS
PINNACLE VALLEY
JOE'S RANCH
STEEL TANKS

STEEP ROUTE THROUGH CRACK
CORRAL 2163
BONELLI SPRING
SANDY
JARVIS RANCH

JIM'S TANKS
SAND
TRAPS
2025

PET
PUMP

1950

PARIA
SANDY TRACK
PLATEAU

BONELLI SPRING
TROUGHS 2163
CORRAL RUINS
1950
PET

SAND HILL CRACK
2066
PET
PINNACLE
PET
HANCOCK SP. 1800

STEEP PLACE STAY LEFT
PIPELINE TRAIL

VERMILION
CLIFFS
SAND HILL CRACK
2066
PET
PINNACLE

WATER TROUGHS 1625
HANCOCK SP 1800

RACHEL'S STONE HOUSE RUINS
EASTERN CRACK 2057
PET

HOUSE
WILDERNESS BOUNDARY
1585
HONEYMOON TRAIL
OLD ROAD
RACHEL'S POOLS

JACOB LAKE FREDONIA KANAB
ROCK
JACOB POOLS 1589
P

561
VALLEY
HONEYMOON WILDERNESS BOUNDARY
TRAIL

560
HOUSE ROCK VALLEY BUFFALO RANCH
559
89A
558
1524
557

ESCALANTE-DOMINGUEZ INTERPRETIVE SITE

SAND HILLS
VERMILION CLIFFS
NAVAJO S.S.
KAYENTA F.
MOENAVE FORMATION
HOUSE ROCK VALLEY
CHINLE F.
OWL ROCK M.
PETRIFIED FOREST M.
SANDSTONE M.
SHINARUMP M.

N

MARBLE CANYON LEE'S FERRY FLAGSTAFF PAGE

SCALE
0 1 2 3 4 5
KMS

The water trough and barn at the Poverty Flat ranch site, located just southeast of Coyote Buttes.

The Jarvis Ranch house in 1987. It looks like new, but was first built in 1935.

Bonelli Spring. Alex Cram originally blasted out part of the wall to get the water out easier.

Bonelli's Pump sits half buried in sand near Bonelli Spring.

The Story of John D. Lee and Mountain Meadows Massacre

A book on the Paria River cannot be written without including the life story of John D. Lee. Nearly all Utah and Arizona residents know of him, but people from other parts of the country probably haven't. This chapter is a brief summery of Lee's life, and is intended to let the reader understand events leading up to the Mountain Meadows Massacre and why John D. Lee was sent to the lower Paria to establish Lee's Ferry. The author used, with permission, a book by Juanita Brooks, *John Doyle Lee, Zealot-Pioneer Builder-Scapegoat,* as the primary source for this chapter.

John D. Lee was born on September 12, 1812, in Kaskaskia, the capital of the territory of Illinois. He lived in Illinois throughout his youth, and at age 16, left home to fend for himself. His first job was a mail rider, which lasted for 6 months. He had various jobs in the several years until he got married, which was on July 24, 1833, at age 21. He married Aggatha Ann Woolsey, the first of 19 women he was to marry during his lifetime.

It wasn't long after this he became a convert to the Mormon Church. During the first 5 years of marriage, he was a missionary part of the time and had various jobs. In the period after 1838, he and the Mormons migrated to Missouri. As you might imagine, when the Mormons rode into that state, proclaiming parts thereof to be their Zion, the reception wasn't too cheery. They had problems, and later had to leave, winding up in Illinois and eventually to Nauvoo where they built a temple.

Because Lee was a very religious man and totally devoted to the church, he became one of the unofficial leaders. Because he was so good at things like farming, building homes, and working with machinery, he was called upon throughout his life to go out and help settle new colonies. He was never a high ranking church authority, but was a major cog in the church settlement program for about 30 years.

From Nauvoo, Illinois, the Mormons headed for the Missouri River in the winter of 1946-47 and the region around Council Bluffs, Iowa, and near the present-day Omaha & Florence, Nebraska. Since it was to take a year or two to get all the Mormons to Utah, they needed to set up several temporary encampments enroute, in preparation for the long haul to the Great Basin. John D. was much involved in building these temporary settlements.

While in Iowa, the Mormons were called upon to send a battalion of soldiers to California. This they did, but then President Brigham Young asked Lee to follow the group to Santa Fe, and collect the soldiers pay and bring it back to their families, who needed it a lot more than did the soldiers.

Because Lee was needed along the Missouri River area in Iowa and Nebraska, he was not chosen to accompany the first Pioneer Party to Utah in 1847. He instead followed in June of 1848. Upon arriving in Utah and the Salt Lake Valley, he immediately began to build a home for his wives. At the time he left Nauvoo, he had 10 wives; Brigham Young 17.

In one of the church meetings on December 2, 1850, in which Lee attended, Brigham Young mentioned they were going to send a group of volunteers south to what is now Cedar City, and establish an Iron Mission. There was a group of Englishmen who had the knowledge and skills to do the iron work, but they needed support in the venture. After the meeting, Young told Lee, that when he had asked for volunteers, he meant Lee. Young said, "*If we are to establish an iron industry there, we must have a solid base of farming to help support it.*"

The next thing Lee knew, he was leader of a small group heading for southern Utah in the dead of winter. On December 11, 1850, the wagons rolled out. Lee took two of his wives. As one can imagine, it wasn't an easy journey. There were no roads, just a trail, and snow was deep at times. They arrived at the present-day site of Parowan, in February of 1851. Parowan was the first of several new settlements Lee was to set up in the next 20 years.

Things went well for Lee and the church for several years, but in 1857 things began to change. News of an impending crisis came to the leaders of the church on July 24, 1857. This was the 10th anniversary of the landing of the Pioneer Party in the Salt Lake Valley. They had a big celebration up Big Cottonwood Canyon, southeast of Salt Lake City. During the afternoon festival, two men rode into the canyon with news that, "*all mail routes to the east were canceled, and an army was enroute to put down the rebellion in Utah.*" According to the Mormon version, there of course was no rebellion, unless you consider it a rebellion for all the church authorities to have too many wives.

With this news, the church leaders and the people became a little hysterical, and there was a call to arms. Since the Mormons had been run out of several of the eastern states, they gradually became better prepared, in a military sense. The church in Utah was organized not only into wards and stakes(religious groupings), but also in the event of an emergency, such as trouble with the Indians, they were organized into military companies and battalions as well. So preparations began, and in a way, Utah was almost in a state of martial law.

In many ways things went on as normal. But there began to be a very deep distrust for all non-Mormons. There were wagon trains crossing Utah all summer long, most of which were heading for

Map 33, John D. Lee's Country

MAP NOT DRAWN TO SCALE

UTAH

ARIZONA

N

CROSSING OF THE FATHERS (UTE CROSSING)

RIVER

UTAH
ARIZONA

GLEN CANYON DAM SITE

PAGE

ARIZONA

COLORADO

MOENKOPI
TUBA CITY

ROCK HOUSE

ADAIRVILLE

HENRIEVILLE

CANNONVILLE

COTTONWOOD WASH

TROPIC

PAHREAH

PARIA   RIVER

LEE'S FERRY

HONEYMOON TRAIL

NAVAJO BRIDGE

RACHEL'S POOLS

JACOB POOLS

SEVIER RIVER

EAST FORK SEVIER RIVER

SAWMILL

SKUTUMPAH

JOHNSON

HOUSE ROCK

PANGUITCH

JOHN D. LEE'S GRAVE

SEVIER RIVER

ALTON

MOUNT SKUTUMPAH

MOUNT CARMEL

MOUNT CARMEL JUNCTION

FREDONIA

KANAB

KANAB CREEK

ORDERVILLE

ROCKVILLE

PARAGONAH

PAROWAN
FORT LEWIS

JOHNSON'S RANCH

CEDAR CITY

HAMILTON'S FORT

KANARRAVILLE

HARMONEY

SPRINGDALE

GRAFTON

PIPE SPRINGS

STRIP

BELLEVUE

TOQUERVILLE

WASHINGTON

SHORT CREEK

PINTO

HARRISBURG

HEBERVILLE

ARIZONA

MOUNTAIN MEADOWS MASSACRE SITE

GUNLOCK

SANTA CLARA

ST. GEORGE

VIRGIN RIVER

NEVADA

NEVADA

Adapted from Juanita Brooks' book, *JOHN DOYLE LEE--Zealot, Pioneer Builder, Scapegoat*

northern California. But those who came late in the season usually went to California via the southern route. This route ran close to present-day Highway 91 and Interstate I5.

Since Salt Lake City was at about the halfway point between the populated eastern states and the coast, it was an important place to stop, rest and restock supplies. However, because of the impending arrival of Johnston's Army, the leadership of the church issued orders to all settlements not to sell food stuffs to any gentiles. The church leaders also went to great pains to convince the various Indian leaders to join the Mormons to help repel the US Army. The Indians were told to join the Mormons and help fight Johnston's Army, or that army would kill all the Indians as well.

One can imagine the hardships this must have created for those unlucky travelers who were caught up in the middle of this Utah problem. One of these groups of wagons was called the *Fancher Train*. It was a loosely knit group of several independent elements who had joined forces in Utah to travel in greater safety. The leader was Charles Fancher. He had crossed the country in 1855, selected and made arrangements to buy a large tract of land, and returned east in 1856 to bring his family and friends to join him in settling in California. They had a reported $4000 in gold coins, a large herd of cattle and horses and 11 well-stocked wagons. There were 11 families, with 29 children; a total of 65 people. Traveling with the Fancher Train was a group of horsemen with their supply wagons. They called themselves the *"Missouri Wildcats."*

Quoting now from Juanita Brooks' book on John D. Lee; *"This group all arrived in Salt Lake City on August 3 and 4, and mindful of the fate of the Donner Party in 1846, decided to take the southern route. They followed a few days behind President George A. Smith on his journey south ordering the people to keep their grain and not to sell a kernel to any gentiles. The Fancher Train was well-to-do; they had cash to pay or goods to trade, but no one would sell. The attitude of the Mormons all along the way was one of belligerence and hostility, aggravated by the attitude of the group of "Missouri Wildcats", who spoke of the Mormon leaders with scorn, and boasted of what they had done in Missouri."* This was the way things shaped up in Utah in the late summer and early fall of 1857.

As the Fancher Train moved south through the state, one thing after another aggravated the situation. The Mormons wouldn't sell them anything, and the emigrant train, especially the Wildcats, did or said things to upset the Mormons. Finally the emigrants arrived in Cedar City, the last place on the road to California to get provisions. Since the locals wouldn't sell them anything, it's been said some of the Missourians helped themselves to some of the gardens. The local Mormon police tried to arrest some members of the party, but were just laughed at. So things continued to get worse.

"In the Sunday service at Cedar City on September 6, 1857, Stake President Isaac C. Haight spoke with bitterness of the coming of Johnston's Army, which he called an armed mob, and made pointed reference to the Fancher Train which had left only the day before. Following the regular service, a special priesthood meeting(men only) was called at which time the problems connected with the Fancher Train were discussed. Were they mice or men that they should take such treatment? Should they let such braggarts come into their midst and boast of the indignities they had heaped upon them in Missouri and Nauvoo? Should a man who would boast that he had the gun that 'shot the guts out of Old Joe Smith' go unpunished?" Such were the feelings of the people in Cedar City.

Finally at the meeting a resolution was passed, to the effect that *"We will deal with this situation now, so that our hands will be free to meet the army when it comes."* But then there was more discussion. Some wanted to do away with the emigrants who were the chief offenders; others preferring to let them all go and prepare themselves for the real war with Johnston's Army. Another resolution was presented to the effect that they should send a rider to Brigham Young seeking his council. It was passed, and they sent a rider(who returned late, and after the big event was over).

Still later a third resolution was passed, that of sending a messenger to John D. Lee at Harmony asking him to come and manage the Indians. At that time, Lee was an "Indian Farmer", or agent, and was second in command. Jacob Hamblin was the agent, but since he was in Salt Lake City, it was Lee who was called upon for advice. Lee had gotten on well with the Indians, and it's been said he spoke at least some of their language.

In the meantime, the Fancher Train had proceeded to a high meadow in the northern part of the Pine Valley Mountains. This was barely one day's drive from Cedar City. This place was called, and would always be known as, Mountain Meadows. They made camp near a spring and had plans to stay awhile to let their cattle recuperate, until the weather became cooler, so they could cross the desert in more comfort.

Meanwhile back in Cedar City, things were happening at a rapid pace, with horsemen hurrying back and forth between Cedar City and Parowan, and between Mountains Meadows and Cedar City. At that time, there were three men who were the most important leaders in the area. William H. Dame from Parowan, was appointed colonel commanding all the Iron County military. Isaac C. Haight was the Stake President, who lived in Cedar City. And John D. Lee, who was the acting Indian agent, in the absence of Jacob Hamblin.

The Mormons were successful in getting the Indians on their side at this time. It seems both groups had no need for these emigrants, but for different reasons. A band of Indians had followed the Fancher Train south from Holden in central Utah, and had hoped the Mormons would help them attack the wagon train, and steal the cattle and other needed items. This same band of Indians joined others in the area of Cedar City, and had asked Lee to join them for an attack at Mountain Meadows. It seems that Lee had gone back home at Harmony to set things in order, and promised the Indians he would return on Tuesday, September 8.

But the Indians were ready for action, and knowing they and the Mormons were on the same side, made a pre-dawn attack on the emigrant camp on the morning of September 8. The emigrants were caught by surprise, but were well-equipped and repulsed the attack. Later, Lee stated that 7 white men were killed, along with several Indians. When Lee joined the Indians on Wednesday the 9th, they were upset and excited. They insisted the Mormons join them to make another attack immediately. Lee wanted to go south and get help from the Santa Clara and Washington settlements, but about that time a group of whites from those communities came, and they decided to send a messenger to Cedar City and to Haight. Lee left at 2 pm.

In Cedar City, the bell rang out for the militia to gather. A statement was read that some of the emigrants had been killed, and they wanted volunteers to help bury them. But according to Brooks' story, a Nephi Johnson indicated a deception on the part of Isaac C. Haight. Johnson later suggested that Haight had said something to the effect that, *"Lee had suggested that they withdraw and let the emigrants go, and Haight sent word to Lee to clean up the dirty job he had started, and that he had sent out a company of men with shovels to bury the dead, but they would find something else to do when they got there."*

During the night of Wednesday the 9th, the military unit from Cedar City arrived at the Fancher camp. But at the same time, three emigrants had left camp under the cover of darkness and had gone to Cedar City to ask for help from the Mormons. As they neared their destination, and while watering their horses in a small stream, they were attacked by members of the Mormon Militia. One man was killed, and the other two scattered. It was later learned the remaining two men were killed by Indians at the Santa Clara crossing, down the Virgin River a ways. Again in Cedar City, the Mormon leaders gathered for council. It was decided to send John M. Higbee to Parowan in the night for advice from William. H. Dame.

Higbee returned the next day, Thursday the 10th, and delivered the message from Colonel Dame to Lee near the emigrant camp. The message indicated he should compromise with the Indians, allowing them to take all the cattle, then allow the emigrants to go. But then in the same message, he indicated if things couldn't be worked out, *"save women and children at all hazards"*. Lee was in a predicament, and with conflicting orders. What to do? Years later Lee insisted, *"that he had written orders to the effect that the emigrants must be decoyed from their shelter and all who were old enough to testify slain"*. Later in court, Klingensmith testified that "*Lee's instructions came through Higbee from Dame at Parowan"*. Klingensmith must have overheard the conversation between Higbee and Lee, *"Orders is from me to you that they are to be decoyed out and disarmed, in any manner, the best way you can."*

So there Lee was faced with a decision. The Indians and Mormons both wanted revenge. The Mormons felt they had rights to some kind of blood atonement, for the way the Missourians had treated them back in Far West. The Indians also wanted some of the cattle; and the Mormons knew the Fancher Party was a wealthy group and had all those wagons and household goods. Greed must have been a factor in what was to be the final decision.

Lee along with a William Bateman, carried a white flag into the emigrant camp and negotiations began. Lee told them that if those guilty men would come back to Cedar City and face charges, they would all be given protection. But to do this, they would all have to show good faith, and give up their arms. This the emigrants did, but ever since, people have wondered why they would give up their weapons? The day was Friday, September 11, 1857.

After the agreement was reached, all rifles and other weapons of the emigrants were loaded into one wagon, along with all children(17 in all) under the age of about 10 years. This wagon moved out in front. Then a second wagon was loaded up with the emigrants who had been wounded in the previous Indian attack. Some said there were two men and a women; others stated there were some older children in it as well.

Following the second wagon, were the women and older children walking in an unorganized group. Following them were the emigrant men, walking in single file, each escorted by an armed member of the Mormon Militia.

The idea was to save the small children, but have no witnesses. The first wagon went way out in front, so they could not see anything. Lee walked just in front of the second wagon, which was at least half a km behind the first. When the first wagon was just out of sight, somewhere near the marching men, the signal was given, *"Do your duty. Instantly all the guns were fired, and at the same moment the Indians leaped from their ambush and fell upon the women and [older] children. The teamsters with Lee, and their assistants killed the ones in the second wagon and threw the bodies out into the brush beside the road."* The plan was carried out to perfection, and was over with in a hurry. It was estimated 120 people were murdered.

Just after the massacre, the Indians stripped the bodies for clothing and valuables. Then Lee issued the order to let the Indians have what they had, but no more. They were to return to their camp where some beef was ready for supper. The men of the Mormon Militia then heard several speeches by Higbee, Lee and others, to the effect that they had defended Zion and their families well, and that they had carried out *"Gods wishes"*. The men were then ordered to stay the night and bury the bodies before leaving for home the next morning.

The wagon with the rifles and children moved on up the valley to the Hamblin Ranch where Rachel(Mrs. Lee No. 6) was living. She cared for the children and put them to bed. Lee came later, and during the night, Haight and Dame came to the ranch. The next morning, they all went to the Meadows and saw the ghastly site. The bodies were still being buried, in the same holes the emigrants had dug previously to protect themselves from the Indians.

Then there was an argument between Haight and Dame about the orders given. The orders were confusing alright! This is the way Juanita Brooks stated part of the argument in her book.

"We must report this to President Young," Dame was saying.

"How will you report it?" Haight wanted to know.

"I will report it just as it is, a full report of everything."

"And will you say that it was done under your orders?"

"No"

Haight was furious with rage.

"You know that you issued the orders to wipe out this company, and you cannot deny it! You had better not try to deny it! If you think you can shift the blame for this onto me, you're fooled! You'll stand up to your orders like a man, or I'll send you to Hell cross lots."

About this time Lee interrupted to tell them it was done now and that we should go on from here. When the men finished with the burial, they gathered at the nearby spring and washed up. Then they all gathered around and Isaac C. Haight addressed the men. They were to say nothing to anyone and block it from their minds. Then they gathered in a circle, with Dame, Haight, Lee and Higbee at the four corners, and pledged they would never discuss it with anyone. Finally everybody left, including Lee, who wouldn't return to Mountain Meadows until the day he died.

A few days later they all met in Cedar City, and since John D. Lee was closest to Brigham Young, he was assigned to travel to Salt Lake City with the news of the killings. He left September 20, and arrived on the 29th. He reported the event to Brigham Young, which was written down by Wilford Woodruff. At that time John D. reported it as a job done by Indians.

The emigrant children were put into different homes and cared for. As far as they were concerned, it was Lee and the other Mormons who had saved *them* from the Indians--the Indians being the ones who killed their parents. The wagons and other contraband were placed in the Bishops warehouse to be given out to needy Mormon families.

In the months and years after the massacre everything went about as normal, given the circumstances. Lee took wife Number 17, a 22 year old girl from England, on January 7, 1858, when he was age 46. This was Emma Batchelor, the one who would accompany John D. to the bottom end of the Paria River in 1871, to set up a home at Lonely Dell, later to be known as Lee's Ferry.

Later on, Lee was involved in setting up the Cotton Mission on the Santa Clara River, near present day St. George. While in the area, John D. stopped in Washington(just east of St. George), and bought some land, including a house in town, where he soon had two of his wives. And speaking of wives, still later in 1858, Lee seemed to be courting a young girl named Mary Ann. He apparently proposed to her, but she refused. She even wrote two letters of protest to Brigham Young. In January of 1859, he mentions in his diary, that she wanted instead to marry John D's oldest son, which she did.

It was in August of 1858, and after peace had finally been arranged between the Mormons, and Johnston's Army and the Federal Government, that a George A. Smith and James McKnight, both church officials, went to southern Utah, and made out two reports on the massacre. The reports didn't amount to much, because everyone remained silent.

In the mean time, Lee lived at the fort in Harmony most of the time, where he had about four of his wives. Since there were lots of travelers passing through Utah at that time, he took advantage of the situation, and set up a *caravansary or way station,* to accommodate the wagon trains. Harmony was in the right place. They got most of their business in the fall and early winter. For a couple of years after the massacre, things went well for John D., but then things gradually changed.

According to Juanita Brooks, in *"April [1859] word came that Judge Cradlebaugh was on his way to investigate the Mountain Meadows Massacre, accompanied by a force of two hundred soldiers. Jacob Forney, the new Indian agent, came ahead to gather up the surviving children that they might be returned to their relatives in the east. They took Charley Fancher from the Lee household, although he was reluctant to go, and in line with the policy followed by all who had kept any of the children, Lee made out a bill to the government for his care."* With this, the beginning of the federal investigation, John D. Lee went into hiding, and was on the run for most of the next 18 years.

Judge Cradlebaugh and his group arrived at Cedar City in May of 1859, and set up camp in a big field about 2 1/2 kms from town. His assignment was to *"collect and bury the bones of the slain emigrants, and to arrest as many participants in the massacre as he could catch."*

The judge brought warrants for the arrest of a half-dozen of the leaders, and he wanted information concerning others who were involved. He found the local people reluctant to talk, for none knew anything for a certainty, and if they did, they would not betray their brethren into the hands of the enemies of the church.

A few did want to talk, but feared the consequences. At least one participant came to the judge secretly late at night and told the story of that tragic day, giving some names and details, and begging for protection and anonymity. The burden of the crime was more than he could bear."

Because many of the participants were either in hiding or had gone to different states, the judge was unable to make a single arrest. There was eventually a reward of $5000 offered for the arrests of Dame, Haight, Higbee, Klingensmith, or Lee. But no one ever turned any of them in. After spending a month in the area, the judge gave up the search, and returned to Salt Lake City.

In the years of 1860 and 1861, things went well for John D. He had two homes; one in Harmony, the other in Washington(near St. George), and nearly all the wives he wanted. Both places were opened as caravansaries and taverns, and business was good.

Right at the end of 1861, there was a stormy period which lasted from December 25 until the beginning of February, 1862. This was a disaster for everyone in the region, and especially for John D. Lee and his families. The fort they had been living in at Harmony was made of mud, and it literally melted away. During the first part of February, they were all trying to move out of the Harmony Fort, and into some new dwellings at nearby New Harmony. But before they could all get moved, the roof of part of the building caved in, killing two of Lee's children.

Down at Washington, things were just as bad. John D. had just recently erected a molasses mill, which had earned him good money the previous fall. It had been swept away, and the machinery buried in sand and mud. Because of this 40-day-storm, it took Lee about four full years to get back to the financial position he had been in before the floods.

In 1866, John D. finally was on his feet again and doing better. In that year he took his last wife, Ann Gordge, who was from Australia and just 18 years of age. Later in the same year, he lost his first bride, Aggatha, who died of a lingering illness. This was a sad occasion for Lee, and seemed to be a sort of beginning of the end for him.

It was about this time that the people of Harmony began giving him untold misery. *"Whisperings about the massacre continued; the stories became more numerous and highly colored. In many ways his neighbors showed their disapproval--by turning their cattle into his grain fields, interfering with his water ditches, and making snide remarks to his wives or children. He always attended church, he was first to fill the assignment made by Brigham Young to get out poles for the new telegraph line, he was prompt in paying his tithes. At Parowan and Cedar City, he was often called upon to speak at church, and at Kanarra he was held in high esteem. Perhaps his very industry, his driving use of his family and hired help, his shrewd trading, his ability to amass property and to live well made his neighbors all the more critical of him."*

In the fall of 1867, he made a trip to Salt Lake City, with a herd of goats belonging to Brigham Young, his adopted father. When he returned in December, he found his estate falling apart. Without Aggatha, and with his two oldest sons away on missions, there had not been the same enthusiasm as had been the case earlier.

It was in the late 1860's, that trouble began to brew for Brigham Young and the church leadership, and since John D. was always a strong supporter of the President, he began to feel the pinch as well. In 1868, there appeared in Salt Lake City a new publication, the *Utah Magazine*. This, as it turned out, was a voice for those who were becoming discontented with the church leaders and their policies. Some of the unrest resulted in a number of excommunications in the northern part of the state. Many of these people wanted to be members of the church, but were simply critical of the leaders; thus they were booted from the church.

The original complaint against Young was, he got too involved with their financial dealings; but later they condemned Young for condoning murder. During this period, there were some mysterious deaths in Salt Lake City. Dr. K. Robinson was assassinated in 1866; John V. Long, former secretary of Brigham Young, was found dead in a ditch in April, 1869; and Newton Brassfield was murdered on one of the main streets of Salt Lake in April 1866. These men were part of the group generally known as the *Godbeites*, after it's chief spokesman, W. S. Godbe.

One of their worst complaints was that Brigham Young gave public recognition to men who had participated in the Mountain Meadows Massacre. The *Utah Reporter*, published in Corrine(in the middle of northern Utah's gentile country), *"ran a series of open letters addressed to Brigham Young, demanding that those guilty of that outrage be brought to justice. The articles were signed by "Argus," who claimed to have lived in Southern Utah and learned the facts from some of the participants."*

During the winter of 1869-70, Lee defended Brigham Young by visiting many communities in southern Utah, to as far north as Fillmore, and by making speeches in Young's behalf.

In September of 1870, Brigham Young led a small group of men to explore areas east of the southern Utah settlements. Lee joined this group, and was assigned the jobs of locating the best route(as they were heading into new country without roads), and making camps along the way. William H. Dame was in charge of preparing meals.

Their route went through Panguitch, south to Roundy's Station(now called Alton), then down Johnson Canyon. At some point along the way, Brigham Young had a private talk with John D. He was urging Lee to move. Quoting again from Juanita Brooks book, Young said, *"I should like to see you enjoy peace for your remaining years. Gather your wives and children around you, select some fertile valley, and settle out here."*

John D. Lee. Picture was taken December 26, 1857, not long after the Mountain Meadows Massacre. (Edna Lee Brimhall foto)

Along the way they met, and were joined by John W. Powell. The party traveled east from the bottom of Johnson Canyon to the Paria River. They got to as far as the Peter Shirts(Shurtz) settlement of Rock House, and found a small patch of green corn and some squash. Lee was not impressed and made the statement, *"I wouldn't bring a wife of mine to such a place as this."* After the visit to the Paria River, they came to the conclusion there was little there to attract future settlements, and left. On their return, the party surveyed and laid out the site of Kanab, to be settled by some of those same men(one group had already tried to settle Kanab in about 1865, but had left on account of the Black Hawk War). After the lots were numbered, the settlers each drew a number from a hat to select his home site.

Brigham Young wanted Levi Stewart to set up a sawmill to make lumber to build Kanab. Levi stated he had worked with Lee before, and would like to have him as a partner again. John D. reluctantly said yes, out of sheer obedience to the church leader. The group then returned to the southwest Utah settlements via Pipe Springs.

Lee immediately set to work to sell his property and settle accounts. He put up for sale and sold his holdings in Harmony, but kept the Washington property; leaving several of his wives there until he could get back later. He started the trip to Kanab with wife Rachel and her children, 4 wagons, and 60 head of stock. The route taken was up through the canyon via Rockville, then over the plateau, and finally down to Kanab. It took 10 days to travel the very rough 150 kms.

From Kanab they moved on to the east to what is today Johnson, about 16 kms east of Kanab. They then went north up Johnson Canyon to a moderately high grassy valley now called Skutumpah. This was to be their new home, but they were to live temporarily a little above Skutumpah where the sawmill was to be located. It was about 15 kms to a site on Mill Creek where they built a camp. It was in late October, 1870, that he first built a cabin for Rachel.

When the engineer and surveyor arrived, they quickly set up the sawmill, but almost immediately it broke down. Someone would have to return to Parowan for a new part. With Rachel safe in the new cabin, Lee left to get another part of his family. He met a second family group at Pipe Springs--it was one of his son-in-laws and several children, along with 3 wagons and 40 head of cattle. At that time, in mid-November, 1870, he was handed a letter which had to do with his excommunication from the Mormon Church! It was dated October 8, 1870. At that time he mentioned it to no one.

The group went straight for Skutumpah, set up a tent for a temporary home, and went upcanyon to Rachel's cabin. Help from Kanab finally came in early December, and they worked fast and furious, because of the coming winter. The work at the sawmill was so fast the wagons coming and going from Kanab couldn't keep up. On December 13, news came of a disastrous fire in Kanab; the fort had burned to the ground, and 6 members of the bishop's family were killed. That ended the winter logging operation in the upper Skutumpah area.

John D. left Rachel and the others, and made a trip back to Washington, where he had a cold reception from his wives and children. The next morning he went to St. George to speak to Brigham Young, who was in his usual winter home, about his excommunication. He pleaded his case saying that he had been loyal to him and the church, and that now he was being singled out to bear the guilt of the massacre. He also stated that the decision to attack the Fancher Train was a mutual agreement between the highest church leaders in the area. After the meeting, Lee left and returned to Harmony, where he was invited to speak in church on Christmas Day, 1870.

Upon his return to Washington, he received a note from a high church official, stating, *"If you will consult your own safety & that of others, you will not press yourself nor an investigation on others at this time least you cause others to become accessory with you & thereby force them to inform upon you or to suffer. Our advice is, Trust no one. Make yourself scarce & keep out of the way."*

After these kind words, and on January 2, 1871, John D. set out once again for Skutumpah, this time with Caroline(Mrs. Lee No. 4), and her 8 children. It took them 15 days to reach Skutumpah this time, because of the heavy snows and poor travel conditions. Upon arriving, the whole family set to work cutting trees and sawing lumber in order to build and finish a large home for Caroline. When that was completed, they dismantled Rachel's cabin, and reconstructed it again down at Skutumpah. By the first of March, they began the third house, but about that time, Emma, wife No. 17, came up in an empty wagon. She was distressed, trying to decide which way to go--whether to stay with John D. or leave him for someone else. She decided to stay with her husband.

Soon after this and as the sawmill was roaring full blast, Lee sold his interest in the site. With all the lumber he needed, he continued to work at Skutumpah, until he had finished four homes, each with wood floors, shingle roofs, and glass windows. In June, 1871, he made another quick trip back to St. George to attend to business. While there he worked to sell out his Washington property, and bring the rest of his family to Skutumpah.

Enroute, and in Johnson Canyon, he met Isaac C. Haight, who was also in hiding. Together they went to Kanab, but waited outside town, while Jacob Hamblin and John Mangum brought them food, and more importantly, news. The news this time was that the federal authorities were clamping down on polygamists, and they were advised to transfer all their property to their wives. Lee set out to do this at once, naming Rachel Woolsey, Polly Young, Lavina Young, Sarah Caroline Williams, and Emma Batchelor as recipients. All of his other wives had deserted him by that time. But the real heart breaking news was that he was *ordered by the church* to take one or two of his wives, and move down to the Colorado River at the mouth of the Paria River. That was in August of 1871.

This was John D. Lee's greatest decision. But he would obey. He had 5 wives; which two would he take? He was heading for some wild country, and would end up in the middle of the desert and be in country controlled by Navajos. Problems would be immense, but even though he had been excommunicated, he still had the secret backing of Brigham Young. After all, it was Young who had ordered him to go.

The first wagons rolled out of Skutumpah in November of 1871. It consisted of 3 wagons, 57 head of livestock of various kinds, and Caroline and her family. At their first camp in lower Johnson Canyon, Jacob Hamblin joined them. He knew the country better than anyone, and he and Lee had a long discussion on the best route to take. It was decided to have the wagons head down what was to be called later the *Honeymoon Trail*, while John D. and 14-year old son Ralph, would take the cattle to the Paria, and drive them straight down the canyon.

At the Paria River, and perhaps it was at Rock House(?), he met Tom Adair and John Mangum, and was happy to have these two men join him. The going downriver was more difficult than anyone had anticipated.*"They spent 8 days on the trail, much of the time in water. Two days and one night they traveled without stopping because there was no place to camp When their provisions were gone, they shot a cow that had become hopelessly mired in quicksand and cut steaks from her, living for the next few days on a meat diet."*

Upon arriving at the mouth of the Paria, they found no wagons. Brigham Young had sent out a work crew to build a road, but neither the work crew nor Caroline had reached the Paria. Adair and Mangum return up the Paria River to Rock House via the Ute, or Dominguez Trail, while Lee and Ralph headed around the Vermilion Cliffs hoping to meet their wagons enroute. Because it was unfamiliar country, John D. got lost himself, and ended up returning all the way to Skutumpah.

The next day John D. and wives Emma and Rachel, and several wagons, headed out to find Caroline. Below Johnson, they found one broken-down wagon, and knew she had gone to Kanab instead. She had changed her mind, and had decided to go and stay there the winter and to give birth to another child, rather than go into the wilderness alone.

Back on the road again, the new contingent made it to the Colorado River on December 23, 1871. The next morning, when they all had a chance to look around, Emma said," oh what a lonely dell". And for ever more the name of the small settlement or ranch at the mouth of the Paria has been called Lonely Dell.

The first thing to do at the lower Paria was to build a house. The first shelter was a dugout up against the hill, made of rock, and would later be a cellar. The second was a rock building with a door and two windows. When the two shelters were finished, John D. rode upcanyon a ways to check on his cows. When he returned, he found Emma with a new baby, which was born on January 17, 1872. They named her Francis Dell Lee.

The very next day, January 18, they saw Navajos across the river. They wanted Lee to help them across. John D. and Rachel first had to work on one of John W. Powell's boats, which had been left there in 1869 on his first Colorado River Expedition. After repairs, Lee and Rachel made the first ferry crossings. It took three trips to get all the Navajos across. They later made some trades, Lee and the families ended up with blankets, cloth for making clothing, and other needed items. The Navajos got two horses, a mule and a colt.

In April, 1872, a group of miners came into camp, and the Lee family helped accommodate them. Emma cooked, in exchange for their help in building up the place, and for some needed tools. It was at about this time it was decided they would build two places; one at Lonely Dell, the other at the springs known as The Pools, or Jacob Pools, and later Rachel's Pools. They were 32 kms apart, but Jacob Pools would be a welcome stop for travelers who were making the long journey from Utah to Arizona. It must be remembered that Lee was sent there to set up a ferry and provide food, shelter and accommodations for travelers, many of who would be Mormons. The church at that time was expanding into Arizona, and Lee, although officially excommunicated, was instrumental in this expansion.

By early May 1872, Rachel moved. The first shelter at Jacob Pools was of mud and willows, and didn't give much shelter. On June 2, a group of engineers of the Powell Survey, passed through the area and fotographed Rachel's first little willow shack. This was a different group than Powell's river expedition.

In was on July 13, that Major Powell and his survey crew landed at Lonely Dell with the boat Cañonita, and were out of about everything except coffee and flour. Emma cooked for them and both groups shared what they had; the expedition members enjoying Emma's vegetables.

John D. was in and out of Lonely Dell and Jacob Pools. He had to help build shelters and go north to get supplies from the settlements. This was all fine, because as long as he was on the move, it would be difficult for the authorities to track him down. At that time the federal people were always after the "cohabs", or polygamists, and a bit later they were after Lee especially for the Mountain Meadows Massacre.

On December 16, 1872, a man named Heath came with a load of lumber for the purpose of building a ferry. While he and a crew were in the process of building a boat, John D. was at Rachel's place making a fine home. He had hired Elisha Everett to help do the rock work, for there was no other material there with which to build. This new home was mostly completed on Christmas Day. It measured about 9 x 11 meters, had two doors, two bedrooms, a kitchen, a parlor and covered with a wooden roof. Nearby was a cellar. If you're there today, you can still see the remains of this 1872 dwelling, just above one of the springs north of Jacob Pools. Most people call this place at the springs Rachel's Pools, as opposed to Jacob Pools, which is about a km to the south, southwest of her home site. At least the USGS maps put Jacob Pools out in the valley a ways, and on what was likely the actual route of the Honeymoon Trail. See the hiking section and Map 29, Sand Hill Crack, for the location.

The ferry boat was completed by January 11, 1873. Counting the Lee family and work crews, there were 22 people in all at the ferry site, and they all took a ride in the new boat, which they called "The Colorado." A little later, on February 1, a group of 12 men used the ferry for the first time. They were heading south to explore the Little Colorado River country for the church. From February 1873 until about November 1874, John D. Lee was the ferryman at what then and now is called Lee's Ferry. The first company of settlers on their way south arrived in April, 1873. They were charged $3.00 a wagon, and $.75 a horse for the service. For those who didn't have the money, payment was made in food or supplies, so things worked out well for the new ferryman.

In the summer of 1873, a message came from Kanab that a unit of 600 soldiers were on their way to Lee's Ferry to set up a permanent camp. This spooked Lee pretty bad, so he swam a horse across the Colorado River, and headed south to Moenkopi. While at Moenkopi, John D. met Jacob Hamblin and later they made a deal for a swap. They agreed to trade places; Lee's or rather, Rachel's home and holdings at

The Pools, for Jacob's claim at Moenave, near Moenkopi. In the fall, Jacob would help Rachel make the move down into Arizona. As it turned out, the story of the soldiers coming to Lee's Ferry wasn't true.

For about a year, things went well and uneventful. Then came the fall of 1874. A sheriff Stokes had warrants for the arrest of eight men who were the leaders of, and had participated in, the Mountain Meadows Massacre. By then the name of John D. Lee was at the top of the list. The Sheriff was familiar with Lee's habits, and was aware of where his wives lived. At the time, Caroline lived in Panguitch. It was on a visit to this wife, that Lee was captured. This was in November of 1874. They took John D. to Beaver in a wagon. He was there in jail from November 10, until July 23, 1875, when the trial for the massacre at Mountain Meadows began.

At the trial, the indictment included William H. Dame, Isaac C. Haight, John D. Lee, John M. Higbee, George Adair Jr., Elliot Wilden, Samuel Jukes, P.K. Smith, and William Stewart. Because everybody involved had sworn to secrecy, no one would testify except Philip Klingensmith. As it turned out Klingensmith's testimony was rather accurate and precise. The defense made the point, *"that while Lee was present and might have participated, he was there by command of his superiors, both military and ecclesiastical, whose orders in this time of military rule would be death to disobey. While they admitted the facts of the massacre and all its unbelievable horror, they placed the responsibility upon the Mormon Church and its doctrine that men were justified in 'avenging the blood of the Prophets' as a part of their duty to God."*

In the end it was a hung jury. The eight Mormons being for acquittal, the four gentiles for conviction. This meant another trial. This time Lee would be held in Salt Lake City. But this meant hardship for his families. Rachel left Moenkopi for the Utah settlements; Caroline was in Panguitch; Lavina and Polly remained at Skutumpah; and Emma stayed on at Lonely Dell. As for the ferry, the church sent Warren Johnson and his family to Lonely Dell to take charge of that operation.

John D. Lee left Beaver on August 9, 1875, and was taken to Salt Lake City. He was kept in the state penitentiary, which at that time was in the area of present-day Trolley Square. As one might expect, Lee was a model prisoner, and ended up with many privileges. At various times he taught other inmates how to read, was a kind of doctor, and was even entrusted with some keys to the place. For some reason, he was released on May 11, 1876, on $15,000 bail. He was to appear in Beaver in about four months for the trial.

In the period before the second trial, John D. traveled around visiting his various wives and families. He was at Lonely Dell in August. His sons had tried to talk him in to going to Mexico to escape, but by doing so he had insisted, he would be admitting guilt. In late August of 1876, he left the ferry and headed for Skutumpah via the Ute or Dominguez Trail. Just after he left, a messenger came via the Honeymoon Trail, with word from the church authorities counciling Lee to jump bond and leave the country. The church would assume the full responsibility to the bondsmen. But he missed the message.

In Beaver, the second trial began in September, 1876. For some reason the atmosphere of this trial was totally different. Twelve jurors were selected, all in good standing in the church. During the trial, seven witnesses were called, again all good members. They were all now willing to talk about the whole thing. The witnesses told of John D. Lee's participation, and that of Klingensmith's, but he had immunity since he had turned state's evidence. They also spoke of how Haight and Higbee were involved, but they were both dead at the time of the trial. It was very clear that something had been worked out so that everyone pointed the finger at John D. Lee. To resolve the issue, perhaps it was necessary to have a scapegoat, so that life for the church could go on as normal(?). Lee never did take the stand or defend himself. He sat through the trial in silence.

At the end and when the jury came back, the statement read; *"Guilty of murder in the first degree."* Lee immediately wrote to Emma for more money, to take the case to a higher court. His attorney, W.W. Bishop felt he had been sold out. Meanwhile two petitions were circulated in southern Utah, asking that the Governor give him clemency. The Governor said he would consider the move, if Lee would speak up and tell all, and make an attempt to implicate those above him. But Lee remained silent, and there was no clemency.

So on March 23, 1877, John D. Lee was taken back to Mountain Meadows, the scene of the crime. There were a number of people there, including James Fennimore, the fotographer, who Lee had known and made friends with at Lonely Dell. A foto of the place shows John D. sitting on his coffin. Lee was blindfolded, but his hands were free, when the five shots were fired. He fell back in the coffin, and it was closed and loaded into a wagon. He was then carried to Panguitch and buried in the cemetery just east of town and south of the highway.

To get to Mountain Meadows today, drive west out of Cedar City toward Beryl Junction and Enterprise, then turn south on the road running toward St. George. About halfway between Enterprise and Central, and off the paved road a ways to the west, is a new memorial built in 1990. From this hillside overlook, drive west down a good gravel road to a monument where a number of those killed were buried. From St. George, drive north toward Veyo and Central, in the direction of Enterprise. The original plaque placed there in 1932 reads:

MOUNTAIN MEADOWS
A FAVORITE RECRUITING PLACE ON THE OLD SPANISH TRAIL

In this vicinity, September 7-11, 1857, occurred one of the most lamentable tragedies in the annals of the West. A company of about 140 Arkansas and Missouri emigrants led by Captain Charles Fancher, enroute to California, was attacked by white men and Indians. All but 17, being small children, were killed. John D. Lee, who confessed participation as leader, was legally executed here March 23, 1877. Most of the emigrants were buried in their own defense pits.

In 1990, there was a new memorial erected on a hill overlooking Mountain Meadows with the names of those who died in the massacre. There was also a new plaque put on the old monument where the Fancher Party had camped and where some of those killed are buried. A dedication ceremony took place on September 15, 1990. The new plaque on the old monument reads:

MOUNTAIN MEADOWS MASSACRE

This stone monument marks the burial site for some of those killed in the Mountain Meadows Massacre in September 1857. The Baker-Fancher Party camped here--a well-known stopping place along the Old Spanish Trail.

The first monument was erected at this location in May 1859 by Brevet Major James H. Carleton and 80 soldiers of the first Dragoons from Fort Tejon, California. Assisting were Captains Reuben P. Campbell and Charles Brewer, with 270 men from Camp Floyd, Utah. The bones of about 34 of the emigrants were buried here. The remains of others were buried one and one-half miles to the north, near the place of the massacre.

The original monument--consisting of a stone cairn topped with a cedar cross and a small granite marker set against the north side of the cairn--was not maintained. The Utah Trails and Landmarks Association built a protective wall around what remained of the 1859 monument and, on September 10, 1932, installed a bronze marker. That marker was replaced with the present inscription in conjunction with the dedication of the nearby memorial on September 15, 1990.

During the dedication ceremonies of the new plaque and memorial, no apologies were given and it seemed everyone, especially the Mormons, were trying to put this one behind them as far as possible. It also seems that who ever made the new plaque is trying to put the blame for the massacre as far behind them as possible too.

At Mountain Meadows, March 28, 1877. John D. Lee sits on his coffin awaiting execution by a firing squad. At his left the Deputy U.S. Marshal reads the death warrant. On horseback in the background are Lee's sons. They were kept at a distance as it was feared they would attempt a last minute rescue of their father. The firing squad is hidden under the canvas at far right.
(Library of Congress)

The tombstone of John D. Lee in the cemetery at Panguitch, Utah.

The monument to the Fancher Party at Mountain Meadows.

History of Ghost Towns of the Paria River

Bryce Valley Ghost Towns

One of the best sources for the history of the first settlements in the upper Paria River drainage, which today is called Bryce Valley, is *The Geology and Geography of the Paunsaugunt Region-Utah*, by Herbert E. Gregory. The following account is adapted from his early geologic explorations and travels throughout the region.

In the 1860's and 1870's, there were surveying parties traveling across parts of the upper Paria and Escalante Rivers, and they noted several large valleys which looked promising for settlement. One of the surveyors was A. H. Thompson, who said the upper valley of the Paria River was well-watered, had good soil, and a good climate. He also noted there were coal beds close by and good range for grazing livestock.

Because of such reports, the first pioneer white settlers in the upper Paria Valley were the families of David O. Littlefield and Orley D. Bliss, who on December 24, 1874, laid out farms near the junction of the Paria River and Henrieville Creek. With the arrival of eight additional families in 1875, the original cluster of log houses at the base of the red cliffs grew into a small settlement called Cliff Town. Since those earliest days, the name gradually changed to **Clifton**. The old Clifton townsite is located about 3 kms due south of Cannonville.

One of the new settlers, Ebenezer Bryce, who is said to have come to Clifton in 1875 or 1876, decided they needed more room and looked for another location to farm. He selected a site farther upstream in what was known then as Henderson Valley. This new settlement was first called **New Clifton**. Bryce, in association with a Daniel Goulding and others(1878-80), constructed an irrigation canal 11 kms long, planted orchards, and took up livestock raising.

It was during this time, and when Eb Bryce ran cattle into the canyons to the west, that Bryce Canyon received it's name. An early-day saying around the region, which Bryce is given credit for, makes a statement about herding cattle into the area which is now called Bryce Canyon National Park. That statement was, *"It's a hell of a place to lose a cow"*.

Bryce left New Clifton in 1880, while Goulding left in 1883, selling their holdings to Isaac H. Losee, Orville S. Cox, and Ephraim Cottall. They renamed the site **Losee**. The Losee townsite is located about 3 kms due east of the present-day town of Tropic, in what is now called East Valley.

About two years after settlement, the people in the little town of Clifton found themselves too closely hemmed in between the cliffs and the bank of the Paria, and their farm lands in the process of destruction by flood water. So in 1877 Clifton was abandoned, with most of its settlers going to a new site about 3 kms north. This new town was named **Cannonville,** after a high dignitary of the Mormon Church, George Q. Cannon.

Only seven graves are in the Losee Cemetery.

Map 32, Bryce Valley Mines and Ghost Towns: Georgetown, Clifton and Losee

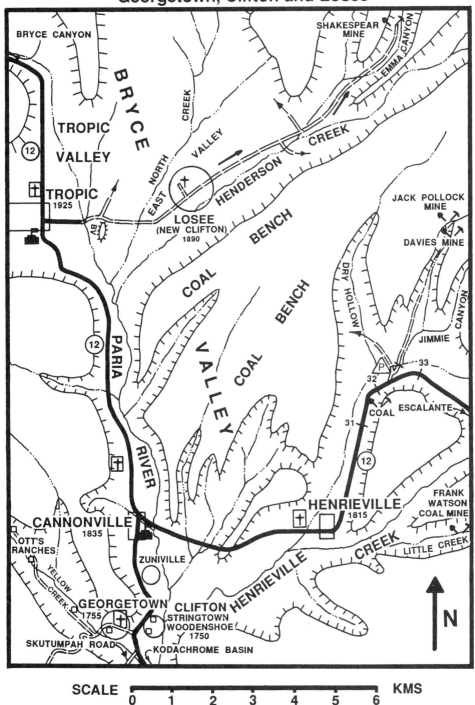

BRYCE CANYON

SHAKESPEAR MINE

EMMA CANYON

BRYCE

TROPIC VALLEY

(12)

NORTH CREEK

EAST VALLEY

HENDERSON CREEK

✝ TROPIC 1925

BV

X

LOSEE (NEW CLIFTON) 1890

COAL BENCH

BENCH

JACK POLLOCK MINE

DAVIES MINE

(12)

PARIA

COAL VALLEY

COAL

RIVER

DRY HOLLOW

JIMMIE CANYON

P
32   33

31   COAL   ESCALANTE

(12)

✝

HENRIEVILLE 1815

FRANK WATSON COAL MINE

CANNONVILLE 1835

OTT'S RANCHES

ZUNIVILLE

✝

HENRIEVILLE CREEK

LITTLE CREEK

YELLOW CREEK

GEORGETOWN 1755

✝

CLIFTON STRINGTOWN WOODENSHOE 1750

N

SKUTUMPAH ROAD

KODACHROME BASIN

SCALE   0   1   2   3   4   5   6   **KMS**

While some of those who abandoned Clifton went to and settled Cannonville, three families headed east instead, and settled on Henrie Creek, about 8 kms east of Cannonville. This is present-day **Henrieville** and **Henrieville Creek,** named in honor of James Henrie, then-president of the Panguitch Stake of the LDS Church.

In 1886, Seth Johnson, Joseph and Eleazer Asay, Richard C. Pinney, and other stockmen took up lands on lower Yellow Creek about 5 kms southwest of Cannonville and thus became the pioneer settlers of **Georgetown.** Like Cannonville, this new ranching community, was named after George Q. Cannon.

It was during the early 1880's, Cannonville became center of prosperity for the entire valley. That's where the Mormon Church Ward was set up, and where the most prosperous cattlemen lived. Later on, in the early 1890's, people were beginning to move out of Georgetown on account of the lack of water. Shortly after 1894, the town was so small, it became part of the Cannonville Ward of the LDS church. A year or two later, it was all but deserted except for a ranch or two.

About the same time Georgetown was thriving, there were some families who moved back into the areas left abandoned in the former Clifton settlement. Perhaps it wasn't totally deserted in the first place. In the late 1880's and/or early 1890's, this small area received the nick-name of **Stringtown**. It seems there were a number of separate ranches strung out along the road between Cannonville and Georgetown; thus the name Stringtown. It was never incorporated into a town or an organized LDS ward or congregation.

If you talk to old timers in the Bryce Valley about early day settlements, they will always mention the name Woodenshoe. The man who knows a little more about it than anyone else, is Kay Clark of Henrieville. He recalls stories and history of his grandfather, Owen W. Clark. After the Clarks had moved into, then out of, the White House Cabin on the lower Paria, then had attempted to resettle at Adairville, they moved north again to Pahreah for several years. That place wasn't as promising as they had hoped, so again they moved, this time north to what was then Stringtown, which was actually part of Cannonville at the time. They lived there until 1896, then sold the farm to some Dutch people. This family was poor and often wore wooden shoes; thus the name **Woodenshoe** was attached to the area of the original settlement of Clifton.

Another interesting story about an early Bryce Valley settlement comes from Wallace Ott of Tropic. When he was a wee small boy of just two or three years of age, he remembered an event and place just south of Cannonville, in the same general area as Clifton, Stringtown and Woodenshoe. It seems that in about 1914 or 1915, there came into the valley a wagon train of Mormons who had fled Mexico. It was in August of 1912, that the Mormons of Chihuahua and Sonora had to leave, because of the Mexican Revolution and Poncho Villa. It must have taken them a couple of years to make it north to the Paria Valley, otherwise Wallace wouldn't have remembered the time.

They came in the fall of the year and asked if it was OK to make a temporary camp about one km south of Cannonville. Permission was granted and they simply made a half circle with their wagons and camped for the one winter. They were the poorest people Wallace had ever seen. Many were of large polygamist

Old cars rusting away at a ranch near the old site of Georgetown.

families and the church had to help out for a time. In the spring, they all set out in different directions looking for new homes. In the meantime, their camp had gotten the local nick-name of **Zuniville**.

Going back in history for a moment. By 1886 the increasing population of the valley was using about all the fields the available water would irrigate, but north of Cannonville there remained a large fertile valley of unirrigated land that was otherwise suitable for cultivation. To increase the arable area, in 1889 the people of Cannonville revived an old scheme outlined by Ebenezer Bryce back in 1880. That plan was to divert water from the East Fork of the Sevier River on top of the Paunsaugunt Plateau(top of Bryce Canyon) through a ditch or canal that would pass over the Pink Cliffs to the land in the upper Bryce Valley.

At the instigation of William Lewman, the locally financed Cannonville & East Fork Irrigation Co. was organized. A reservoir site was selected and a survey made for a feeder canal about 16 kms long. Maurice Cope was made boss of the project, and work began May 15, 1890. Anticipating the successful completion of the project, James Ahlstrom, C. W. Snyder and others, began building houses on land that the proposed ditch was intended to water. In 1891 a townsite was laid out called **Tropic**, allegedly after it's fine climate. On May 23, 1892, the new-found water was flowing through the townsite and onto the adjoining fields. This date marks more than a century of continuous habitation of Tropic, which is truly a man-made oasis.

This canal, known locally as the Tropic Ditch, is still used today, as it is the life blood of Tropic. It took two years of voluntary labor and hard work by 50 men, women and boys from Cannonville and the neighboring communities, to finish the project. It was mostly hand work with pick and shovel. The only payment received was a reliable water supply and a better place to make a home. The canal can be seen about 100 meters south of Ruby's Inn as you drive toward the entrance to the Bryce Canyon National Park; or in the middle part of Tropic Canyon, as it crosses under the highway.

Today in the area of Georgetown, one can find the cemetery which is just north of the road. It's still used today by some people who reside in Cannonville. It has some old graves dating from the last century. A little further down the road to the west, you'll see the remains of an old ranch, but this one dates from the 20th century, and isn't that historic. However there are a couple of old 1920's cars hidden in the sagebrush out back. Just across the road from this old homestead(to the northwest), are the foundations of an even older home, complete with the remains of a wooden pipeline.

There's nothing remaining of anything historic in the area of Clifton, Stringtown or Woodenshoe, however there are two very old cabins east of the paved road as you drive south out of Cannonville. They are out in the fields a ways and are clearly visible from the road. These may date from the later days of the Woodenshoe era, and are still used today as barns for livestock and storage.

If you drive due east out of Tropic and past the "BV" on the hillside, you'll be in the general area of New Clifton or Losee. There's nothing there today except the old Losee Cemetery. The author counted seven tombstones, only three of which could still be read. Two belonged to young children, the other an older woman. They all had died in 1889 or 1890.

To get to the cemetery, drive to about the middle of East Valley, and locate a narrow lane running north

Old cabin located in the area which was Clifton, Stringtown and Woodenshoe. This cabin may date from the Woodenshoe period.

from the main graveled road. To the left of this lane is a line of cottonwood trees. About 200 meters along this narrow lane from the main road and to the right, is the small cemetery site with a one-meter high fence around it. If you park on the road, then walk to the site and disturb nothing, no one should care if you cross their private land. The local farmers occasionally find stones or other old debris in the Losee area, but this graveyard is really the only thing to see.

Middle Paria River Ghost Towns--Pahreah

It was in December of 1869, when Jacob Hamblin was sent out by the Mormon Church to head a group in organizing an Indian farm somewhere on the Paria River. These first settlers did well and they built a guard house and a small corral, where men could cook and have safe lodging. By March, 1870, they had 2 1/2 kms of ditches and 800 meters of fence built, and had 8 Indians there helping and learning about agriculture. Some of the first information about this settlement comes in the form of a letter from Jacob Hamblin to Erastus Snow of the LDS church. It was dated March 27, 1870. Trouble is, the letter doesn't state where they settled; at the site of Pahreah, or at Rock House, where Peter Shirts(Shurtz) had made his homestead earlier. It was probably at Rock House(?)

In the story of John D. Lee, mention is made of a trip to the Paria River in September of 1870 by John D. Lee and Brigham Young. At Peter Shirt's settlement of Rock House they found some green corn and squash, but John D. didn't like the looks of the place and apparently refused to go there to live. The people there at that time must have been part of Jacob Hamblin's group.

Herbert E. Gregory thinks they went to Rock House, 8 or 9 kms below the later townsite of Pahreah, and settled there. Then three years later they were driven out by floods, and couldn't get water in their ditches or on the fields. At that time, about 1873 or 1874, they relocated; some went downstream as did Thomas Adair, to settle at what was to be known as Adairville, while others went north through The Box of the Paria River and founded the settlement of Pahreah.

Everyone seems to agree that a William Meeks was the leader and first bishop at Pahreah in the early years. The community did very well at first. They grew nut orchards, vineyards, vegetable farms, and raised cattle and sheep. In 1877, Pahreah was large enough to have organized an LDS ward by itself, and was part of the Kanab Stake. According to most accounts, by the spring of 1884, the number of people reached an all time high. At that time, there were 107 members of the Mormon church, plus a number of other cattlemen and about 20 Piute Indians living at Pahreah.

But there were a series of floods, the first of which was in 1883. It was followed by the severe winter of1883-84, then more flooding in the summer of 1884, which washed away farm houses and fields and converted the narrow stream channel into a wash that extended in places from canyon wall to canyon wall. This spelled doom for Pahreah. People started leaving. By September of 1884, only 48 people remained. The next year, 1885, the church ward was disbanded.

In the following years, people came and went, but mostly left. However, even in its declining

About the only thing left at the old Pahreah townsite in 1997, was this old chimney.

Map 33, Middle Paria River Mines and Ghost Towns: Pahreah, Rock House and Adairville

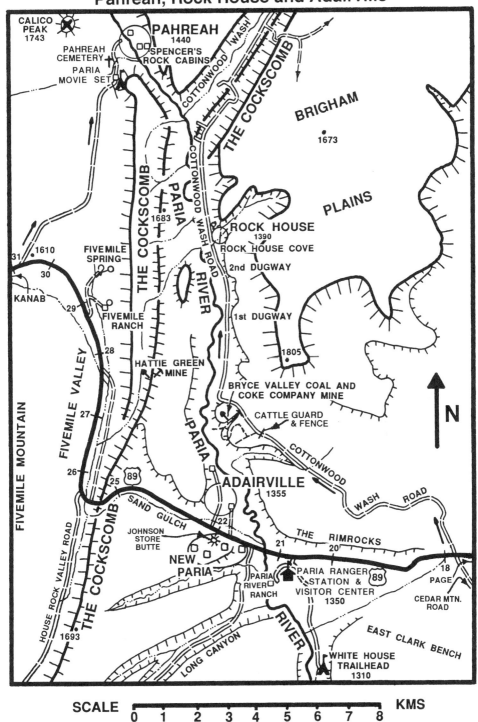

CALICO PEAK 1743
PAHREAH 1440
PAHREAH CEMETERY
SPENCER'S ROCK CABINS
PARIA MOVIE SET
COTTONWOOD WASH
THE COCKSCOMB
BRIGHAM
•1673
PLAINS
THE COCKSCOMB
PARIA
COTTONWOOD WASH ROAD
•1683
ROCK HOUSE 1390
ROCK HOUSE COVE
2nd DUGWAY
1st DUGWAY
RIVER
FIVEMILE SPRING
31 •1610
30
KANAB
29
FIVEMILE RANCH
28
HATTIE GREEN MINE
•1805
FIVEMILE VALLEY
FIVEMILE MOUNTAIN
27
PARIA
BRYCE VALLEY COAL AND COKE COMPANY MINE
CATTLE GUARD & FENCE
N
26
25 89
COTTONWOOD
WASH ROAD
ADAIRVILLE 1355
SAND GULCH
THE COCKSCOMB
HOUSE ROCK VALLEY ROAD
JOHNSON STORE BUTTE
22
NEW PARIA
THE RIMROCKS
21 20
PARIA RIVER RANCH
PARIA RANGER STATION & VISITOR CENTER 1350
89
18 PAGE
CEDAR MTN. ROAD
1693
LONG CANYON
RIVER
EAST CLARK BENCH
WHITE HOUSE TRAILHEAD 1310

SCALE   KMS
0 1 2 3 4 5 6 7 8

years, Pahreah received a post office on July 26, 1893, and Emily P. Adair became the first postmaster. Finally things got even worse, and the post office closed on March 1, 1915.

In 1912, promoter Charles H. Spencer brought his miners up from Lee's Ferry, and tried unsuccessfully to extract gold from the very colorful Chinle clay beds. This after the gold mining failure at the Ferry. In 1921, Spencer once again returned to Pahreah, this time to do some surveys for a proposed dam to be located in The Box of the Paria River, just downstream from the Pahreah townsite. Add this to the long list of failures for Spencer.

Throughout the early years of the 20th century, there were only one or two families living in or around the town. Their source of income was from farming and ranching, and to supply sheepmen who had large flocks in the region. One of the last settlers was a John Mangum. He lived in the area until about the mid-1930's, then finally left for Idaho. In the same time period as the Mangums, was a Jack Seaton who ranched and was the sheep supplier for awhile. According to Leola Scheonfeld of Kanab, Jack lived in a dugout just southwest of Pahreah for several years. Then on April 2, 1932, Jack Seaton traded his holdings at Pahreah, for a home and land in Henrieville. This trade was with Jim Ed Smith. For three years, the family of Jim Ed Smith, including his son Layton, lived in Pahreah.

Layton recalls the family then sold Pahreah to Roy Twitchell in March of 1935, after living there for only three years. Roy was old then and most of the work was done by his son Cecil. The Twitchells stayed on for several years, but it was a tough life. Finally, after a long winter in the early 1940's, the Twitchells moved out. In 1942, at least some of the land around old Pahreah was purchased by a man named Burge, but he never did live there. It was Cecil Twitchell and Herman Mangum who spent the last winter there. After 1942, no one ever lived in Pahreah.

Calvin C. Johnson of Kanab, mentions an interesting event at Pahreah during the summer of 1943. Movie makers went there and filmed a picture about Buffalo Bill and Geronimo. They had 300 Navajos, plus Joel McCrae, Anthony Quinn and Murene O'hara. They build a little dam across the Paria inside The Box to back water up during the shooting. You may still be able to see parts of that dam.

At old Pahreah today, is a corral, some fences and a couple of rock cellars. Just to the south less than half a km, are several rock structures and some remains of the sluicing operation dating from Spencer's time. One of these rock buildings is in relatively good condition.

To get to Pahreah today, drive along Highway 89 about halfway between Kanab and Page. From between mile posts 30 and 31, turn north and drive about 8 kms to the 1963 Paria Movie Set and a small campground with toilets and picnic tables(but no water). After another km or so, you'll come to the Pahreah Cemetery on the left. The one large tombstone lists 13 people buried there. The original grave markers are unreadable. Another km beyond the cemetery, is the end of the road at the edge of the river. Park at the sign, and walk across the river to the sites. Wear an old pair of shoes, or remove shoes, to wade in the usually ankle deep water of the Paria.

This is the monument located at the Pahreah Cemetery.

Rock House--Peter Shirts(Shurtz) Homestead

The very first white settler to make a home in the Paria River drainage was a man by the name of Peter Shirts(sometimes spelled Shurtz). Most of this information comes from an unpublished family document, **History of Peter Shirts and his Descendants,** by his grandson Ambrose Shurtz.

Peter was born in 1908 in St. Clair, Ohio. He married for the first time in 1831, then became a Mormon convert in 1832. In 1835, he worked on the Kirkland LDS Temple, and became a high

From the steep dugway on the road to old Pahreah, one can see the Paria Movie Set, and the site of Pahreah in the far background.

From the top of the Carlo Ridge, one has a fine view of the Pahreah Valley.

ranking church leader in 1844. Later he lived in Nauvoo, Illinois where he worked on the temple there.. He came to Utah in 1849, and became part of a group to settle in Parowan in 1851. In 1852, he helped built Shirts Fort just south of Cedar City. With John D. Lee, Shirts helped settle the area now known as St. George, but then helped survey the site for the future Las Vegas in 1955. He was apparently not part of the Mountain Meadows Massacre and was not a polygamist. Peter had 4 wives altogether, but only one at a time.

Shirts migrated to the Paria River in the spring of 1865 with his family--a wife and two children. The presumed site is about 8 or 9 kms downstream from the old Pahreah townsite, and on the east side of the river. In the back side of a cove he built his home up against a cliff, behind which was a cave. He walled up the front part with rocks, partly because rocks were so abundant, and logs weren't; and partly it's been said, so the Indians couldn't burn him out. The roof of the home was covered with flat slabs of rock, called flagstone, of which there is an abundant supply in the area. He enlarged the rear end of his cave to store grain and produce. This is how the place got the name Rock House.

One story says he built his house right over the ditch, so he could have water if under attack. But in the story by Ambrose, he says Peter dug a hole down to the water table right in the floor of his house. After he raised a good crop that first year, the Black Hawk War broke out, and hostilities erupted between Indians and white settlers all over the region.

On November 12, 1865, Erastus Snow, one of the leaders of the Mormon Church, wrote to all settlers in the region reminding them of the impending crisis and to obey their church military leaders. One of the main events which signaled the beginning of the Black Hawk War, was the killing of a Dr. Whitmore and Robert McIntyre by Indians at Pipe Springs, located southwest of Kanab. This happened in January of 1866. At the time of that attack, Peter Shirts was already besieged by Piute Indians, who killed or ran off all of his livestock. A militia force stationed in St. George, under the command of Col. MacArthur, attempted to rescue Shirts, but deep snows prevented a speedy march.

The military never got to the region until later, but in the meantime Shirts had outlasted the Indians, and by winter's end, was apparently in better condition than the attackers, who were half starved. He talked to the Indians, explaining that since they had run off and killed his oxen, he could no longer plow his ground. When the militia force arrived, they found Shirts behind a plow pulled by 6 Piutes. However, Shirts and his family returned, or were removed unwillingly, to Toquerville. On March 10, 1866, he gave a report of his adventures to Erastus Snow.

According to one story of the history of Rock House, March 1866, was the last time anyone lived at the Shirts Homestead. Later, on December 7, 1869, Jacob Hamblin headed a small group of settlers to organize an Indian farm of some kind on the Paria River. Some think they settled at Rock House.

The Paria Movie Set is now a tourist stop. A small water-less campground is nearby.

However, there's a little different story about Rock House, as told by Herbert E. Gregory, the geologist who did a lot of exploring in that part of the country in the 1920's. He claims that Shirts stayed right there on the land for three full years, instead of being marched off by the military in 1866. (Perhaps he went back after reporting to Snow in Toquerville?). He then picked up and left the country for the San Juan River. Gregory also states that Rock House was relocated in 1871(probably 1870?), by six families, who did well for a short time. In 1872, 11 more families came in and grew corn and sorghum. He quoted someone as stating," *In 1874, trouble with the ditches, caused the 15 families at Rock House to relocate above the hogback, at the present site of Pahreah.*"

To finish the story of Peter Shirts, he apparently was in the Cedar City area in the late 1860's, then by 1877, was wandering alone around the Four Corners area. He attempted to settle on lower Montezuma Creek near the San Juan River. Some of the Hole-in-the-Rock Expedition members met him somewhere in the Bluff, Utah, region during the winter of 1879-80, then he was with his son Don Carlos in Escalante in 1882. In the spring of that year he left with his burro packed with supplies and headed for Fruitland, New Mexico. Later that same year he got sick and died. He apparently is buried in the Fruitland cemetery.

To reach Rock House, or the Rock House Cove as it's now called on some maps, drive north from Highway 89, from between mile posts 17 and 18. This is the Cottonwood Wash Road. Drive about 15 kms. As you near the cove, you will pass along part of the road which is pushed up against the hillside by the river. About 1 1/2 kms past the first dugway, you'll pass still another, which is again pushed up against the hill on the east by the river. Just after this second dugway(less than one km), and on the right or east, is the Rock House Cove. It's in the western part of Section 4, T42S, R1W, on any USGS map.

You'll know you're there when you see one single cottonwood tree just east of the road, which is at the northern end of a large flat area. That tree is also near the north end of a 200 meter-long line of tamaracks. In this case, they're so large, they're almost like trees. No one can say for sure if this is the Shirts Homestead, but those tamaracks are the biggest this author has seen and in a line too straight for it to have occurred by accident. The author has never found any sign of the rock house, but most people who have seen the cove are convinced this is indeed the place. However, it's probable the tamaracks got there much later, because they were first known to exist in St. George only in 1880. Kay Clark, formerly of Henrieville, once stated he remembered a pile of rocks towards the south end of the line of tamaracks, but they're covered by sand now.

Adairville

Adairville is another of the tiny farming and ranching settlements along the middle Paria River. The site of this little cluster of ranches is just north of mile post 22, on present-day Highway 89, about

Looking west at the straight line of tamaracks in Rock House Cove. The Cockscomb
and Paria River are in the background.

halfway between Kanab and Page. This place is just east of The Cockscomb, whereas old Pahreah is just to the west of this same cockscomb ridge.

All sources agree that the year Adairville was first settled was in 1873 or 1874, by a group of cattlemen, led by Thomas Adair. Some of these settlers came down from Rock House, where Adair had originally settled. In the beginning, it too was prosperous, as they farmed the land, planted gardens and raised livestock. According to Gregory, there were 8 families at Adairville in 1878, but they had some of the same problems as the earlier settlers had upstream at Rock House and Pahreah. They had some minor floods, and couldn't get water to their fields, and the water in the river in the heat of summer didn't reach their settlement. Water in the Paria is reliable down to where it crosses The Cockscomb, but below The Box, it gradually seeps into the sands and disappears during early summer. So in 1878, those 8 families left, most of whom went upstream to Pahreah.

In the years after 1878, there was nearly always a rancher or two in the area. Kay Clark, said his grandfather built the cabin, which was later known as the White House, in 1887. This is downstream a ways from where the trailhead to the Lower Paria is today. After a year or two there, they moved upstream to the area of Adairville and lived there for a couple of years. After that, the family moved upstream to Pahreah for a while, then on up to Bryce Valley in the early 1890's.

After the Clarks left Adairville, it's not certain just what happened to the place for a number of years, but the late Elbert(Farmer) Swapp of Kanab, remembered some of the later history. Elbert believed the land around Adairville was abandoned from the 1890's until the 1930's. However, the Cross Bar Land and Cattle Company filed on water rights in the area in 1912.

Finally the Adairville area was homesteaded by Charley Cram and Charley Mace in the 1930's, but they sold out to Elbert and Orson Swapp in the early 1940's. From that point on, the Swapps have owned most of the land south of Highway 89. The Swapps built the brick and cement ranch house just to the southwest of the Paria Ranger Station & Visitors Center in the 1940's. Most people refer to this as the Paria River Ranch.

Some of the land just north of the highway, and right where Adairville was founded, was homesteaded in the late 1930's by a Sandal Findlay. He later sold out to Fay Hamblin and Floyd Maddox. Finally, the Frosts bought them out, and have owned that land ever since, leasing it to the MacDonald family in the 1980's. After Merril MacDonald passed away, his sons got out of the business. Just south of the place MacDonalds used to lease, is the Hepworth place. It's just north of the former rest area along the highway and northeast of the Johnson Store Butte. In the 1990's, Hepworth also leased some farm land from the Frosts, in conjunction with his public lands grazing rights.

Today, there's nothing left to see at the original Adairville townsite, except perhaps for some of the old trees, just west of the Hepworth place, and just north of mile post 22 and Johnson Store Butte. There is one grave in there somewhere, but it's private land, and permission would have to be granted

Looking south at the bridge over Bull Valley Gorge.

before entry can be made.

Across Highway 89 to the south, are now 6 or 8 or more new homes forming a rural settlement generally called **New Paria**. Those people commute to Page or Kanab to work each day.

This is the cave with pictographs in Starlight Canyon.

The Rimrocks, in the area just north of old Adairville and the Paria
Ranger Station & Visitor Center.

Geology of the Paria River Basin

While most people aren't really interested in geology, it's only a matter of time and one or more trips to the Colorado Plateau, before many begin to be hooked. All you have to do is look at a map of the lower 48 states, and you can see that many of our national parks and monuments are found on the Plateau.

The Colorado Plateau is a vast physiographic region covering the southeastern half of Utah, the northern half of Arizona, the northwestern corner of New Mexico, and the western fifth of Colorado. In other words, it covers the middle third of the Colorado River drainage system.

What makes the Colorado Plateau so unique are the flat lying rocks. During millions of years while the sediments were being laid down, the land remained relatively flat. Some times it was below sea level or was under the waters of a fresh water sea or lake. But always it remained relatively flat, even during this last time period when the entire region was uplifted to create what we have today. And what we have today, is a colorful and majestic canyon country unequaled anywhere.

Because much of the Plateau is dry and has very little vegetation, the rocks are laid bare, and can be examined by all. This is why so many people become interested in geology when visiting this part of the country.

The Paria River drainage is near the middle of the Colorado Plateau, and has at least its share of unique geologic wonders. It starts out at Bryce Canyon National Park and Table Cliff Plateau. Then there are canyons like Bull Valley Gorge, Round Valley Draw, the Buckskin Gulch, and the Lower Paria River Canyon. Perhaps the most interesting geologic feature of all is The Cockscomb. All these areas combine to make a fascinating geology field trip.

Geologic Formations and Where They're Exposed

If we follow a line from the top of the Table Cliff Plateau, south to Lee's Ferry on the Colorado River, we'll pass along all, or most, of the formations which are exposed in the drainage. Let's begin at the top of the Table Cliff and run down through the different formations, and where they are prominently seen. At the end of this list are three formations which are exposed in Kaibab Gulch, just west of the Buckskin Trailhead. Two of these are not exposed along the lower Paria River.

Tuff of Osiris It's found only on top of Table Cliff Plateau just north of Powell Point. It's of volcanic origin, as is the top of the Aquarius Plateau, located further north and east.

Variegated Sandstone Member--Wasatch Formation This is usually considered the top of the Wasatch Formation, and seen only in a few places on the rim of Bryce Canyon N.P. and on top of Table Cliff Plateau. It's more weather resistant; therefore a capstone.

White Limestone Member--Wasatch Formation This is prominently seen all along the rim of the Pink Cliffs in Bryce Canyon, the Sunset Cliffs on the west side of the Paunsaugunt Plateau, and along the top part of Table Cliff Plateau. This and the Pink Limestone below, look nothing like ordinary limestone.

Pink Limestone Member--Wasatch Formation Seen on the lower slopes of Table Cliff and on Canaan Peak, as well as in Bryce Canyon. In this member are found the famous *Hoodoos*, for which Bryce Canyon is famous. It's the same member as is seen in all the Pink Cliffs, the Sunset Cliffs, and in Cedar Breaks National Monument. This is a crumbly limestone formation full of iron, which gives it it's color.

Pine Hollow Formation An indistinct mudstone strata immediately below the Pink Cliffs of Bryce Canyon and Table Cliff Plateau.

Canaan Peak Formation Another indistinct formation below the Pinks at the bottom of the Table Cliff Plateau. Made up of cobble, pebble, and sandstone conglomerate.

Kaiparowits Formation A slope-maker, made of sandstone, limestone, siltstone, and clays, and is seen most prominently to the east of The Cockscomb, or between Henrieville and the pass between Table Cliff Plateau and Canaan Peak.

Wahweap Formation This is a cliff-making formation, most prominently exposed as the east side ridge of Cads Crotch, one of the features of the upper end of The Cockscomb. It's a brownish-yellowish sandstone, mudstone, siltstone and shale.

Straight Cliffs Formation This formation is another cliff-maker. It's best seen as the highest ridge of The Cockscomb east of Hackberry Canyon and Cottonwood Wash. It also forms the western ridge of Cads Crotch, which is a prominent valley within the larger structure called The Cockscomb.

Tropic Shale The name tells the tale; it's mostly the gray clay beds you see around the town of Tropic, the type location. It's also the grays you see above Henrieville on the way to Escalante. Another location is in the lower end of the valley of The Cockscomb. You'll be driving along this gray clay area in the bottom 16 to 18 kms of the Cottonwood Wash Road. It begins just north of Highway 89, and is slick as hell when wet.

Dakota Sandstone This one is made mostly of a light brown sandstone, which makes a prominent cliff, but it also has siltstone and some shale. You'll see this as one of the prominent and intermediate ridges within The Cockscomb Valley. Remember, it's the first and very prominent ridge just west of the gray

Geology Cross Section
Table Cliff Plateau to Lee's Ferry

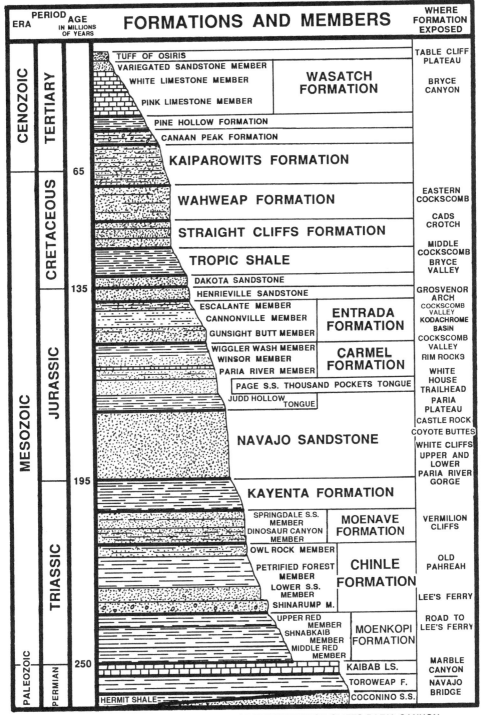

ERA	PERIOD	AGE IN MILLIONS OF YEARS	FORMATIONS AND MEMBERS	WHERE FORMATION EXPOSED
CENOZOIC	TERTIARY		TUFF OF OSIRIS	TABLE CLIFF PLATEAU
			VARIEGATED SANDSTONE MEMBER — WASATCH FORMATION	
			WHITE LIMESTONE MEMBER — WASATCH FORMATION	BRYCE CANYON
			PINK LIMESTONE MEMBER	
			PINE HOLLOW FORMATION	
			CANAAN PEAK FORMATION	
MESOZOIC	CRETACEOUS	65	KAIPAROWITS FORMATION	
			WAHWEAP FORMATION	EASTERN COCKSCOMB
			STRAIGHT CLIFFS FORMATION	CADS CROTCH
			TROPIC SHALE	MIDDLE COCKSCOMB BRYCE VALLEY
		135	DAKOTA SANDSTONE	
			HENRIEVILLE SANDSTONE	GROSVENOR ARCH
	JURASSIC		ESCALANTE MEMBER — ENTRADA FORMATION	COCKSCOMB VALLEY
			CANNONVILLE MEMBER — ENTRADA FORMATION	KODACHROME BASIN
			GUNSIGHT BUTT MEMBER — ENTRADA FORMATION	COCKSCOMB VALLEY
			WIGGLER WASH MEMBER — CARMEL FORMATION	RIM ROCKS
			WINSOR MEMBER — CARMEL FORMATION	
			PARIA RIVER MEMBER — CARMEL FORMATION	WHITE HOUSE TRAILHEAD
			PAGE S.S. THOUSAND POCKETS TONGUE	
			JUDD HOLLOW TONGUE	PARIA PLATEAU
			NAVAJO SANDSTONE	CASTLE ROCK COYOTE BUTTES WHITE CLIFFS UPPER AND LOWER PARIA RIVER GORGE
		195	KAYENTA FORMATION	
	TRIASSIC		SPRINGDALE S.S. MEMBER — MOENAVE FORMATION	VERMILION CLIFFS
			DINOSAUR CANYON MEMBER — MOENAVE FORMATION	
			OWL ROCK MEMBER — CHINLE FORMATION	OLD PAHREAH
			PETRIFIED FOREST MEMBER — CHINLE FORMATION	
			LOWER S.S. MEMBER — CHINLE FORMATION	LEE'S FERRY
			SHINARUMP M. — CHINLE FORMATION	
			UPPER RED MEMBER — MOENKOPI FORMATION	ROAD TO LEE'S FERRY
			SHNABKAIB MEMBER — MOENKOPI FORMATION	
			MIDDLE RED MEMBER — MOENKOPI FORMATION	
PALEOZOIC	PERMIAN	250	KAIBAB LS.	MARBLE CANYON
			TOROWEAP F.	NAVAJO BRIDGE
			HERMIT SHALE — COCONINO S.S.	

ADOPTED FROM: BUSH--GEOLOGY MAP OF THE VERMILION CLIFFS-PARIA CANYON
SCALE 1:62,500, MAPS USGS MF-1475 A, B, C, & D

Tropic Shale Valley along The Cockscomb Valley, which in this case is called Cottonwood Wash.

Henrieville Sandstone The type location for this one is near the town of Henrieville. It's seen in only a few areas, from the head or northern end of The Cockscomb, up through Butler Valley and at the head of Round Valley Draw. It's a yellow cliff-making massive sandstone. It's best seen at the Butler Valley Arch, more commonly known as Grosvenor Arch. It's that part of the wall from the top of the arch down to ground level.

There's a question on whether or not the *Morrison Formation* is exposed in this area, especially along The Cockscomb. In the lower end of The Cockscomb, the author sees no gap between the Dakota and the top of the Entrada, but there may be a thin layer of Morrison in there somewhere. Some reports place it in, but those are not detailed reports. Thompson and Stokes leave it out in their report.

Escalante Member--Entrada Sandstone An indistinct, and mostly sandstone member of the Entrada Formation seen in the upper slopes of Kodachrome Basin.

Cannonville Member--Entrada Sandstone This is a mostly fine grain white sandstone, but looks nothing like the real thing, the Navajo Sandstone. Its type location are the slopes around Cannonville, but the best place to see this one is in Kodachrome Basin. It's the white upper slopes and cliffs you see above the more scenic red sandstone in the park.

Gunsight Butte Member--Entrada Sandstone This is the reddish brown sandstone layer you see in Kodachrome Basin. In this member, are found most of the *sand pipes* in the park. Another good place to see this one is in The Rimrocks, which are seen just north of Highway 89 and Paria Ranger Station & Visitor Center. It is the white capstone which forms the top of The Rimrocks, which is just above the colorful Winsor Member of the Carmel Formation. In this location it's pure white. You can also see this member in the bottom part of the Cottonwood Wash and just east of the road. It's the white sandstone monoliths you see standing up alone like icebergs.

Wiggler Wash Member--Carmel Formation The type location for this strata is in the southern part of Kodachrome Basin where it's a thin gypsum layer, just below the red Gunsight Butte Member.

Winsor Member--Carmel Formation This is a mostly sandstone layer you can see just north of the Cottonwood Wash Road in the southern part of Kodachrome Basin. It's largely indistinct there, but the author believes this is the very colorful beds of clayish-looking deposits you see just north of Highway 89, between the eastern side of The Cockscomb to just east of the Paria Ranger Station & Visitor Center. These are the purple and white banded layers forming the lower part of The Rimrocks.

Paria River Member--Carmel Formation These are indistinct beds of mostly sandstone, mixed with thin layers of siltstone, as well as some limestone and gypsum. This one may be seen between the Paria Ranger Station & Visitor Center and the White House Trailhead.

Thousand Pockets Tongue--Page Sandstone This is a massive sandstone layer, once considered a part of the Navajo. It's type location is in the area just east of the top of the Dominguez Trail or Pass, in the lower end of the Paria. It's the smooth white sandstone you see at the White House Trailhead and around the town of Page. White House Spring comes out of the bottom of this tongue. (On the BLM map-guide-booklet called, *Hiker's Guide to Paria Canyon*, it shows a geology cross section on page 31. It shows the **Temple Cap Sandstone** immediately above the Navajo Sandstone. However, in the source they used, the UG&MS Bulletin 124, 1989, it states, the Temple Cap Sandstone exists only to the west of Johnson Canyon, which is a few kms east of Kanab.) (?).

Judd Hollow Tongue--Carmel Formation This tongue separates the Page Sandstone from the Navajo below, and is easily seen all along the Cottonwood Wash. It's the first layer above the massive white and yellowish Navajo Sandstone on the west side of the road along Cottonwood Wash. You'll also see it as you walk downstream from the White House Trailhead and into the Lower Paria River Gorge. The type location for this member is in Judd Hollow, which is just above where the old Adams Pump still sits in the middle part of the Lower Paria.

Navajo Sandstone This formation is probably the most famous and most seen of any formation on the Colorado Plateau. This is the one in which many of the fantastically narrow slot-type canyons are made. It is a massive sandstone, up to 600 meters thick, and is considered by many to be one large fossil sand dune. It was created by wind-blown sand, therefore it has lots of crossbedding. The Navajo is seen as the White Cliffs between Highway 89 and Cannonville, and in the narrows of Bull Valley Gorge, Round Valley Draw, Castle Rock, the Buckskin Gulch, and the Lower Paria Canyon. It's the Navajo Sandstone which forms the fantastic slopes and colors of the Teepees and The Wave in the Coyote Buttes. It's also seen as the top most part of the big cliff making up the Vermilion Cliffs just south of the Sand Hills or Paria Plateau. Elsewhere, you see the Navajo in the big walls of Zion N. P., all the canyons of the Escalante, throughout the San Rafael Swell, in the Moab area, and all across the Navajo Nation, which is the type location.

Kayenta Formation Where ever you see the Navajo, you'll see this one just below. Frankly, the author can't remember seeing a geology cross section without these two together. It's usually a deep reddish brown formation made of mudstone, sandstone and siltstone layers. It usually forms the series of benches just below the Navajo.

Moenave Formation This is the red cliff-maker just below the Kayenta, and above the Chinle. To the east of the Echo Cliffs Monocline, this one phases into, and is called the Wingate Sandstone. But between the

Paria and Zion National Park, it's the Moenave filling the same slot. This formation forms the lower cliffs just above the talus slopes along the Vermilion Cliffs and in the lower end of the Paria River drainage.

Owl Rock Member--Chinle Formation An indistinct, mostly sandstone layer just below the Moenave cliffs along the base of the Vermilion Cliffs and just above the varicolored banded slopes around old Pahreah.

Petrified Forest Member--Chinle Formation This is the same formation where all the petrified wood is found in northern Arizona. It's also full of petrified wood in Utah. This is the very colorful and fotogenic banded layers of clay you see around the old town of Pahreah and the Paria Movie Set. It's this red, purple, green, pink and white layered formation which have attracted movie makers to old Pahreah throughout the years.

Lower Sandstone Member--Chinle Formation Another indistinct sandstone bed in the lower part of the Chinle. Probably best seen in the lower end of the Paria around Lee's Ferry and just above the prominent Shinarump Bench.

Shinarump Conglomerate Member--Chinle Formation A white and very course sandstone and pebblestone conglomerate, which forms a very prominent ridge, cliff or bench throughout Utah and northern Arizona. It's white only when disturbed, otherwise it's covered with desert varnish and very dark colored. In other parts it's called the *Black Ledge.* It's best seen around Lee's Ferry, where it forms what is called Lee's Backbone, which is on the south side of the Colorado River. The original wagon route south from the ferry, went along the edge of this layer, which made a very rough road. This member is also full of petrified wood.

Moenkopi Formation This is the chocolate brown strata you'll see all across Utah and Arizona, wherever the Chinle's Shinarump member is found. It makes up the slope below the Shinarump and is composed of claybeds along with sandstone and siltstones. You drive upon it as you make the side trip to old Pahreah. It's also seen along the road running between the Navajo Bridge & Marble Canyon, and Lee's Ferry.

Kaibab Limestone This formation is seen at the land surface just west of the Buckskin and Wire Pass Trailheads, and on Buckskin and Fivemile Mountains. It's the capstone along the rim of Kaibab Gulch(that part of the gulch, wash or canyon just above the Buckskin Trailhead). It's this limestone which forms the top layer throughout the House Rock Valley. You are driving atop the Kaibab as you approach Marble Canyon and Lee's Ferry along Highway 89A from either direction. It forms the top layer in Marble Canyon, as seen at the rest stop at Navajo Bridge. You can also see the *Toroweap* and *Coconino Formations* in Marble Canyon if you stop at the Navajo Bridge on your way to Lee's Ferry.

Toroweap Formation In the Paria drainage, this formation is only seen in Kaibab Gulch, just upcanyon from the Buckskin Trailhead, where the channel cuts deep into Buckskin Mountain.

Hermit Shale This is the lowest or oldest of all formations found in the Paria River system. It's the red rock seen only in the very bottom of the Kaibab Gulch, just upcanyon above the Buckskin Trailhead. Normally the **Coconino Sandstone** is in that slot, but it's missing in Kaibab Gulch. However, the Coconino is seen just emerging in Marble Canyon below the bridge.

Looking north, northeast, from Red Top toward Yellow Rock and the Yellow Rock Valley.

Mining in the Paria River Drainage

Coal

Very little mining has occurred in the drainage of the Paria, but in the early days of settlement, coal was mined and used mostly in the blacksmith trade. If you look at the maps of Bryce Valley, and the Middle Paria River Ghosts Towns, you'll see coal mines near each of the former or present townsites. Most of the coal mining has occurred in the upper reaches of the Paria northeast of Tropic and north of Henrieville.

The coal mined in Bryce Valley comes from the bottom part of the Straight Cliffs Formation, while that coming from the mine above Adairville, comes from the Dakota Sandstone. There are also coal beds in the Tropic Shale, but they're so thin it has always been too uneconomical to mine.

The most northerly coal mine in the valley is usually called the *Shakespear Mine*, but sometimes it's referred to as the *Emma Canyon Mine*. It's located about 11 kms northeast of Tropic, in a little side drainage of Henderson Valley, called Emma Canyon.

The late Herm Pollock believed it was his grandfather William W. Pollock and his brother Jack, who may have been the first to dig coal out of this mine. They were among the earliest settlers to the valley and were both blacksmiths. They needed coal to do their work; on the other hand, Obe Shakespear, long time Tropic resident, told the author he never knew coal in his life, until an uncle started mining it not too many years ago. Bryce Valley families always used cedar(piñon-juniper) wood in their stoves, even though coal was there for the taking.

After the earlier blacksmith days, nothing happened in the mining business until the late 1930's. This is when Lewis and Vern Ray(father and son) came into the valley from Orderville, and filed on the mineral rights to the coal in Emma Canyon. They mined coal for 5 or 6 years, until about the mid-1940's, then sold it to Alton and Vernal Shakespear. They are the ones who did more mining than anyone. They shipped it to as far away as St. George and Panguitch, but most of it stayed in the valley. The mine was active until perhaps the late 1950's, then business slowed down and it was not used after about 1960. One person thought the state closed it down because of water and safety problems?

Finally in 1964, Alton Shakespear sold the old Shakespear Mine for a reported $75,000 to a man from Denver. This new owner was hoping to invest more money in the business and make big profits, but nothing ever happen to the scheme, and coal hasn't been mined there since.

The Shakespear Mine is located in the bottom part of the Straight Cliffs Formation, where there's a total of nearly 4 meters of coal in four separate seams. Today, it appears there are two tunnels to the mine, the openings of which are protected by the installation of large galvanized steel pipes which prevent cave-ins.

To get to this site(in the NW corner of Section 22, T36S, R2W), drive east out of Tropic toward the old

The Davies Mine in Coal Canyon north of Henrieville.

Map 34, Mine Locations of the Paria River Drainage

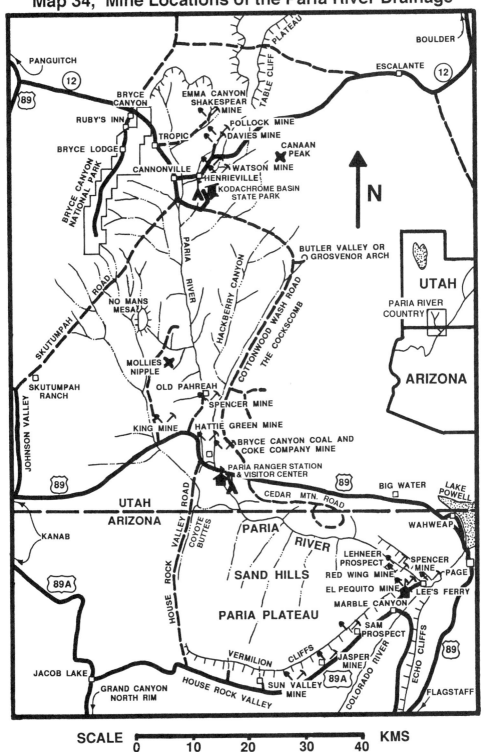

townsite of Losee and into East Valley. There are several side roads, but continue in a northeast direction and straight into Emma Canyon. Stay on this main road, which is generally good for any vehicle all the way.

In the area north of Henrieville, are the Pollock and Davies Mines. These are both in the Straight Cliffs Formation, and presumably across the narrow canyon from each other. Everyone in Henrieville calls the one place the *Jack Pollock Mine*. He was one of the earliest settlers in Henrieville and he used the coal for blacksmithing. Today there is little or no evidence this old mine ever existed, but the one just across the canyon did operate for awhile and is clearly visible. This was the Davis or *Davies Mine*.

Wallace Ott recalls a time he took Byron Davies up Coal Canyon and showed him the veins of coal. That was in the early 1940's and after Davies had tried, apparently unsuccessfully, to mine coal from a mine downcanyon around Adairville. It was Davies who did some mining here in the 1940's. He ran a shaft into the beds for 30 to 50 meters, but didn't have the money to go into mining big. The Davies Mine has one vein nearly 3 meters in thickness; another about 2 meters thick. The mining that was done was more for a promotional than anything else. Davies and Ott and others, including Alfred Foster, organized the Garfield Coal Company in about 1960, but as yet nothing has happened. Selling it is still a possibility, and they still have money invested in the project.

To get to these two old mines, which are nearly side by side, drive north out of Henrieville on Highway 12 in the direction of Escalante. After about 5 kms, turn left, or north, from between mile posts 32 and 33. The mines are almost due north of that point in Coal Canyon, which is in between Jimmie Canyon and Dry Hollow. See the *Map 32, Bryce Valley Mines & Ghost Town* on page 195. From the highway to the mines, it's about 3 kms(located in the north half of Section 36, T36S, R2W). However, you can't take a vehicle past the first wash and gate. So you might as well park on the highway and walk as the road just into the mouth of the canyon is totally washed out anyway. Walking will take about 45 minutes, and you have to jump or climb around some deep gullies. The Davies Mine is on the south side of the canyon, and there is still a pile of coal and a chute at the site. Across the canyon north, one can just barely make out a faint line indicating the possible location of the Pollock Mine.

Not far south of the Pollock and Davies Mines is another old coal mine one old timer called the *Jack Pollock Mine?* Maybe Jack Pollock had several mines, one near each town. It's right on Highway 12, between mile post 31 and 32, and about 4 kms north of Henrieville. No one in Henrieville today knows much about the history of this mine, except that one cold winter day, two boys from Henrieville, went into the mine and started a fire to get warm. When they left, they failed to put out the fire properly and it started the coal to burning. Later the state of Utah had to send men and equipment down to cover the shaft and smuther the fire. You can still see some of the coal from the highway.

There's still another old coal mine not far east of Henrieville. If you hike on some old roads about 5 kms east of town and into Little Creek, you may see the *Frank Watson Mine*. This is the same man who built the

North of Adairville, is the Bryce Canyon Coal & Coke Company Mine.

cabin in the lower end of Hackberry Canyon. After he left the Hackberry country, he went to Henrieville for awhile, then ran a small store out on Watson Ridge just south of Kodachrome Basin. His hottest selling item out there was rot-gut whiskey known locally as *Jamaica Ginger*. After he left the store, he started working a coal mine in Little Creek, but he only worked there for one winter.

In the Adairville area is still another old abandoned coal mine. About 2 1/2 kms due north of the site of Adairville, is the site of the *Bryce Canyon Coal & Coke Company Mine*. This old mine is located in the center of Section 21, T42S, R1W, and in the Dakota Sandstone. See *Map 33, Middle Paria River Mines & Ghost Towns*.

This mine was first opened in the late 1930's by Byron Davies of Cannonville. It's been said he took some good coal out by truck in the direction of Kanab, but apparently he couldn't find a market for it. They mined it for just a couple of years, then was sold to David Quilter in about 1940. No mining ever took place after that and it was abandoned.

To get there, you could walk up the Paria River bed from the highway, but you can also drive almost to it. Drive along Highway 89 to between mile posts 17 and 18, about 5 kms east of the Paria Ranger Station & Visitor Center. At that point turn north onto the Cottonwood Wash Road and drive about 10 kms. At that point you'll be about half a km west of the only fence and cattle guard around. This is just before you drop down into the Paria Valley. Park right on the road in the dry creek bed.

From where you park, walk 50 meters to the southwest, and look right down on the mine, which has one collapsed shaft and a tumbled-down loading chute. On the east side of the drainage, you can walk right down the steep slope to the mine, or you could walk along an old track which circles around to the south and comes back to the Cottonwood Wash Road near the cattle guard.

Copper

Prospecting for copper has been carried on at a number of places in the Paria River drainage, but only a small amount of low-grade copper ore has been shipped from the Hattie Green Mine. The history of this mine goes back to the late 1800's. It was March 8, 1893, that George J. Simonds filed a claim or notice of location on what was called the Hattie Green. Just a few days later, there were several other locations registered in the area just to the north. They were the Silver Queen and Gold King claims which are about one km north of the Hattie Green and evidently on top of The Cockscomb. These were filed by several members of the Ahlstrom family. In the same time period, Tom Levy, Oren Twitchell and Murphy Alexander filed on what was called the Red Bird Claim. This was just south of The Box of the Paria. Of all these claims, only the Hattie Green produced.

According to Kay Clark of Henrieville, two brothers named Clint and Pat Willis, worked this mine in the late 1910's and early 1920's. They are the ones who did most of the work on the tunnels and adits, and who lugged out most of the copper ore. Kay Clark did some poking around the place and filed on the old claims

Just off the Nipple Ranch Road is this loading chute near the King Manganese Mine.

in the 1960's, but nothing came of that.

To get to the Hattie Green, located in Section 18, T42S, R1W, stop on Highway 89, just south of mile post 28. Then walk due east across the gully, and locate a track first running east, then south, then north inside a minor draw within The Cockscomb. From where you turn north, it's about one km to the mine, which sits atop The Cockscomb Ridge on the right. Read more on route details under the hiking section and *Map 21, The Hattie Green Mine Trail.*

At the mine there are two tunnels, one coming in from the east side, the other from the west. The west side tunnel has wooden tracks which supported small ore cars within the mine. Right on top of the ridge is an ore heap with the blue-green stained rocks still lying there. About 20 meters inside the east side tunnel is a door way. There are also three other adits or test prospects in the area.

Manganese

Another mining operation took place not far south of Kitchen Corral Point and along the Nipple Ranch Road. This is the King Mine and it's primary mineral was manganese.

According to Calvin C. Johnson of Kanab, this operation first began sometime in the late 1930's. It was on November 15, 1939, that John H. Brown filed a claim and started mining. It was soon found they couldn't separate the manganese from the bentonite clays of the Petrified Forest Member of the Chinle Formation. After Brown gave up, several Johnson brothers from Short Creek, Arizona, worked it for 6 or 8 months. This was in the early 1940's. Then it was abandoned for about a decade.

In 1954 or 1955, a bigger outfit came in with a guy named Bennett in charge. In the year or two they worked the area, they spent upwards of $250,000 to develop it. They made five small dams in the one little canyon where most of the mining took place. They then built another dam across Kitchen Corral Wash and caught flood water; plus they used water from some nearby springs. They then pumped this water up the canyon to the five reservoirs, and used the water in the attempt to separate manganese from the clays. At the height of the operation, 20 to 25 local men worked there. But they also had troubles with separation, and soon closed down.

To see this old abandoned mine operation, drive along Highway 89 about 45 kms east of Kanab. Right at mile post 37, turn north onto the Nipple Ranch Road and drive about 5 or 6 kms. At that point look for a couple of roads running northeast into a minor canyon. Drive about half a km from the main road and park under a large cedar tree. From there, you can walk upcanyon on an old and partly washed out road about 200 meters to the old ponds, one mine tunnel, and some loading chutes(it's in the middle of Section 2, T42S, R3W). When you return to the Nipple Ranch Road, turn north and drive about one km, and on your right or to the east, you'll see on a low hillside, some mining scars and an old loading chute.

The entrance to the Red Wing Uranium Mine, just south of the Wilson Ranch.

Uranium

In the very lower end of the Paria River Canyon in the vicinity of Lee's Ferry, and along Highway 89A just under the Vermilion Cliffs, are a number of uranium mines and prospects. These all go back to the 1950's uranium boom days.

If you're coming downcanyon out of the Lower Gorge, you'll pass the *Red Wing Mine*, about 6 1/2 kms up from Lee's Ferry, and about half a km south of the Wilson Ranch site(in the north side of Section 3, T40N, R7E). This mine has two adits, 13 and 17 meters long. The adits were tunneled into the Shinarump Member of the Chinle Formation, but the vegetal trash heaps where the uranium is concentrated, are right at the contact point of the Shinarump and the Moenkopi. About half a km upcanyon from the Wilson Ranch is another adit, called the *Lehneer Prospect*. Not much happened there.

Near Lee's Ferry is the *El Pequito Mine*. It's found about 2 kms west of the Lonely Dell Ranch, at the head of a minor canyon just north of Johnson Point. El Pequito is in the Shinarump, and at the contact point of the Moenkopi. Mineralization occurs in an old stream channel in the Shinarump. This mine is found in the northwest corner of Section 14, T40N, R7E.

Going southwest from Lee's Ferry, you'll find the *Sam Prospect* in the southeast corner of Section 2, T39N, R6E. It's about 3 kms west of Vermilion Cliffs Lodge, along Highway 89A, and in the south side of Badger Creek. This adit is in the upper part of the Petrified Forest Member of the Chinle Formation. Not much went on there.

Further along to the southwest, is the *Jasper Mine* in the southwest corner of Section 27, T39N, R6E. It's about half a km northeast of Cliff Dwellers Lodge, and about 100 meters from the highway. It too was located at or near the contact point of the Shinarump and the Moenkopi. They found small amounts of many minerals, including copper staining, but not much else.

The only real uranium mine in these parts, was the *Sun Valley Mine*. It's 5 kms southwest of Cliff Dwellers Lodge, and in the south half of Section 6, T38N, R6E. At the time it was studied by Lane and Bush, this mine was owned and operated by Intermountain Exploration Co. The mine was started in 1954 during a period of intense uranium exploration in the area. An inclined shaft was sunk on a Shinarump outcropping, with the ore being on the contact with the Moenkopi. Several hundred tons of high grade uranium ore was shipped before the shaft was filled with mud from a flash flood. Later, a vertical shaft was sunk, and a drift was driven to connect with the old, sand-filled workings, but there was no further production. The Sun Valley Mine has been worked in recent years on a sporadic basis. Today all of these old mines and prospects are included in the Paria Canyon--Vermilion Cliffs Wilderness Area.

Gold

The story of gold mining along the Paria River, is also the story of Charles H. Spencer. As one writer

Lee's Fort, once used by Charles H. Spencer and his mining crew.

The boiler used by Spencer's crew to power a water hose, which washed the Chinle clays down to a sluice box.

The steamboat *Charles H. Spencer* as it appeared in August, 1915.

Charles H. Spencer's stone house just south of old Pahreah.

All that remains of the sunken steamship *Charles H. Spencer* can be seen in the Colorado River just southeast of Lee's Fort at Lee's Ferry. Note the crystal clear river water which is also very cold, even in the middle of summer.

put it, "*he seemed to enjoy the pursuit more than the gold itself, especially when it meant spending other peoples money looking for it.*"

Spencer first arrived in the canyon country in 1909, where he set up an operation on the lower San Juan River far upstream from Lee's Ferry on the Colorado. There he was trying to separate gold from the Wingate Sandstone. During that stay, a couple of prospectors told him about the possibilities of the Chinle Formation at Lee's Ferry, and that coal existed north of the Colorado River a ways. With that tip, he made tracks for Lee's Ferry, arriving there in April, 1910.

On arriving at the Ferry, Spencer looked things over and decided the Chinle clays 300 meters from the river could be a possibility. He speculated that a boiler could power a high pressure hose, which could wash the clays and shales down to the river, where gold could then be recovered with the help of an amalgamator. But his first job was to send his men out to look for the promised coal field. It was found in a side drainage about 45 kms upstream in Glen Canyon. The site was is Warm Creek.

While the hunt for coal went on, Spencer began experimenting with power dredging at Lee's Ferry. At first he used wood to power the boiler. He then set up power hoses to wash the gold bearing clays down to a sluice and amalgamator at the river. Gold is indeed in the Chinle, but it's in the form of very fine dust. The method used, was to run the muddy water over the amalgamator which had mercury in the bottom. The mercury was supposed to absorb and trap the gold, allowing other materials to pass over. But instead, the operation merely clogged the amalgamator, and the mercury did not absorb the gold. While chemists worked on the problem, Spencer was thinking about how to get the coal from Warm Creek to the Ferry.

At first it was thought coal could be brought in by mule, using an old trail called the Ute or Dominguez Trail, which entered the canyon about 5 kms above from the Ferry. Because of the extra distance, it was decided to make a shortcut route directly above the operation on the Colorado. So in the fall of 1910, Spencer and his men constructed the Spencer Trail from the river to the top of the cliffs. From there it was hoped they could head northeast with mules for the Warm Creek coal fields. But the trail was never used to bring in coal, instead it was more of an promotional scheme than anything else. Spencer finally decided to bring coal downriver in a boat.

The next job was to build a wagon road right down the dry stream bed of Warm Creek to the Colorado River. While workers were building the road, others were building a barge on the banks of the river. This all went well--they brought coal down the canyon, loaded it onto the barge, then floated it down to the Ferry. But then the problem was to get the barge back upstream again.

This problem, it was thought, could be solved by a tugboat of some kind. So with more investor's money, a 9 meter-long tug boat called the *Violet Louise,* was purchased and brought to Lee's Ferry. As it turned out, it was too far underpowered to push a large barge upstream against the current. The current wasn't that fast, but pushing a barge wasn't easy.

While Spencer worked on problems at the Ferry, the managers of the Chicago company he

Rainwater pool and teepee-shaped rocks at what this author calls Coyote Buttes Overlook.
It's located in the southwest corner of the West Clark Bench.

worked for, ordered a steam powered boat from San Francisco. The boat was built in 1911, dismantled, and shipped by train to Marysvale, Utah, the end of the railway line at the time. It was then put onto large wagons for the rest of the 320 km trip to the mouth of Warm Creek. There it was reassembled in the spring of 1912. It was the biggest thing to sail the Colorado River above the Grand Canyon. It measured 28 x 8 meters, was powered by a coal boiler, and had a 4 meter-wide stern paddle wheel. Even though this part of the project wasn't one of Spencer's ideas, the boat was named the *Charles H. Spencer*.

The next problem was to find a crew for the boat. This wasn't easy in the middle of the desert, but they found a crew anyway, with a fellow by the name of Pete Hanna at the helm, the only crew member who had any experience with boats. They loaded the deck full of coal for the trial run. But almost immediately, they hit a sandbar. Then another. Finally Hanna turned the boat around and allowed it to sail down the river backwards, which gave it better maneuverability. They spent one night in the canyon, then next morning finished the 45 km run to Lee's Ferry.

They then had to figure out how to get the *Spencer* back upstream against the current, which was stronger than anyone had expected. Hanna decided to keep most of the coal which had been brought down on board, to insure passage back up to Warm Creek. This was a good move, because they barely made it back upstream. They again loaded the boat as full as possible, and returned to the Ferry, where it sat for a couple of months. All this, while the chemists and the workers figured out what to do about separating the gold from the Chinle clays.

Finally it was decided to try something different. They ended up towing the original barge upstream with the *Spencer*. This worked fine. They then loaded up both the barge and the steamer with coal. The barge was then allowed to drift downstream with several workers guiding it around the sandbars, with the *Spencer* following. This worked fine too, and it appeared they had this part of the gold mining problem solved. The only thing left to do, was to find a successful way to get the gold out of the clay. This Spencer was never able to do, and the steamboat had made its last run.

Spencer left Lee's Ferry later in 1912, bound for the nearly abandoned settlement of Pahreah. Meanwhile, the steamship *Charles H. Spencer* sat on the river tied to the bank. In 1915 the combination of high water and piles of drift wood, put the boat on its side and it sank in a meter of water. Later, parts were stripped off and taken away, and some of the lumber from its decks was used for various projects. Today, you can just barely see the sunken remains of the boat just upstream from Lee's Fort, at the bottom end of the Spencer Trail. Near the old fort is the boiler and parts of the stern paddle wheel. Just north of the boiler one can still see scars where they operated the power sluicing machinery. Perhaps the best source of information about all the subjects of Lee's Ferry is found in the books, *Desert River Crossing* and *Lee's Ferry*. See *Further Reading*, in the back of this book for more details on these two books.

The Pahreah Cemetery located between the Paria Movie Set and the townsite of old Pahreah.

This old cabin is located at The Meadows, which is not far north, or above, the Deer Spring Ranch, which is along the Skutumpah Road.

From high above, one can see Adair Lake, the fault line, and the old corral.

Map 35, Bryce Valley and Skutumpah Road Ranches

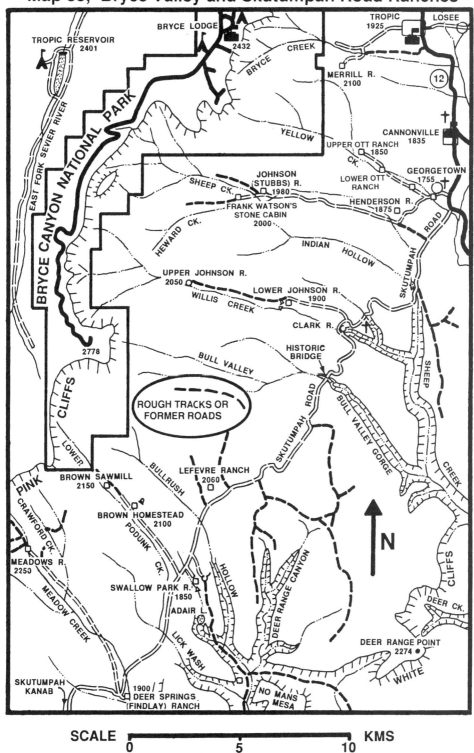

TROPIC RESERVOIR
2401

EAST FORK SEVER RIVER

BRYCE LODGE

2432

BRYCE CREEK

TROPIC
1925

LOSEE

YELLOW

MERRILL R.
2100

12

BRYCE CANYON NATIONAL PARK

CANNONVILLE
1835

UPPER OTT RANCH
1850

CK.

JOHNSON
(STUBBS) R.
1980

SHEEP CK.

LOWER OTT
RANCH

GEORGETOWN
1755

FRANK WATSON'S
STONE CABIN
2000

HENDERSON R.
1875

HEWARD CK.

INDIAN HOLLOW

SKUTUMPAH ROAD

UPPER JOHNSON R.
2050

LOWER JOHNSON R.
1900

WILLIS CREEK

CLARK R.

SHEEP

2778

HISTORIC
BRIDGE

BULL VALLEY

CLIFFS

ROUGH TRACKS OR
FORMER ROADS

CREEK

LOWER

SKUTUMPAH ROAD

BULL VALLEY GORGE

PINK

BROWN SAWMILL
2150

BULLRUSH

LEFEVRE RANCH
2060

N

CRAWFORD CK.

BROWN HOMESTEAD
2100

PODUNK CK.

MEADOWS R.
2250

DEER RANGE CANYON

CLIFFS

MEADOW CREEK

SWALLOW PARK R.
1850

HOLLOW

DEER CK.

ADAIR L.

DEER RANGE POINT
2274

LICK WASH

SKUTUMPAH
KANAB

1900

DEER SPRINGS
(FINDLAY) RANCH

NO MANS
MESA

WHITE

SCALE

0   5   10

KMS

221

Further Reading

History Books

Desert River Crossing, Historic Lee's Ferry on the Colorado River, Rusho-Crampton, Peregrine Smith, Inc.

Emma Lee, Juanita Brooks, Utah State University Press.

Golden Nuggets of Pioneer Days--A History of Garfield County, Daughters of Utah Pioneers, Panguitch, Utah.

History of Kane County, Daughters of Utah Pioneers, Kanab, Utah.

John Doyle Lee, Zealot-Pioneer Builder-Scapegoat, Juanita Brooks, A.H. Clark Co.

Lee's Ferry, A Crossing of the Colorado River, Measeles, Pruett Publishing.

Lee's Ferry and Lonely Dell Ranch Historic Districts, Grand Canyon Natural History Association, South Rim-Grand Canyon, Arizona.

Mountain Meadows Massacre, Juanita Brooks, University of Oklahoma Press.

Some Dreams Die, Utah's Ghost Towns, George A. Thompson, Dream Garden Press.

Utah Ghost Towns, Stephen L. Carr, Western Epics.

Geology

Chinle Formation of the Paria Plateau, J. P. Akers, Masters Thesis, U. of Arizona, 1960.

Geology of Bryce Canyon National Park, Lindquist, Bryce Canyon Natural History Association.

Geology of Kane County, Utah, Doelling, Davis & Brandt, *UGMS Bulletin 124,* 1989.

Geology of Table Cliff Region, Utah, Bowers, *Bulletin 1331-B, USGS,* 1972.

Mine and Prospect Map, Vermilion Cliffs, *USGS Map MF-1475-D, Miscellaneous Field Studies*(also contains maps A, B and C).

Map-Geology of the Kaiparowits Plateau, Carter and Sargent, *USGS Map I-1033-K.*

Sandstone and Conglomerate-Breccia Pipes and Dikes of the Kodachrome Basin Area, Kane County, Utah, Cheryl Hannum, *Masters Thesis,* Brigham Young University, 1979.

Stratigraphy of the Dakota and Tropic Formations, Lawrence, *Bulletin 19, Utah Geological Survey,* 1965.

Stratigraphy of the San Rafael Group, Southwest and South Central Utah, Thompson and Stokes, *Bulletin 87, UGMS,* October 1970.

The Geology and Geography of the Paunsaugunt Region, Utah, Gregory, *Professional Paper 226, USGS.*

The Kaiparowits Region, Gregory and Moore, *Professional Paper 164, USGS.*

Magazines and Unpublished Manuscripts

An Episode of Military Exploration and Surveys (A survey party's account of riding up the Paria River Gorge) *The United Service,* Vol. 5, Number 119, October 1881.

Biography of John G. Kitchen(unpublished manuscript), J. G. Kitchen Jr., 1964.

California Condors, Updates on restocking public lands with condors: from *Arizona Desert Digest, Arizona Game & Fish Department,* and *The Peregrine Fund.*

Desert Bighorn Sheep Restocking, Arizona Game and Fish Department, *Wildlife Surveys and Investigations,* 1984.

First Motor Sortie into Escalante Land, Breed, *National Geographic Magazine,* September, 1949.

History of Deer Spring Ranch(unpublished manuscript), Graden Robinson, Kanab, Utah.

History of Peter Shirts [Shurtz] and his Descendants, Ambrose Shurtz, 1963, Unpublished family history, but available at Special Collections, BYU Library, Provo, Utah. (By about the year 2000, a real book may be published?)

Historic Utilization of Paria River, Reilly, *Utah Historical Quarterly,* Vol. 45, Number 2, 1977.

Lee's Ferry at Lonely Dell, Juanita Brooks, *Utah Historical Quarterly,* Vol. 25, 1957.

Vegetation and Soils of No Man's Mesa, Utah, Mason and others, *Journal of Range Management,* January, 1967.

Other Guide Books by the Author

(Prices as of January, 1998. Prices may change without notice)

Climber's and Hiker's Guide to the World's Mountains (3rd Ed.), Kelsey, 928 pages, 447 maps, 451 fotos, ISBN 0-944510-02-7. US$34.95 (Mail orders US$37.50).

Utah Mountaineering Guide (3rd Ed.), Kelsey, 208 pages, 54 hiking maps, 142 fotos, ISBN 0-944510-14-0. US$10.95 (Mail orders US$13.00).

Canyon Hiking Guide to the Colorado Plateau (3rd Edition), Kelsey, 288 pages, 116 maps, 159 fotos, ISBN 0-9605824-1-5. US $12.95 (Mail orders US$15.00).

Hiking and Exploring Utah's San Rafael Swell (2nd Ed.), Kelsey, 160 pages, 35 mapped hikes, plus lots of history, 104 fotos, ISBN 0-944510-01-9. US$8.95 (Mail orders US$11.00).

Hiking and Exploring Utah's Henry Mountains and Robbers Roost, *Including The Life and Legend of Butch Cassidy,* Revised Edition, Kelsey, 224 pages, 38 hikes or climbs, 158 fotos, ISBN 0-944510-4-3. US$9.95 (Mail orders US$12.00).

Hiking and Exploring the Paria River (3rd Edition), Kelsey, 224 pages, 32 different hikes from Bryce Canyon to Lee's Ferry, 177 fotos, ISBN 0-944510-15-9. US$10.95 (Mail Orders US$13.00).

Hiking and Climbing in the Great Basin National Park--*A Guide to Nevada's Wheeler Peak, Mt. Moriah, and the Snake Range,* Kelsey, 192 pages, 47 hikes or climbs, 125 fotos, ISBN 0-9605824-8-7. US$9.95 (Mail Orders US$12.00).

Boater's Guide to Lake Powell (2nd Updated Edition), with emphasis on hiking, Kelsey, 288 pages, 256 fotos, ISBN 0-944510-10-8. US$13.95 (Mail Orders US$16.00).

Climbing and Exploring Utah's Mt. Timpanogos, Kelsey, 208 pages, 170 fotos, ISBN 0-944510-00-0. US$9.95 (Mail Orders US$12.00).

River Guide to Canyonlands National Park & Vicinity, Kelsey, 256 pages, 151 fotos, ISBN 0-944510-07-8. US$11.95 (Mail Orders US$14.00).

Hiking, Biking and Exploring Canyonlands National Park & Vicinity, Kelsey, 320 pages, 227 fotos, ISBN 944510-08-6. US$14.95 (Mail Orders US$17.00).

Life on the Black Rock Desert, *A History of Clear Lake, Utah,* Venetta B. Kelsey, 192 pages, 123 fotos, ISBN 0-944510-03-5. US$9.95 (Mail Orders US$12.00).

The Story of Black Rock, Utah, Kelsey, 160 pages, 139 fotos, ISBN 0-944510-12-4, US$9.95 (Mail Orders US$12.00).

Hiking, Climbing & Exploring Western Utah's Jack Watson's Ibex Country, Kelsey, 272 pages, 224 fotos, ISBN 0-944510-13-2. US$9.95 (Mail Orders US$12.00).

High to the southeast, one has a good look at the southeast buttress of Castle Rock.

Distributors for Kelsey Publishing

<u>Primary Distributor</u>   If you'd like to order any book, please call or write to the following address. All of Michael R. Kelsey's books are sold by this company.
Publishers Distribution Center, 805 West 1700 South, Salt Lake City, Utah, 84104, P.O. Box 27734, Salt Lake City, Utah, 84127. Tele. 1-801-972-6570, or for Book Orders 1-800-922-9681.

<u>Many of Kelsey's books are sold by each of the following distributors</u>
Alpenbooks, 3616 South Road, Building C, Suite 1, Mukilteo, Washington, 98275, Tele. 1-206-290-8587, or for book orders 1-800-290-9898, Fax 1-206-290-9461.
Anderson News, 1709 North, East Street, Flagstaff, Arizona, 86001, Tele. 1-520-774-6171, Fax 1-520-779-1958.
Big Horn Booksellers, 1813 E. Mulberry Street, Ft. Collins, Colorado, 80524, Tele. 1-970-224-1579, Order Line 1-800-433-5995, Fax 1-970-224-1394.
Canyon Country Distribution, P. O. Box 400034, Highway 50-6 West, #100, Thompson Springs, Utah, 84540-0034, Tele. 1-801-285-2210.
Canyonlands Publications, 4860 North, Ken Morey Drive, PO Box 16175, Bellemont, Arizona, 86015, Tele. 1-520-779-3888, or 1-800-283-1983, Fax 1-520-779-3778.
Crown West Books(Library Service), 575 E. 1000 S., Orem, Utah, 84058, Tele. 1-801-224-1455.
High Peak Books, PO Box 703, Wilson, Wyoming, 83014, 1-307-739-0147.
Many Feathers, 2626 West, Indian School Road, Phoenix, Arizona, 85012, Tele. 1-602-266-1043, or 1-800-279-7652, Fax 1-602-279-2350.
Nevada Publications, 4135 Badger Circle, Reno, Nevada, 89509, Tele. 1-702-747-0800.
Peregrine Outfitters, P.O. Box 1500, 105 South Brownell Road, Suite A, Williston, Vermont, 05495, Tele. 802-860-2977, or 1-800-222-3088, Fax 1-802-860-2978.
Recreational Equipment, Inc.(R.E.I.), P.O. Box C-88126, Seattle, Washington, 98188, For Mail Orders Tele. 1-800-426-4840 (or check at their local stores).
Treasure Chest Books, 1802 West Grant Road, Suite 101, PO Box 5250, Tucson, Arizona, 85703-0250, Tele. 1-520-623-9558, Fax 1-520-624-5888, or Order Toll Free Tele. 1-800-969-9558, or Fax 1-800-715-5888. Credit Cards Accepted.

For the UK and Europe: CORDEE, 3a De Montfort Street, Leicester, England, UK, LE1 7HD, Tele. 0116-254-3579, Fax 0116-247-1176.
For Australia and New Zealand: Macstyle Media, 20-22 Station Street, Sandringham, Victoria, Australia, 3191. Tele. International+61-39-521-6585, Fax International+61-39-521-0664

Another look at the narrows and small cascade in Starlight Canyon.